A GOOD RUNNING AWAY

MISPLACED MERCENARIES BOOK ONE

KEVIN PETTWAY

Cursed Dragon Ship
P U B L I S H I N G

Cursed Dragon Ship Publishing, LLC

4606 FM 1960 Rd W, Suite 400

Houston, TX 77069

captwyvern@curseddragonship.com

This books is a work of fiction fresh from the author's imagination. Any resemblance to actual persons or places is mere coincidence.

Cover © 2019 by Lena Shore

Developmental Edit by Kelly Lynn Colby

Proofread by Shannon Winton

ISBN 978-1-951445-02-7

ISBN 978-1-951445-01-0 (ebook)

✿ Created with Vellum

To my wife Lena.
For encouraging me to be as bad as I wanted to...
then putting up with it.

1

A THIEF IN THE HAND

KEANE

Bright noonday sun warmed the broad grassy glade, providing no comfort at all to a shirtless Keane as his fellow mercenaries threw him into the wooden-barred prisoner cart. Over four hundred freemen of Wallace's Company laughed and waved their spears in the air as they engaged in their third-favorite pastime, turning on their own.

Banging shoulder first onto the hard boards, Keane winced and sucked in his breath against the sharp pain. He rolled forward and stood, dodging the butts of spears that jabbed at him between the bars. His brown skin purpled where rough hands had torn the shirt from him.

"Rabbit-dicked cowards," he yelled, trying not to think of all the times he had been one of those holding a spear. "Anyone wanna climb up in here and—Oldam's cock ring—ow!" A poke in the small of his back sent him against the rear bars where another haft glanced across his temple. He knew better than to try and grab a spear. That would only cause the others to get turned around before coming back in, point first. But it was hard not to do, and he couldn't take a lot more of this.

He knew how much more was coming.

Someone else's scream climbed above the din of the mercenary army from in front of Keane, and a wave of quiet swept out across the throng. The man who hit Keane in the temple, thin and bedraggled with crisscrossing scars on his forehead and cheeks, was flung to the ground, his broken spear tossed on top of him. A huge woman stood behind the unconscious man, bringing a bloody grin to Keane's face.

At six-foot-two, Sarah stood above most of the assembled mercenaries, which alone did not account for the looks of fear thrown her way. She too was Pavinn, her brown skin only slightly darker than Keane's. Her black hair was pulled behind her head in braids and run through a leather sleeve. She was a year or two younger than he was, though he couldn't be sure exactly by how much. Neither of them knew their own ages for certain. Keane's arms showed hard muscle, but he had seen Sarah break a man's forearm by accident in a wrestling match just by grabbing him with her hand. And right now, she stood watching the crowd with grim brown eyes, a naked broadsword in her fist.

A circle formed as soldiers moved away.

The mail of her hauberk jingled as Sarah stepped up to the back of the prisoner cart, and one side of her mouth quirked up. Her dark green cloak rustled in the breeze.

"I take it you haven't seen Harden yet," Sarah said to Keane as if not surrounded by hundreds of evil men, "since your guts are all, you know, still inside you."

"Can we have this conversation while we're running away, please?" Keane asked, brushing blood from the wound on his temple out of his eye. He turned his head in a slow arc to take in the assembled soldiery. "I'd like to leave before *anyone scary* shows up."

"Too late there, ya weedy little shit," came a gravelly voice from over Keane's left shoulder. Captain Eli Whister, foremost of the Wallace's Company captains, strode into the empty ring around the prisoner cart. Eli was a grizzled old veteran, bald with an iron-gray beard and unexpectedly kind eyes. He was Andosh, light-skinned and powerfully built, but short for his people. His black leather armor, mail peeking out in the joints, was faded along the curves and creases from exposure to the elements.

"Sarah, you just leave now. This don't concern you."

"I think that depends on what the old man has in mind for my friend," Sarah answered. Tension crept up along Keane's spine at the menace flowing from the two relaxed warriors. His chest burned, and he realized he was holding his breath.

The empty circle grew as the mercenaries scented the potential for *real* bloodletting in the air.

"I don't know what Harden's got in his mind," Eli said, holding out his hands in a gesture meant to show openness but was actually an old swordsman's trick to distract from a sudden blade draw. It didn't fool Keane, and it wouldn't fool Sarah. "Whatever it is, I'm sure he'll wanna talk it over with you first, won't he? This ain't gotta end the sharp way."

"You know everything the old man is thinking." Keane found his voice and rounded on Eli. "You're his brain, that's why he keeps you in his ass. You haven't had a thought in the last twenty years that wasn't clenched in there by the old man's bowels. He wants me dead, and that means you want it too."

His one chance at getting out of here was to get under Eli's skin so much the veteran captain lost his cool and came after him. That way, he might be distracted enough for Sarah to jump in and get a fast kill. Once they were running, none of these other cowards would stand against them.

Well, not against Sarah, at any rate.

"Children, children," said Harden Grayspring, Lord Marshal of Wallace's Company as he stepped out of the crowd. He hopped between Eli and Sarah. "Sarah, put the blade away, and we'll talk like civilized murderers."

Tall and lithe, Harden wore his near-fifty years well, his honey-brown eyes full of light and energy. His clothes, on the other hand, were all onces—a once-purple coat, once-brown pants, hat, and shirt —long ago faded to gray. His brown skin stretched tight over his bones. He could have been Andosh or Pavinn. Most people mistook him for whatever they were.

"Only one way you get to make an example out of Keane," Sarah said. She did not sheath her broadsword. "And the rest of your captains don't seem to be backing you up. How do *you* want to play this out?"

"I can't have insurrection in the ranks, my girl," Harden said, sweeping an arm to indicate the mercenaries. "If we don't have our rules, then we're no better than the animals."

"You're really making this too easy," Keane said, thinking of a dozen animal-rectal comparisons for a mercenary lord marshal.

"Then change the rule," Sarah offered. "What's the benefit of being the boss if you can't be the one to tell everyone else what to do because some *rule* is more important than you are?"

A few chuckles broke out amongst the crowd.

Harden removed his wide-brimmed gray leather hat and scratched at his scalp through stringy gray hair. "Eli," he asked over his shoulder, "was the intestine thing for not obeying an order one of my rules or one of Wallace's?"

"Neither, sir," Eli answered. "That'd be from Burrfist's time."

"Really?" Harden twisted and stared at Eli. "It just sounds so much more like something Wallace would have done."

Eli shrugged.

"Regardless," Harden said and returned to Sarah, "it wasn't my rule, so it *should* be changed. Keane, for disobeying a direct order, you will be confined to the prisoner cart for three days. Do it again and I'll likely kill you on the spot. Do you understand me?"

"If I disobey another order, don't get caught," Keane replied.

"He's just impossible *not* to want to kill," Harden said to Eli.

"He gets it," Sarah replied, brows drawn and mouth downturned at Keane. "He'll do what he's told, *and* he'll shut his yap and make it easier for me to save his life,"—one eyebrow went up—"won't he?" Her sword disappeared beneath her cloak.

Keane looked away and waved a hand, dismissing the conversation. Harden would just try and find a different way to kill him when Sarah wasn't around. He wasn't the type to accept a denial for long.

No sense in prostrating himself to the old bastard just for a knife in the ribs.

Harden led Eli away, shaking his head and chuckling to himself. With the failure of any entertaining violence appearing, the soldiers walked off in search of their first two favorite pursuits—drinking and fucking.

As soon as she could no longer be overheard, Sarah leaned against the cart. "Do you think you can keep from making anyone else want to kill you for a few hours? I need to make arrangements."

Keane pulled himself upright and looked down at Sarah. "You can't tell me what to do. How many opportunities have I ever had to make fun of people from the safety and comfort of a place like this?"

"Do you want me to count?" She glanced around. "Where's Simon?"

"Oh no, not *that* halfwit." Keane shook his head. "We can't be that desperate."

"See you later. I'll bring some food or something in a couple hours. We'll discuss it more then."

"No more boiled leek and cabbage dinners, please," he called after her, retreating back. "All the beatings and threats have me gassy enough already."

2

DOGS OF WAR PLAYING POKER

ELI

Even a late-summer night could get cold in Northern Greenshade, and the rosy fire that warmed his face left Eli's backside cold and brittle feeling in the still air. He and the lord marshal sat together at one of the mercenary camp's few still-lit campfires and shared a bottle of whiskey while they tried to play cards. Everyone else had moved into their tents for the night.

The big glade more than accommodated the sprawling camp and seemed pleasant enough when they found it. Now it smelled like a cesspit.

"Stop frowning," Harden said. "You're making me constipated." He drew another card and flipped it over onto the pile between them. "You're a frost cock who can't stand the cold and a soldier who doesn't like camps. You're kinda disagreeable, you know that?"

"It weren't right to change the rules like that," Eli said, arranging his cards for the third time and making a draw. He put it into his hand and placed another on the pile. "Your go."

"It's my call if I want to keep Sarah alive. I'll thank you to keep your withered dick out of it unless you want it cut the hell off."

"Sarah?" asked Eli. "Keane's the one inna box. We coulda got

Sarah outta there. Probably. Anyway, it's Keane's life you saved, not his giant woman-thing protector."

"I hate that asshole," Harden said, frowning into his cards. "Hey, let's go kill him, and in the morning, everyone will think he just died in his sleep—which will be true if he's asleep when we stab him to death."

"You're drunk."

"So're you," Harden responded. "We kill Keane come morning, and you make sure Sarah stays well clear of it. Well clear."

"Sure, but you ain't making sense," Eli said. "Why change company law to save a guy you hate, if'n you're just gonna go kill him anyways?" Eli rubbed at his bleary blue eyes. "Crosscut," he announced, putting his hand face up beside the pile of cards. "Ain't like you to be stupid, so what's the move? Is all this just to kill Keane? Why do you care what happens to Sarah?"

Harden arranged his cards. "What do *you* care? Maybe I want to promote her. She'd make a better captain than you. Easier to look at, anyway. Capture." Harden put his fanned-out hand over Eli's and gathered the coins between them.

"Hagrim's stinking armpit. You led me into that on purpose, you old crag lion."

Tapping the side of his head, Harden said, "That's why I am the high and mighty lord marshal, and you are the lowly, crawling captain."

Opposite the fire and behind a line of dirty white tents, a bottle skittered across the ground, finding stones in the grass to bounce over. Both Harden and Eli looked up, but the fire rendered them both night-blind.

"Put that back," Harden said, his brows drawing together.

"You're a damn cheat," Eli said, pulling the coin out of his pocket and putting it back in the pile.

Harden's grin showed every tooth in his head. "That's *also* why I'm in charge."

3

AMADEO TAKES A LONG NAP

KEANE

"Where is Amadeo?" whispered Keane. Two hours before sunup the camp was silent—if you ignored the snoring, farting, and occasional crying sounds coming from the hundreds of small, dirty tents. Starlight shone through wispy clouds and lined Sarah's shape beside the prisoner cart, but their third conspirator was nowhere to be found.

"I don't know," Sarah answered. "We'll stop by his tent on the way out."

Keane tapped his fingers against iron studs in the wooden bars. "He was supposed to have gathered all the supplies. And a shirt for me. I told you we should have picked Simon for this."

Examining the lock on the door of the cart, Sarah turned her head and leaned down. "When I brought your food, you said Simon was 'too stupid to catch a fish out of his own asshole,' and that you'd rather work with someone unreliable and smart than someone loyal and stupid." She took hold of the lock and twisted, slow and steady.

"Well you went along with it."

"So I'm unreliable now, am I?" said Amadeo, stepping from the darkness. "You chickens got everything tied up without me? Maybe I should just go back to sleep."

"You've been napping long enough," Keane said. "Keep an eye out while Sarah unlocks the—"

A soft cracking noise interrupted Keane, and Sarah took a step back. The cart door swung open several inches.

"Thought you had a clever plan for getting the key off of Eli," Keane said.

Sarah dropped the big padlock, door hasp, and a fist-sized piece of torn wood to the ground. "I stand by that plan. It would have worked if I'd decided to do it."

Keane hopped out of the cart and stepped over the unconscious guard Sarah had coldcocked. He slipped on the shirt Sarah handed him but stuffed the folded leathers and scabbarded sword under one arm.

The three of them picked their way past soiled tents and discarded waste. In the still night air, the stink of stale alcohol rode the smells of unwashed bodies and urine, uniting to create an amazing stench.

"This way," Keane said, turning right.

"The horses are straight ahead," said Amadeo, stopping on the trampled grass between several haphazardly placed tents. "That's where the track is. Behind the tree line just there. You're going the wrong way."

"Oldam's kidney stones, Am, calm down," Keane whispered. "We're just making a little detour first. Ah, there we go."

Eighty feet or so to the left, Harden and Eli sat at a low campfire drinking and playing cards. Dead ahead loomed the object of Keane's attention, Harden's big command tent. Ten-by-fifteen feet, the sun-bleached blue canvas pulled against its frame, smelling of must and old beer.

"This is a good idea," Sarah said. Keane heard her smirk in the dark. "I like this idea."

"What are we doing?" asked Amadeo. "Why aren't we getting on the horses?"

Keane pulled Harden's tent flap open and waved the others in.

Dim orange light from a hanging hourglass-shaped jar of emberflies, along with the additional smell of spoiled meat, greeted them inside the lord marshal's tent. Keane ducked beneath Harden's map table and rolled up the filthy red rug that lay beneath it. He chuckled and hauled a battered wooden box with bronze fittings out of the hole dug into the dirt. Ten inches high, a little over a foot deep, and two feet wide, the box was heavy as hell with all the coinage inside it.

He pulled the box out of the hole and ran his hand across it. The back of his head pressed against the underside of the big map table. This seemed like the perfect compensation for nearly getting his guts yanked out.

"I can't believe Harden never considered that anyone might notice a hole under his tent in the exact same place every time we leave a campsite. I mean, the average mercenary *is* pretty goddamn stupid, but—ow, hey!"

A scuffle had broken out in the tent above Keane, and a dagger fell, narrowly missing his leg. An instant later, Amadeo's body fell to the ground, eyes wide and chest bloodied. Keane snatched the dagger and rolled backward, coming out from under the table with the blade in front of him.

Sarah wiped Amadeo's blood from her broadsword and glanced up. "Sorry. He was trying to stab you in the head. I guess he really wasn't that reliable." Her mouth went up in that half smile of hers, and she sheathed her sword. "You really *should* have picked Simon for this."

"Treacherous little fuck. He wanted to go back to bed anyway," Keane said, pushing Amadeo's fancy dagger behind his belt.

Sarah lifted the heavy wagebox onto her hip, making the coins inside slide to one end. With the tip of the broadsword in her other hand, she pushed aside the tent flap to make sure no one outside heard the commotion.

"You son of a goat-whoring shitsnake," whispered Keane. "You sand-brained... *traitorous*... tunny asshole!" He punctuated the sentence with hard leather-booted kicks to the corpse's stomach. "We"— *kick*—"got you"—*kick*—"this job! You were"—*kick*—"one of us!"

Leaning forward, Sarah looked out at the smaller tents sitting quietly in a haze of cold night air, cheap alcohol, and sweat. "I think he gets the point. Hide him and let's get going."

Keane kicked the form on the ground one more time. "Jerk," he said, dropping the dead man's head against a table leg. "All right." Keane stood up straight and wiped his hands on Harden's bed linens.

"Wait, let's roll him under the table," Sarah said, waving her heavy blade toward the bed. "If anyone wanders in before light, they might not see him. Could give us a little extra time."

Keane nodded and pushed Amadeo's body beneath the big table where it thumped into the shallow hole the wagebox had been in and replaced the threadbare rug over everything but Amadeo's head, which lolled against a table leg.

He stood, staring at his handiwork. No chance that Harden wouldn't notice the corpse there eventually, but it was a lot funnier for Keane to picture the old man finding a dead Amadeo where his money should be.

"There," Sarah said, "Now he's all comfy."

"You know, he was one of the best men in our squad. Hell, he still is for that matter, even dead," Keane said, lifting one of Amadeo's arms from under the rug and letting it drop. "The rest of them are pretty shitty. Simon's all right." Thinking of Simon, Keane smiled to himself. That kid would do anything to please, but he just wasn't a violent man. It took a special kind of bastard to be one of Harden's mercenaries. Like Amadeo... was.

Shoulda picked Simon.

"Stupid prick."

"You wanted him."

Keane frowned at her. "You can be right without being smug about it, you know."

"Does he look more... peaceful to you? Now that he's dead?" Keane asked. His leg bounced, betraying his eagerness to be gone.

"No, not really," Sarah answered. She turned her head sideways and frowned, her dark brows furrowed.

"I didn't think so either," Keane said. "I'm beginning to believe that's a myth."

"He looks kind of... like he ate some bad crabs?" said Sarah.

"I'm pretty sure I'm well past giving a shit *what* might be wrong with that stupid, dead catfucker," Keane said. "I'm leaving. I never even liked this guy."

"Hang on," Sarah said. She placed the battered box on the floor. With careful, practiced motions she wiped her blade again on her cloak and sheathed it. "Almost there," she said and grabbed a lengthy lock of black hair to stuff behind her braids. Reaching back, she checked the leather sleeve and pulled it up a little tighter.

"All pretty now?" Keane asked. "This is the slowest getaway I've ever been involved in."

By way of reply, Sarah narrowed her eyes and scowled. She picked the wagebox back up. "You want to carry it?"

"You're the beefy one," Keane said.

With careful and composed movements, Keane left the lord marshal's dust-and-sweat-smelling tent and slunk around the soldier's smaller tents and the guttered fires of the mercenary camp. Sarah, wooden wagebox under one thickly muscled brown arm, followed. They moved opposite the smoldering bonfire at the center of the camp where Keane could just see the gray-colored Lord Marshal Harden and the bald-headed Eli. The two old mercenaries sat colluding with a bottle of rye in the dark, their cards left in the dirt in front of them. Eli scowled in irritation.

Keane remembered when he and Sarah first ran into Harden. After years together as kids on the streets of Levale, they met up with Wallace's Company and decided to graduate from street urchins to mercenaries. The pair took Amadeo and as many of the old gang with them as would go and never looked back.

Not until recent events forced them to, at any rate.

Sarah stepped behind one of the soldiers' tents out of view of Harden and Eli. Her foot landed on the edge of an empty rum bottle, sending it skittering off into the dark. Both old men looked up at the noise and glared straight at Keane. His nerves jangled and froze his muscles stiff, leaving him standing in the open between a pair of tents, one with a wide brown smear of old blood across the back of it. His only chance was that the light of their fire, the dark he stood in, and their old eyes would prevent the two of them from recognizing him.

Keane gave them a sort of sick smile and waved, but the two men just scowled and went back to their conversation.

Thank Oldam's swinging stone cock, Keane thought.

"You're gonna get me killed," Keane hissed at Sarah, once he was out of sight. "And I don't *wanna* get killed."

They whispered to each other as they traversed the darkened campsite.

"You won't be any more killed than if we'd stayed," she said. "And this way would probably be quicker too. They *were* going to tie your guts to the prison cart, and then—"

"Aren't you a ray of sunshine?" Keane interrupted. "Can we please leave the murderous cutthroats now?"

"You never minded being amongst murderers before you thought they wanted to murder *you*," said Sarah.

"Well, I do now," Keane answered. "Oldam's rocky balls, come *on*."

Keane and Sarah left Wallace's Company camp and stepped through the tree line where their horses waited for them—unattended. Amadeo's horse and all of the supplies for the trip that were supposed to accompany it were nowhere to be seen.

"Shh." Keane tapped Sarah on the shoulder and pointed. Not fifty feet away, on the other side of a line of trees, stood three mercenaries watching the camp. The route Amadeo had been leading them toward would have carried them straight into an ambush.

"Asshole was trying to lead us straight into an ambush." Keane couldn't believe what thieves some people were.

Frowning, he considered his options. There was no way they could lead the horses away without attracting the three thugs' attention. That left removing them. But...

"Oh, right," Keane whispered to himself as he tiptoed behind Sarah, already stalking toward the ambushers.

While just as smart as Keane, Sarah's thinking tended to proceed in a more linear fashion. He thought in circles and she in sharp straight lines.

Keane clubbed his man in the back of the head with the silvered pommel of Amadeo's dagger and went to help Sarah. One man lay unconscious at her feet while the second pried at the steel-sinewed arm covering his mouth. His struggle was short-lived, and Sarah dropped him beside his companion. After satisfying himself that there were no more soldiers lying in wait, Keane returned to their horses.

Robert, an energetic chestnut stallion, nuzzled Keane's face as if to say that while Keane had been lollygagging about in a prison cart, apple time had *definitely* come and gone.

"Sorry, boy," Keane said, scratching the horse's neck. "I'm hungry too."

They led the animals another twenty feet through the trees and onto a double-rutted track dappled with moonlight falling through the leaves above. While Keane slipped into his leathers, Sarah secured the small but heavy wagebox to her mount, an even-tempered draft horse named Brownie, and wrapped a blanket around it. The two of them climbed up and rode away into the night.

4

THE JOYS OF FARMING AND WASTE-MANAGEMENT

KEANE

The pair spent the night riding their horses as fast as was safe through the woods along the narrow track. Neither spoke much. Sarah yawned constantly, but Keane was wound up. Every step jingled with Sarah's mail or the coins in the box, keeping him nervous.

"Just pisses me off, is all." Keane couldn't keep his thoughts off of Amadeo. "Making us kill him like that. Who does that to their friends?" The truth was he still felt guilty over misjudging which conspirator to enlist, and pointing out how unfairly treacherous Amadeo had been made him feel like it was less of his own fault.

"I know," Sarah said. "If he had started yelling instead of making a go for you, I might not have killed him, and he would have brought the whole camp down on our heads." They were both silent a moment, contemplating that thought.

"I bet he was reporting to Eli," Keane said, still unmoving. Keane used to like Captain Eli—looked up to him even. But the old man kept a paranoid close watch on anyone in the company who held a flicker of brains, and that included Keane and Sarah.

"Maybe," Sarah said. "But I'm hoping we never find out."

As the late-summer sun dawned, filling the sky with white light that did not yet crest the trees, the two of them broke from the woods and rode into a tiny hamlet.

Maybe two dozen wide wattle-and-daub structures lined either side of what might charitably be called a road ahead of them with a broad square in the middle. Long rows of growing vegetables— mostly beans and peas animated with toiling farmers—stretched out behind the dwellings. Typical of Greenshade, the farmers were white-skinned, strong-backed Andosh people. And typical of such places everywhere in the Thirteen Kingdoms, they looked dirty and joyless. In the distance beyond the working farmers, the wood bounded the fields.

From the stink, it had to be fertilizer day.

"You know," said Keane. "I bet these people would get more visitors to their village if they didn't fertilize everything in sight with their own personal waste. It smells like the bottom of a latrine in here."

"Maybe they don't want visitors," said Sarah. "Not everyone is as extroverted as you are."

"I'd settle for them just being as not covered in crap as I am," he answered. "I hope no one tries to shake my hand. Ugh."

Sarah looked over the little berg as the horses started nosing about for grass or unattended vegetables. "Waste not, want not. Let's rest the horses and get back on the track. Harden can't be that far behind."

"Harden can slide his own ass straight into the Undergates, for all I care," Keane said. "He has to be hours behind at least, *if* they even know we're gone yet, which I doubt." Whether it was true or not, it made Keane feel better to say it out loud.

"Did you forget where we left Amadeo?" Sarah asked. "You know how Harden is about his money. You think he'll walk in, check for the wagebox and say, 'Look at that. Dead guy under the table. I'll ask someone about it tomorrow.'" She stretched her long brown limbs, reaching up into the air, muscles taut.

Keane smiled and said, "Maybe we should have put him in Eli's bed. Could have bought us even more time if the old tunny was feeling randy." Keane turned to glance meaningfully at the familiar old wagebox behind Sarah's saddle concealed with a blanket. "Even money that Harden spots the wagebox not being in the hole before he notices the dead man on top of it. You know his priorities."

Harden counted out each mercenary's pay from that box once a month. Every man in the company spent long minutes staring at it, memorizing its beaten-up wood and dented bronze corners while waiting in line for their coin.

"No bet," Sarah said, leaning down and patting Brownie on the neck. "I don't see a water trough anywhere. Do you? These two have got to be thirsty."

Keane flicked the reins, causing Robert to dance sideways and away from Sarah. "You look for water. I'm going to go tell these fine people the truth about the terrible danger on its way and lie to them about what they can do to stop it!" Tapping the Wallace's Company insignia stitched to his leather jerkin, Keane whirled and rode into the village square, yelling for attention.

"See if you can get..." Sarah yelled after him, but Keane lost the rest of what she said under his own shouts. She didn't follow, but that was all right. The big warrior woman was absolutely the only person he needed on his side when the knives came out, but taking food and maybe a few coins from rubes was more Keane's bailiwick. His stomach rumbled at the thought of actual, cooked food, and a little graft was what he needed to take his mind off his nervousness about being followed.

"You there," Keane said as he rode up on a plain-dressed farmer carrying a conical basket of beans. The woman wore one of the gray-green felt acorn hats so popular in Greenshade, peaked on top in the woman's style, not rounded as a man's would be. Keane had once heard a nobleman refer to the commoners as mushrooms. "Hello, my dear. Could you please tell me where the hell I am?" he asked her with an ingratiating smile.

"This is Sheaf, sir," the graying woman said. Keane thought the "sir" came more from the sword on his hip than from any perceived status. "Nothing here to interest a great man such as yourself." She blinked as if expecting Keane to disappear. "Yellowbells comin' soon. Prob'ly wanna be movin' on afore they git here," she added with a hopeful smile.

Half moth, half bird, and all hungry, yellowbells swarmed the wood and grasslands of north and west Greenshade for three days every year, devouring the treetops and long grasses in gigantic, curling swaths. They ate anything made of vegetables but shunned animal materials. Thus, they would eat a cotton shirt right off your back, but a wool cloak would keep them at bay.

Mostly.

"That so?" asked Keane. He hated yellowbells, but he wasn't going to be chased off by them. "Where's your head man, or leader, or whatever?"

"Villein Grenan is in his rows," the woman said, putting down her basket and pointing into the working men and women laboring over their plants. "That one. Straw hat."

"Oh. Thanks," Keane said, his face screwed up in distaste. No one wanted to enter the crops while the fertilizing was going on, especially with the sun coming up, but that was the way his life went these days. Keane directed Robert onto the strip of grassy divider between the villein's rows and his neighbor's, and the horse gingerly plucked his way toward a sturdy man bent over a procession of tiny pea plants.

"Ho there," Keane said, trying to sound friendly. "You the villein of this... um... town?"

The man straightened and turned to Keane, raising his head to see beneath the wide brim of a ratty straw hat. The man's large red face made Keane think of a boiled fist.

"I am," Villein Grenan answered.

"Right then, I am Captain Keane. The large, muscular woman over there is Captain Sarah," Keane said, giving himself and Sarah a field promotion on the spot. "Afraid we're going to have to ask you to pull all these people out of the fields for a little while." He brushed travel dust off his leather leggings. "My partner and I are the vanguard for Wallace's Company. Perhaps you've heard of us?" Keane tapped the insignia on his breast, a pair of yellow golden coins, and waited for the inevitable panic.

"Nope," said Grenan.

"Really?" asked Keane, taken aback. "Wallace's Company? Four hundred bloodthirsty mercenaries? Scourge of the Thirteen Kingdoms?"

"Sorry. Maybe you're too new?"

"Oh, come on!" Keane said, slapping his thigh. "We've been in Greenshade for *six years* now. You do know you live in Greenshade, right?"

"Sure, yeah," the villein said. "Sorry, I thought you said *Waller's* Company. But no, Wallace's Company. Right. Very scary guys."

"Now you're just trying to placate me," Keane said, frowning.

"You seemed upset."

"No, I'm fine," Keane said, waving it off. "But we need to get everything of value together now, so it's all out in the square before the company gets here. Otherwise, they'll tear the tits off the whole place looking for it."

With a frown of his own, Villein Grenan said, "Yeah. You know, no offense, but I hope the King's Swords catch and hang the lot of you."

Keane sighed and slumped in his saddle. "I know how you feel."

An hour later, the farmers were still piling possessions in the square, but Sarah had convinced Keane to call a halt to the slow and orderly ransacking. He ordered the villagers to make piles according to types of goods with anything he and Sarah might want to take being put in a wagon yoked to Robert and Brownie.

This included none of the fecal-smelling vegetables.

While he supervised the work, Keane noticed a young man, perhaps fourteen or so, approaching with a pitchfork. It was the boy's stance that turned Keane's head. Tense. Hostile.

Just before the boy raised his weapon, Keane spied Sarah twenty feet away with her hand on Villein Grenan's shoulder. The boy's round eyes stared out from his wide red face, and his jaw worked in worried frustration.

"We don't need a pitchfork, boy." Keane sidestepped the thrust, and iron tines bit into the wooden side of the wagon. The boy squinted and heaved, effort reddening his face further and making it look like a boiled fist. He yanked and pulled the pitchfork free, hitting himself in the chest with the haft.

Keane took the opportunity to hop in and break the boy's nose with a single careful punch. The kid screamed and dropped his pitchfork. His hands flew to his bleeding face. Tears covered his ruddy cheeks, and he turned and ran into one of the homes where an older, roundish woman took him in her arms and pulled him inside.

Villein Grenan turned to Sarah. "Thank you. He's a stupid boy."

Sarah smiled back at him. "He really is."

In short order, Sarah and Keane were on the wagon, prepared to leave. He stood to give the villagers a warning about what was coming next.

"Good work, everyone. You should be very proud of yourself—" A wrinkled old woman with a patched blue dress and a faded kerchief over her hair reached up and pushed an uncommonly adorable black and pink piglet into his arms.

"Oh, thank you. Right, uh... good then," Keane said as Sarah reached over and took the wriggling animal from him. "So, just leave all of this stuff out here. Don't be goddamn dumbasses when Wallace's Company shows up, and they probably won't kill anyone."

Leaning out the other side of the wagon, Sarah whispered to the villein, "If you can, I'd get everyone out of the village until the company is long gone, just in case."

Grenan nodded his fist face in answer. "I'd say thanks, but well... not really."

5

YELLOWBELLS

KEANE

"That was an interesting waste of time," Sarah said, shifting on the seat and moving her shoulders around to keep her mail from constricting. The piglet on her lap dozed, its tiny hooves in the air. Absently, she played with the creature's feet with a fingertip.

"We needed supplies. They had supplies," Keane answered, pointing into the cart with a thumb. "Plus, wagon."

"We could have just taken a few things and been on our way. There was no need to make such a production out of it." Sarah looked up, one brow arched and a half smile on her lips. "You wanted them to be ready when Harden got there."

"They aren't ever gonna be ready for that," Keane said, narrowing his eyes and gazing at the track ahead. Trees leaned out of the way, chopped back and pushed aside by generations of nameless farmers riding the same twin ruts they now did. "But I guess there's a chance now he might take pity and not burn the whole thing down."

"Whatcha looking at? Worried about big folk out here?" Sarah asked. "We're hardly in the wild lands."

"Me? No," Keane said, still looking ahead. "I doubt anything that horrific could get close without you smelling it first. Unless it was hiding behind a farm like that last one, that is. Just... looking."

He caught sight of a woodswife. Her wide eyes and shy smile following his movement. This one towered a good seven feet, and her long, willowy limbs swayed in the breeze. If he mentioned the fey creature to Sarah, it would jump back into the roots of its oak. They did not seem to like women, and most members of the opposite sex thought them lies invented by drunken or foolish men. As far as Keane knew, no one had ever gotten close enough to determine if they were dangerous.

Just another of the world's mysteries to ponder.

The trip continued for nearly an hour in comfortable, lazy silence. At some point, they left the woods behind for the tall grasses.

Starting from her languid doze, Sarah stretched, inhaled deeply, and asked, "So... genius, what kind of name for a horse is *Robert*?"

Keane shook his head to clear it. He had been dozing at the reins. "What's wrong with Robert?" he asked back, yawning. "My dad's name was Robert."

"You hate your dad."

"Well, yeah," said Keane. "He was a goddamn asshole. But what about *Brownie*? That's just silly. You might as well call her Cookie. Or Sandwich. Oo... we have sandwiches." He twisted around to ransack their food packs.

"That horse is a bay, anyway," he said as he pushed aside a salted ham hock.

Sarah rolled her eyes. "Ugh. No way. Brownie sounds a *lot* better than Bay-ie."

Keane pretended to consider it, but then another thought popped up. "Maybe we should go back to one of the Pavinn countries now that we're on the run. Plenty of fighting that way. Must be mercenaries around."

They would fit in well there. Mercenaries, as a rule, gave little thought to race, but Keane and Sarah's brown Pavinn skin would not stick out like it did in Greenshade. Sarah often talked about visiting the Pavinn parts of the world, the Paradisal Islands in particular.

Sarah frowned. "Pirates, maybe. In the islands, but I don't know how to sail."

"You could learn," Keane said. "We've spent so much time up here with the frost-cocked Andosh, I think we've forgotten what jackasses they are. Sure be a lot easier for you anywhere else than here. Greenshade's the *least* misogynist of all of them, and they still think a person's only value is the weight of his pecker." He scratched his head. "And they all wear those stupid little hats. What's *that* about —mushrooms"

"I've never been to the Paradisals," Sarah said. Keane had never been to the island nation either, although its lawless reputation seemed inviting.

"Sure," he said. "Or Sedrios, or Arlea. Even Rousland is half Pavinn. That'd have to be an improvement."

"You think mercenary companies in Rousland would have more than one woman?" Sarah asked. "It'd be nice to have some company"—she sighed—"if we are set on being mercenaries."

"I wouldn't think they'd have anyone like you," he answered. "You are one of a kind. And I wouldn't be good for anything besides mercenary work." He glanced at her sidelong. Sarah was an attractive woman if you were a man who didn't scare too easy—large brown eyes, full lips that smiled often, and big, round shoulders that could lift that man up over her head and toss him off a cliff if he got too familiar. She wasn't normal, he knew, but they had been inseparable since they met on the streets when he was around seven.

"One of a kind," Sarah said with a smile. "As are you, thank Al-Dagos."

"It's why we're so well suited to one another," said Keane.

"Maybe we are," Sarah said. "We both seem to have pissed off the leader of the biggest active mercenary company in the Thirteen Kingdoms without a clear plan of escape."—she frowned and looked around, squinting—"or apparently, any idea where we're going."

"That stone licker deserved it," Keane said, his face drawing tight. "If killing him would have hurt him half as much as taking his money, I'd have done that instead."

"He wasn't being fair," she said.

"*Of course* he wasn't being fair," Keane said. "Did I disobey an order? Yes, I did. Has everyone else in the whole besotted company done the same thing? Yes, they have. They got fines. I got the intestines-and-cart thing. We should've left a long time ago. He did us a favor if you think about it."

"I wish you'd tell me what he said to you. You know, before," said Sarah. She reached out to touch him on the shoulder but withdrew the hand before she did. Her face drew up, pensive.

"You really don't," he responded.

Sarah said nothing and stared at the occasional trees passing them by in the fields of tall grass. They were making better time now that they were out of the dense woods. Of course, so would Wallace's Company when *they* got to the grasslands. "Every time I think of—"

"Then don't," Sarah interrupted, still looking at trees. "Think of it, I mean. I'm not. And Keane, I'm *glad* we left."

Neither of them spoke for the next few minutes. The piglet yawned, arching its back and extending thumb-length legs straight out all without opening its eyes. It slumped back into Sarah's lap. Sarah's face softened, and she smiled a bit as her gaze returned to the infant animal.

"I figure we'll keep straight past the north bend up ahead," Keane said, the piglet's toy-sized yawn having broken the sullen silence. "This track runs up against the Greenshade River west of Pippiton. We can stop and resupply there. Maybe an opportunity will become more obvious if we haven't figured anything out by then... which seems sorta likely."

"We can always cross over and go north," Sarah said.

"Into Tyrrane? No way," Keane said. "That place is horrible."

"It's just a place," said Sarah, shrugging. "Like a pub."

"It's just a place for evil degenerates who worship demons and eat babies," Keane said, furrowing his brow to show Sarah he really meant it. "And they all dress like they're on the way to their own funerals. Even the ground there is black. And it's too cold. I thought we were going south somewhere. Didn't we just decide that?"

"Tyrraneans worship the Alir, just like all the Andosh do," Sarah said. "The same gods they worship here in Greenshade."

"When King Oldam plucked out his eyes and cast them into the heavens to keep watch over Andos, it was Tyrrane he was watching out for," Keane said with the air of a lecturing priest addressing a truculent child. "And when he turned himself to stone on the path to the Alireon to protect the other gods, it was Tyrrane he was protecting them *from*."

"I'm pretty sure the Tyrraneans aren't trying to invade the Alireon and catch the gods with their knickers down," Sarah said.

"Then you *admit* they eat babies."

Sarah rolled her eyes, one side of her mouth curling up again.

"I could eat babies if that's really where you want to go," Keane said as he leaned back against the front wall of the wagon. "Did we get any salt back there in... where were we again?"

"Sheaf," answered Sarah. "And no. What would peasants be doing with salt?" A pound of salt was worth more than a typical Andosh peasant would see in a lifetime.

"Tyrrane's off the table then," Keane said, waving his hand back and forth. "I'm not eating babies without salt. Now *piglets*, on the other hand..."

Sarah gasped and placed her callused hands over the tiny animal's ears. "Don't you dare. Besides, it's too late to eat this pig. She already has a name."

"Oh yeah?" Keane asked. "What's her name?"

"Uh..." Sarah said, stammering for time. "Her name is... uh..."

"What's her goddamn name?" Keane asked again. He tried to look stern.

"Her name is *Pig*," Sarah said, laughing and raising her voice, causing the piglet to jump and wiggle as it attempted to right itself.

"Mm-hmm," Keane said with a sly smile. "Exactly the same name as all of the other pigs we've eaten. There's no help for it. It's the fork for you, little Miss Pig."

"This is so sad," said Sarah, picking up the piglet and rubbing noses with it.

Keane gave a big, showy sigh. "Stop. I am not some heartless Tyrranean baby-eating monster. I shall name the pig and make her safe from being made delicious." He drew himself up in his seat. "Slago's a good name, but she doesn't look much like a flying shark that would eat your soul and transport it to paradise. What about Magda, Hagrim's wife?"

"Magda's an Andosh goddess," Sarah said. "This pig is Pavinn. Also—goddess of insanity."

"And beauty. But alright, no Andosh gods. What about Allz the Shining?" Keane said, smirking.

Sarah gave Keane a flat stare. "Allz is Darrish. *And* a boy. It's like you're not trying at all."

"Wait," Keane said, "I have it. Let's call her... Robert Also."

"Over your dead body," Sarah said, brows coming together.

"Give it up, warrior," Keane said. "Everyone who isn't covered in shit for a living knows Robert is a genius name. And as we both know, I *am* a genius."

Sarah lifted the piglet once more and looked into its eyes. "Your name is Genius Junior. Oh look, Keane, she's got your nose!"

"No," Keane said, though he already knew he was talking to himself.

"And she's got your belly."

"Absolutely no."

"You even *smell* the same!"

"She *is* a beauty, isn't she?" Keane said.

Sarah raised her hand for silence and cocked her head. Keane pulled back just enough to stop their horses. For several seconds they sat that way before Sarah grimaced and said, "Yellowbells."

Keane dove into the back of the wagon and rummaged madly for anything to cover himself and the horses with. Sarah grabbed a long-eared leather hat and a cowhide rug and wrapped herself and Genius Junior in it.

"Dumbass, know-it-all farmer woman," he growled.

"What?" asked Sarah.

Finding a cache of wool blankets, Keane ran up and threw them over the horses. He could hear the yellowbells now—a low, thrumming hum that vibrated in his stomach. They weren't dangerous in and of themselves, but they were...

Well, they were *here*.

Keane dove and rolled under the wagon as the first of the yellowbells buzzed into view. Three inches long with feathered bodies that buzzed on yellow and black moth wings that beat too fast to see, they zipped through the few trees like arrows. At first, there were only two and then twenty. The sky went black as the main body of the swarm, flying low above the trees and grass, moved over—and under—their wagon.

"Ow!" shouted Keane as one of the tiny beasts bit through his collar and into his neck. He'd forgotten to take off the damn cotton shirt beneath his armor, and the feathered fuckbugs were aiming right for it. He tore the collar off his shirt with frantic speed and threw it, already covered with wriggling insect forms, as far away as he could.

Sarah laughed and climbed off of the wagon. She tried to calm Brownie, who whinnied her panic and pulled against the traces. If either of the horses knocked off their blankets, they could get scared enough to do themselves some real damage.

Counting to three, Keane ran out from under the wagon and grabbed Robert's blanket just as it slipped off. He stood still and held the wool around the animal's head, whispering into its flaring nostrils. The yellowbells continued to bite, but other than flinching, he ignored them. Sarah, still grinning and holding Genius Junior against her stomach, threw a heavy arm over Brownie's neck and calmed the more docile beast.

"Ouch—dammit!" Keane yelled. "Shut up. Stop laughing. Why do these stupid things never bite you? That's not normal! Ouch! *Stupidshitsticklittledemons!*"

"Dunno," Sarah said as Keane wriggled and slapped. The noise of the little creatures drowned out anything else she might have said.

Two minutes later, the swarm passed. Keane released his horse. Every bit of exposed skin was dotted with tiny red wounds. He inspected Robert, who stood and stamped with wide, crazed eyes, and removed the yellow-splattered blankets. Sarah did the same for Brownie. The swarming moth-birds ate acres of grass or woodland at a time and excreted at a similar rate. Having ruined everything in their path, they would continue to fly west until sated. Then they would return, docile and full, to burrow beneath the soil and lay their eggs, setting up the whole thing to happen again the next year.

Keane wrinkled his nose and tossed the soiled blankets into the now-leafless trees.

"Why is it not enough that these things swarm all over the place, eat trees down to the dirt, and bite like hell," Keane said, his voice rising with his irritation, "but they also have to shit on *everything*?" All around him spread yellow-spotted desolation. Grass gone. Trees naked and shivering in the wind.

"Oldam's weary stone taint, I *hate* those things."

Sarah, smiling, held a dead yellowbell in one hand and cradled a curious Genius Junior in the other, "People gotta eat, birds gotta fly, yellowbells gotta poop. This has been a real day for you and excrement, hasn't it?" Her smile turned to a frown of concentration as she lifted the small, winged animal to her face. "I wonder if these are birds or bugs?"

"How could anyone possibly care?" Keane asked, wiping off the sides of the wagon to little effect.

"Well, that's a shame." Keane lifted the leather tarp Sarah had thrown over the wagon's contents. "They didn't get any of the mushroom hats the villagers insisted we take."

"They don't really swarm everywhere, you know," Sarah said, turning the yellowbell over in her hand and showing it to the baby pig, who snorted in approval. "It's kinda rare to see them like this. It doesn't last that long, and there aren't many swarms—two or three at the most."

"I feel so lucky," Keane said, his voice flat. Shrugging in defeat, he threw the rag he'd been using on top of the discarded blankets.

"We are," Sarah said. "Lucky, I mean. Most people never get to see yellowbells swarm. I think this must be a good omen."

Keane looked down at his hands, bleeding from a dozen tiny punctures each, and at his yellow bird-bug-poop-spattered chest and arms. "Well this is my fifth time being so 'lucky'—and they only do that for what, three goddamn days a year?" In the wagon, he found a clean dress of blue cotton beneath a crate of shoes—why had those idiots given him a crate of shoes?—and wiped the blood from his face and hands on it. "Do they have yellowbells on the Troll Coast? I bet they don't."

"Just feral Andosh tribes, giants, and, well, *trolls*," Sarah replied.

"Enormous improvement," Keane said, not entirely certain if he was being sarcastic or not. "Let's go be mercenaries *there*."

6

GRAYSPRING HANDLES THE DISCUSSIONS HIMSELF

ELI

The late-afternoon sun turned the world honey colored as Captain Eli and the first of the mercenary company trotted on horseback out of the nearby wood and into the tiny hamlet, an army at their backs.

He rode ahead with the Lord Marshal Harden Grayspring. The afternoon sun shone off Eli's bald head while Harden's greasy gray hair stirred in whatever breeze could reach beneath the wide-brimmed leather hat. The buzzing thrum of yellowbells had only just moved on to the west, but this little farming community had been spared.

Pity the voracious creatures were now the least of their worries.

The other captains preferred to ride well behind, hidden amongst their men, like the cowardly bastards they were. Harden was Eli's commander and his good friend, but to be honest, the man was in the foulest of humors. It would have suited Eli to ride back a bit himself, though his conscience wouldn't have abided it. *A man doesn't abandon his friends in time of need, does he?*

The populace of the little village wisely kept in their homes, betraying no appearance of even existing. Up ahead, a wide-shoul-dered fellow stood in the slanted sunlight between the deepening shadows of the farmhouses. He resembled nothing so much as a great slab of pink stone. He was pale skinned and reddened by the sun. The way he rested with his hands on his hips, seemingly unconcerned by the hundreds of ill-mannered and well-armed men walking into his little mud splat of a nothing town made Eli nervous. The captain had seen a lot in his time, and people who ought to be panicked and begging for their lives who just stood there like you were running late to dinner, smelled like a trap to him.

"Calm down," said Harden as if reading Eli's thoughts. "Even if it is a trap, they're just farmers. I hope they *do* try us."

"Yeah, well..." Eli said, looking left and right, "just don't like killing folk I don't hafta."

The sun over Harden's shoulder cut the man's already gaunt face into stark gold and black, completely obscuring his eyes. "We've never *had* to kill anyone," he said.

Eli hated it when Harden got all philosophical and creepy like that. *That kind of bullshit is for spineless book people and women, not fighters.* He sighed and slowed his horse as they approached the man standing in the square. "Well, let's just see what this dirt face is about 'fore we go making pronouncements on who needs killing," Eli whispered. "Maybe he's up to something, or maybe he's just stupid."

"I hope stupid means I get to live," the man said, removing his ratty straw hat. "I'm here to help."

Eli frowned into his graying beard. The wide man stood in front of—*what was going on here?*—a pile of wooden furniture, a pile of farm implements and metal tools, and a pile of food that rested in the road. Loaves of bread sat stacked beside joints of meat, and those sat next to a long table with a dozen pots of what smelled like cabbage that had been boiling since Oldam tore the world from his mother's breast and threw it spinning into the sky.

He pressed a heel against his old roan, and the stallion walked over to the farmer. Harden's gray followed and stepped up to Eli's left.

"What's going on here?" Eli asked, letting the gravel rattle around in his voice. His men liked to tease him for using the "voice" like that. But it scared the commoners, and that meant fewer folk had to die.

Eli considered it an irritation that this big fellow seemed entirely undisturbed.

"Everything is laid out just the way you like it," he said as if it were the most obvious thing in the world. "Just like your vanguard told us to."

"Vanguard?" asked Eli. Beside him, he could hear a low growl coming from deep in Harden's throat. Behind them, more and more soldiers filtered out of the trees and into the village.

"Aye. A Pavinn pair. Skin like yours," the big man said, indicating Harden. Eli was from Coldspine, where the men were big, pale, and hard as cold steel. "Young man, kinda tall, and a giant of a woman even bigger'n him. Pretty face. Never saw a lady warrior before."

"Where are they now?" Harden asked, his voice, husky and low, coming from beneath the brim of his dusty hat. His skinny nag chuffed at the farmer, warning him against getting too close.

"Oh, they went on ahead," the burly farmer said as if unaware how close to him death now sat. "Took the money and some supplies and said to tell you hi."

Harden turned to Eli and nodded. The balding old mercenary knew what that nod meant, and the weight of it settled on him like a stone on his chest. But it didn't pay to stand against the tide when you knew it was going to carry you along anyway. The man who lived was the man who was right. Everyone else was a body in the river.

"Burn it down!" Eli shouted to the mercenaries already moving amongst the poor buildings. "Pull everyone out inna street and torch the rest. Don't hurt no one you ain't gotta, but them people gave help to the traitors, and now they're gonna pay for it!" He closed his eyes and sighed. The gods, knew he, hated this kind of shit. A fair fight was one thing, and an unfair one was even better, but dragging women and babies out of their beds to be—

"Dammit." The big farmer's face fell when Eli shouted Harden's wishes, and he shook his head from side to side. "We didn't know they was traitors. They said they was with you."

Eli scowled down from his saddle at the burly farmer, as if his face could bring every devil the Undergates had on offer. "You keep your damn mouth shut. You wanna burn too?"

The man paled and took a half step back. He said nothing.

Harden slid out of his saddle and walked his horse forward. Eli followed suit, leading his own. The tiny hamlet—*what was this place even called, anyway?*—was torn open in fury and sadistic glee by the men of Wallace's Company. Never requiring much of an excuse to express violence and greed, they were all too happy to indulge themselves now that they actually had one. The raucous destruction went on for only a few moments, however, before bewildered-looking soldiers were left standing or walking around while they searched the already-flaming debris.

"Is there a problem, Captain Darkling?" Harden asked of a well-dressed Andosh man with a pointed beard. The fellow's careful tailoring attempted to obscure his slight paunch. "Where is the screaming? There is generally screaming at this point."

Darkling pulled at the pointed beard on his chin and leaned sideways, trying to spot something just out of his view. He sighed and looked up at Harden. "I'm sorry, Lord Marshal. The village appears entirely empty of population"—he gestured at the large, white-faced farmer—"other than our good friend here. The men were really looking forward to having some women for the night too."

The big villager's face regained some of its customary red, but he still did not move.

"This'd be Keane and Sarah's doing, sir," said Eli. "The two of 'em musta told these folks to leg it 'fore we got here." Although he could see the situation frustrated Harden, who required a target to focus his anger on, Eli was secretly glad the villagers had fled and gotten themselves safe. Now in his third decade as a mercenary, Eli's conscience was bruised enough.

Smoke from burning thatching rolled out over the rows of foul-smelling vegetables. Flames reached into the sky, stretching to burn it too.

"No, Sarah did this," Harden said as he removed his grayed hat and dug his fingers into his scalp. "She's better than him. Keane isn't the type to care." He slapped the dust from his faded purple coat and massaged his temples through his thinning hair.

Leaning over, he inspected all three piles of the farmers' possessions. "You know," he said, "from such a map speck, this is really some nice loot. We can't use much more than the food, but still, their hearts were in the right place. I think I'm beginning to regret burning their lives down."

The farmer jumped as the timbers from one of the first houses collapsed inward and sent a gout of fire roaring into the air.

"I'm sure they'll rebuild, good as new," Eli said, though he thought that perhaps five minutes ago would have been a more appropriate time for this sentiment, even if it was sarcastic. "Of course, while we's tarrying here, our traitors is gettin' away."

Harden didn't stand, but his eyes flicked up to Eli's face. He picked up a brass mechanical clock and straightened. "I don't suppose you could have thought of that five minutes ago?"

Eli opened his mouth to reply, and then closed it. Shaking his head, he climbed back astride his horse and watched the mercenary army destroy the tiny town of Whatever-It-Was.

7

SARAH AND KEANE TRY TO FEED A
BABY PIG

KEANE

Glowing clouds of stars floated like sunlit dust motes over the field where Keane and Sarah stopped to rest. Although neither of the mercenaries wanted to camp, Robert and Brownie showed no interest in carrying on in the dark, and Robert, in particular, strayed more and more often from the track to munch on the tall grasses and stall out. The decision was reached to sleep for a few hours and head back out before daybreak. It was almost certainly less time resting than Wallace's Company would spend.

Almost.

They traveled a half mile or so southeast of the track to camp and hunkered down behind a slight decline. While they couldn't see the track from there, they also couldn't be seen which Keane judged more important.

Sarah stood in the center of their little circle of beaten-down grass, holding an emberfly jar out in front of her. She spoke to the sky in a happy, sing-song voice.

"Be my light, and I'll be yours. Bring me colors, I'll bring you doors. Don't ask when, I won't ask why. Be my light, pretty emberfly."

Every child in Greenshade and Arlea, and most in Rousland, knew the nursery rhyme to bring the emberflies, although only one in twenty could manage it. Even those capable often required multiple tries to pull one into the hourglass-shaped jars.

Three glowing flies appeared out of the dark and zipped into the jar. Sarah twisted on the metal lid and set the jar in the center of their camp. She sat down next to it.

Keane had never heard of anyone pulling more than a single fly in at a go, but there was a lot about Sarah that wasn't normal. It was one of the few things they didn't talk about.

He untied his jerkin and took it off, frowning down at the tatters of his shirt. The yellowbells had gotten under the leather in places and chewed rents into it, or they'd been crushed and left broad yellow stains everywhere. His leathers chafed now at the holes, and the shirt smelled like sharp, tangy bug guts.

He threw the shirt into the grass.

"Looks like Genius Junior is hungry," Keane said, distracting himself by watching the tiny pig root beneath Sarah's calf. "I don't think we were intended to keep her as a pet." He scratched at the welts on his bare shoulders and chest.

"Well, I'm certainly not going to eat your only daughter," replied Sarah. "Though I'm not sure what I'm supposed to feed her. A lifetime of soldiery has not prepared me for babysitting duty." She picked up the piglet, who squealed in a small, angry voice. "I'm getting tired of calling her Genius Junior. How about Gennie?"

"All those boobs and you can't even feed one itty-bitty pig?"

Sarah scowled. "They don't work that way, moron. I'd have to be... forget it. I'm not explaining this to you. Did the farmers give us a skin of milk?

"No. There's some cheese. Will that do?"

"How do you think cheese is the same as milk?" Sarah asked. "This is a baby. It can't chew cheese. It needs to drink."

"Hey, I have a gross idea," Keane said. He hopped up and rummaged around in the back of the wagon. "Here ya go."

"I said she couldn't eat... cheese." Sarah took the items from Keane. "You know, that could work. Here, you take her for a minute."

While Keane made a show of looking at anything other than

Sarah, the large woman took bites of soft white cheese, chewed them, and spat them into an empty wineskin. When she had enough, she mixed in a little water and poked a tiny hole in the leather with her dagger.

Keane handed the infant animal back. Sarah placed it in the crook of her right arm and pressed the skin up against its snout. For an instant, the piglet appeared confused. Sarah squeezed the skin to push out a few drops of the cheese mixture, and Genius Junior dove right in.

Amid the grunting and smacking, Keane shook his head and smiled. "Gennie is a grand name."

"Hi, um, everybody," came a man's voice from the grass.

Gennie squealed as Sarah leapt to her feet and drew her sword. Keane pulled Amadeo's dagger and barreled into the grass, catching the intruder around the middle and bearing him to the ground.

"Don't kill me!"

Sarah caught Keane's arm as he yanked the dagger down toward the man's face. He stopped pushing when he realized the figure beneath him wasn't fighting back.

"Simon?" Keane asked. "What are you doing out here?" He jumped up and stared out over the tops of the grass. "Oldam's cross-eyed testicles! Is the company behind you?"

Simon, flat on his back, pushed himself up on his elbows. "No, no. You's safe as pillows. They's miles from here. I been scouting ahead. Looking for you two."

"And now that you've found us?" Keane returned his attention to the clean-shaven young mercenary. Simon wore dirty clothing and ragged armor, but his innocence shined through it.

"Uh, I guess I'm telling you the comp'ny's looking for you?"

Sarah sheathed her sword and held a hand out to Simon. "Are you going to tell anyone you found us out here?"

"No ma'am," Simon answered as he grabbed her hand and pulled himself up. "But I was hoping maybe I could come along. We been friends a long time, and I don't really like being a soldier much. I reckon we got that in common, too."

"Too?" Keane asked.

"You know—like how your daddy threw you away, and my daddy threw me away? We talked about it over the fire that night. After Gullhome."

The memory of that night sent chills down Keane's spine. He *did* recall something about a quiet conversation while huddled around the fire. It bothered him that Simon remembered it so well, while for Keane, it was no more than a blurry feeling.

The abusive bastard with the dubious distinction of being Keane's father drank himself to death when Keane reached six years of age. The next morning, the small boy had hidden in a cart full of beets headed for Levale and never looked back. He met Sarah there, and the two of them—and assorted other ne'er-do-wells—grew up on the streets until the day they met Harden.

He really should have picked Simon after all.

Swallowing the lump in his throat, Keane put a hand on Simon's shoulder. "You can't. If you came with us, Harden would know exactly where to look when you didn't return. You have to go back and say you couldn't find anything."

Simon frowned and nodded. "Yeah, that's the smart play, I s'pose. You always was the smartest, Keane."

Sarah stepped forward and hugged him. "It's the only play. Good luck, Simon."

As Simon walked back into the shadows, head hung and shoulders hunched, Keane called after him.

"Hey Simon, you think I could borrow your shirt?"

8

THE WELL-KNOWN HOSPITALITY OF PIPPITON

KEANE

Sarah and Keane stood in the central square of a medium-sized and well-ordered town, surrounded by well-ordered buildings and dozens of busy people in a well-ordered rush. Sarah watched the crowd, calm as a stone in the sun, while Keane fretted and paced back and forth in front of a gray-haired and unamused-looking woman. A noonday sun blazed white and hot in a brilliant blue sky, cotton puffery floating by on a lazy track east.

Some of the crowd, pole arms at the ready, watched Sarah in return.

"Captains Keane and Sarah? I know you are in a hurry, but I am afraid this is going to take at least another hour. Pippiton is not a large town, but to collect *everyone's* valuables requires some degree of organization." The elderly rivan of Pippiton, Evelyn Kibbage was her name, locked gazes with Keane who was at least six inches taller. Yet somehow, standing as they were in the streets of the tidy little township, Keane couldn't help but feel he was the one being talked down to.

"What did I tell you?" whispered Sarah.

It probably didn't help that about a dozen of Kibbage's brown-cloaked and capped soldiers stood at a not-so-discreet distance, scowling at him and Sarah as if they were common thieves. It was unnerving.

Still, Sarah stared right back at them, leaving Keane free to concentrate his nervous attention on the businesslike and portly rivan. With her hair up in a bun, she dressed in prim but functional clothes—a white shirt with a brown vest and skirt. Both her callused hands and well-tanned face told of a lifetime of working out-of-doors.

"What's a rivan?" asked Keane, trying not to think about the soldiers. "I've heard it before, but no one's ever told me what it means."

"Women aren't allowed to be mayors in Greenshade," Kibbage replied, "but the people of this town picked me to run it for fifteen years now. *Rivan* is an old-world term. Means a leader that tears her followers apart. King Rance picked it to describe me, thinking maybe it'd turn folks away. Might've too, if anyone knew what the hell it actually meant."

"You must be something special," Keane said with a smile. "I guess I'm not alone in my stupidity."

Kibbage narrowed her eyes and gave Keane an appraising look. She did not respond.

"You know we're only trying to help you here, right?" Keane asked. Men and women in their felt caps went about their business all around Keane and Kibbage, barely glancing their way. "This is a beautiful place. Nice little shops and houses all lined up like whores when the army gets paid. It looks as if it's hardly ever been sacked."

"We're very close to the border," Rivan Kibbage replied. "Pippiton's welfare is seen to by Greenshade *and* Tyrrane."

Keane meant to be threatening to Kibbage—he didn't expect the older woman to threaten him back. It hardly mattered. He was planning on being gone well before the rivan's implication became relevant. Harden spent years doing just what he and Sarah were doing right now. Roll up to a town, demand everything of value, and move on. Nobody got so much as a skinned knee out of it. The only difference was that when Harden showed up, he had his army with him.

"Maybe we could just collect whatever cash you've already gathered, and you could pile everything else here in the market for when the troops show up," Keane said. The buildings in Pippiton were low, one or two stories at best, and the streets wider than most towns. On a bright day such as this one, Keane felt exposed. "Y'know, if this has to be so goddamn slow..."

The old rivan glanced up at Sarah again, her eyes a pale, clear blue. She'd been doing so ever since Keane and Sarah arrived. People did that. Sarah dominated with height alone and possessed an unnerving amount of muscles beneath her womanly physique.

She was a lot to take in.

"I still have a hard time believing Harden Grayspring would condone this," Rivan Kibbage said. "This is not our arrangement."

"The lord marshal is a bit... fluid in his interpretation of his arrangements," Keane said. "At least no one is getting killed here."

"That's a short stick to measure with, young man," she replied.

"Hey, is anyone thirsty?" Keane said, clapping his hands together. "Sarah?"

"I could drink," Sarah said, never taking her eyes from the Pippiton Watch.

"I suppose I could have some wine brought out, and... Hello? Can we help you?" Kibbage's offer was cut short by the arrival of a thick-browed man in boiled leather armor under a pale-yellow tabard with a green castle on it. A steel helmet covered his skull, and a very conspicuous sword swung at his hip. He was a King's Sword, a soldier of Greenshade.

"Honorable Rivan Kibbage, Lieutenant Falt of the King's Swords, Swift Shields Unit, has asked me to inform you that he will be quartering troops here at Pippiton for the next few days, awaiting a package from Tyrrane." While the man spoke, more and more yellow-liveried Swords entered the market. They stalked about and secured the street corners, established their perimeters, and in general looked intimidating.

"We are six hundred men, and we require provisioning and water. We will see to our own accommodations. The lieutenant will be along presently to explain any additional details you require."

Without answering the soldier, Rivan Kibbage turned and pointed to Keane and Sarah who were both slowly backing away from the exchange. "Guard!" she shouted. "Arrest these two for thievery and coercion and toss them in jail." She gave Keane a thin-lipped smile. "Hardly seems I need to be afraid of your army as long as I have my own here. This is comically terrible timing for you, wouldn't you think?"

Sarah leaned over and whispered into Keane's ear as the Pippiton guard grabbed them from behind, "I *would* say I told you so, but I just want you to know I'm a better person than that."

9

CAPTAIN VANCESS FINGERS HIS SWORD

ELI

"Looks like they've been here a day or two, at most," Eli said as he peered through his spyglass at the King's Swords encamped outside of Pippiton. "Don't seem to be doing nothing, just sitting there." He and Harden stood in a field of emmer, peering into the small town's clean rows of shops and houses. The late-afternoon sun turned the already-yellowed crops a rich gold.

"Well," Harden said, "if they were here for us, they'd hardly just be lying about." He paused for a moment. "Have the men move into this field and set up our camp here. We'll see who comes out to say hello."

They didn't wait long. Within minutes of the main mercenary force moving into the field, about a dozen hard-faced Swords and one squat, elderly woman in working clothes came riding across the grass. They slowed as they approached, and an older soldier who looked as if he were made of rocks and gristle took a few steps ahead. He wore sergeant's bars on his dirty yellow tabard and swordsman's calluses on his knotty muscular hands.

The hard-bitten swordsman scratched at his stubbly gray head and shouted, "In the name of King Eggan Rance of Greenshade, shall the leaders of this force of fighting men now present themselves to

Lieutenant Falt, commander of the Swift Shields Unit of the King's Swords!" Having delivered his mouthful, the old sergeant sat tall in his saddle, casting a withering scowl over the mercenary men.

For several long moments, there was no response. Eli watched Lowger and Darkling, both captains in Wallace's Company, turn and look at the sergeant as he spoke, then return to their own conversation. Eli frowned and thought. That only left...

Captain Vancess stalked forward in his bright armor through the tall grains, several of his own ruffians in tow. Vancess, unlike most everyone else there, had been raised in wealth and could be well mannered when the occasion demanded it. He was also dangerously cracked, believing himself to be on some sort of holy journey. For safety's sake, Eli jogged up behind the straight-backed and delusional Vancess. This was just bad planning.

"Sir." Vancess ran a finger along his forehead to push a stray curl of blond hair out of his handsome face. "You must be the much-esteemed Lieutenant Falt."

"I do be... eh, that is... I am." Lieutenant Falt, a thin young man with no appreciable chin, was having difficulty finding his voice. In Eli's estimation, this was good and bad. A weak commander could be more easily led, but he was also more likely to do something unexpected and stupid with the lives of those under him, if for no other reason than to prove to everyone else that he was *not* weak. More than likely, one of the others here was holding the reins.

As if on cue, the old sergeant coughed, and Falt's eyes darted in his direction. On closer inspection, Eli decided that the career soldier seemed a kindred spirit—which meant he was trouble.

"Ah yes, Sergeant Fingiron. Please deliver my statement." Falt exhaled and smiled at Fingiron, caught himself, and drew his brow together in an effort to look stern.

Eli stood just over Vancess's right shoulder and shook his head. He wanted to avoid this discussion altogether. He didn't like talking to the King's Swords. They made him jumpy in the best of circumstances, which this was nowhere close to.

"This force of men will disperse immediately," shouted Sergeant

Fingiron far too loudly for the comfort of those he was addressing, "and by order of the King's Swords, shall not reconvene for any purpose, under penalty of no less than ten years' hard labor and no more than death by hanging and confiscation of personal goods and estate."

From where he stood, Eli could just see Vancess's attractive grin fixed in place. The mustache twitched.

"Well, Lieutenant Falt"—Vancess ignored the sergeant—"circumstance seems to have thrust we men of great virtue together in both purpose and locale. I am pleased that we can be of such service to one another..."

"What possible use could the Swift Shields have for cowardly dogs such as you?" Fingiron thrust into the conversation.

Falt opened his mouth to speak, but all he managed was an "upp" sound before being cut off.

The sergeant continued, "The King's Swords don't make deals with low men. The King's Swords don't make deals with thieves, nor murderers. And that means that the King's Swords do *not* make deals with the likes of *you*."

Although the man's grin never slipped a whisker, Eli saw Vancess's right hand slide toward his rapier even as the left continued twirling his mustache. "I am dismayed to hear that," Vancess said, his voice stiff through his rigid smile.

With only an instant to act, Eli cocked back his fist and took aim at the back of Captain Vancess's head. Time slowed, and from the edge of his vision, Eli spotted Sergeant Fingiron's happy snarl as he unsheathed his sword and the looks of shocked distress on the faces of Falt and the gray-haired older woman next to him.

"Gentlemen, if I might be of assistance?"

Smooth as a buttered eel, Harden inserted himself between the soon-to-be-fighting groups of men. His voice, as always, was both soothing and commanding. Despite themselves, everyone stopped to pay heed.

Eli dropped his fist, glancing around to see if anyone noticed.

"If I might," said Harden. "In the interest of avoiding considerable

and entirely unnecessary loss of life, I would suggest that our dealings are not with the estimable Lieutenant Falt or his erstwhile
sergeant but with the good Rivan Kibbage here—whom I already
have a healthy acquaintance."

"Very good!" Falt squeaked, his voice rather like a nail sliding
down the side of an iron bell. "You will stay out of the, um... the..."
Falt waved in the general direction of Pippiton. "Stay out of town.
With your, uh... rabble." His hand fluttered to his not-chin, and he
looked over to the sergeant as if he had overstepped his bounds.

Fingiron just rolled his eyes.

"Quite," replied Harden. "Only a fool would disobey the famous
Lieutenant..."

"Falt," whispered Eli.

"Falt. Rivan, if you would be so kind."

Falt's eyes widened at the flattery, and he leaned forward with
what he must have thought of as a fierce grin. Given his gangly body
and lack of chin, the effect was more comedic than intimidating.
Fingiron, his slablike face reddening, shoved his blade back in its
scabbard and massaged his temples.

Rivan Kibbage, stony and unreadable, slid off her horse and
walked a short distance away from the proceedings. Harden and Eli
followed her. Once they were out of earshot, Kibbage turned to the
pair.

"Look, I'm sorry, but I'm not going to give you what you're after.
Your people were here demanding your 'tribute' or whatever, but the
Swords are here now. Your people are in jail, and I don't really see the
need to pay you off just to leave. So cut your losses and go. It's better
for everyone this way."

"My people are in jail, you say?" asked Harden, rubbing at the
stubble on his chin.

"Yes?" Kibbage said, looking confused. "But that's not..."

"I don't think she *do* know what it is we's after, sir," Eli said. He
crossed his arms, feeling a warm satisfaction in his chest. The end of
this mess was in sight, and he could taste the celebratory whiskey
from here.

"Rivan," Harden said with an affable nod, "the two people in your jail, a young man and woman, both Pavinn? The man a handsome, strong lad, and the woman a terrifying and beautiful brute?"

"I think we're talking about the same people," Kibbage answered, lips pursed. Eli watched the old woman working the angles, figuring out where all of this might be leading. A survivor's brain worked behind those blue eyes.

"Those people stole from me, Rivan," Harden said, his voice low. "They are traitors to the freemen of Wallace's Company. If you would have us leave— and in good will—merely return them and whatever they had with them, and the matter will be settled. In fact, I should say I would be in your debt."

"Two prisoners, a box of coin we'd have to turn over to the Swords anyway, a wagonload of junk, and a piglet?" the rivan asked. "That, sir, is a deal, and a damn sight better than the one they were peddling on your behalf."

Eli's mouth opened in a broad grin as Harden and Kibbage shook on it, enjoying his victory for a full three seconds before being startled by Sergeant Fingiron's rough cough, much closer than he should have been.

"As long as the King's Swords are in residence, legal authority belongs to them," the sergeant said, his blunt face incongruous with the particulars of law coming out of it, "and as already stated, the Swords do not make deals with criminals such as yourselves."

Eli's short-lived happiness faded as Fingiron's step closed on Harden, his face inches from the mercenary lord marshal's.

"Now what was this about a box of money?"

10

CHECK SHOES BEFORE ENTERING

ELI

Captain Eli stood looking out across the mercenary encampment as men lounged, drank, fought, and gambled away the little coin they had to one another. The sun had disappeared beneath the horizon less than an hour ago, yet the camp smelled like it had been rotting in place for years. One end of Eli's mouth turned down a bit at the thought.

Wallace's Company and the mercenary existence it represented had consumed most of his life, and as a result, he was good at it. Loved it even, if he was being honest with himself. He felt like an eternal piece of the fighting life, as if he had somehow molded it, formed it up from the dirt. He sighed, spotting his objective. Someday —and someday soon if he could help it—he would bring this whole miserable mess crashing down in ruin.

"Cap'n Darkling!" Eli shouted toward the press of men gathered around one of the larger bonfires. "The lord marshal's got words for you."

After a few seconds more conversation with the men surrounding him, the atypically well-dressed Captain Darkling stroked his pointed beard and detached from his fellows. He worked his way around the short tents and between the bedrolls toward Eli.

"What is this about?" he asked as he came closer. In his fancy black frock coat, gold vest, and britches, Eli thought the man belonged more in some parlor for pampered, inflated jackasses than camping with a pack of mercenaries. Darkling might be clever, but he was shit in a fight.

"Don't know and didn't ask," Eli said, turning and heading back to Harden's tent. "If it were my business, I expect I'd've been told." This was not strictly true. In fact, Eli and Harden hatched this little scheme together as they had many others before. But Eli didn't care for Darkling and considered the conniving fop to be emblematic of everything that was wrong with mercenaries today. Let the ponce wonder a while.

"Ever the obedient dog." Darkling scowled. Eli could feel the taller man's smug smile burning against his back. "Will you receive a treat for summoning your better, I wonder?"

Eli slowed a pace and stepped left, forcing Darkling to stumble a step in that direction. There was a *splatch*, and Darkling shouted imprecations as he hopped on one foot and waved the other, now covered with the feces of a drunken mercenary who had stopped for his business somewhat short of the latrines.

"You did that on purpose, you miserable old bastard!" Darkling roared.

Eli turned and looked at the man, blank faced. Darkling was a schemer and ambitious backstabber who would much rather see a sleeping man chopped in half than step over him on the ground, but they both knew that he was not fit to do the chopping himself. Eli let his sword hand drift toward a pommel.

The snarl fell off Darkling's patrician face. Eli had no intention of butchering him, but a little fear now and again often helped the workings of a successful military enterprise.

"When you say '*yer better*,'" Eli said, his tone at once conversational and devoid of emotion, "I gotta wonder, better at what?"

Darkling was spared having to come up with an answer by Harden who stepped out of the shadows between his two captains. "Evening, gentlemen. Darkling, glad you could make it. Do come in."

Harden stood to one side and held open his tent flap. "Um... better take that boot off first."

Once the three of them were inside his spacious tent, Harden leaned against the map table to face Eli and the one-booted Darkling. He pulled off his wide hat and tossed it onto the bed, his graying hair sticking flat to the sides of his head.

"Captain Darkling, I have need of your particular assets." Harden paused, but Darkling, still fuming, kept silent. "Our quarry, soldiers Keane and Sarah, are but a mile through wood and field in the jail of yonder town. I would like you to kill Keane for me and retrieve Sarah."

Darkling spat on the floor and scowled at Harden. "Why me? Why not your ass-licker here?" He nodded toward Eli. "I assume the two of you are setting a trap for me."

"What is a lord marshal," asked Harden, opening both arms wide, "if not a man who can have others murdered at his command and leisure?"

Eli examined the dirt under his nails. "Coward."

"Oh please," said Darkling He glared at Eli and twisted the end of his pointy little beard. "Is this the best you can muster by way of subterfuge? Name-calling? I should think that of all people, *you* would be aware that appealing to the bravery of a mercenary was a fool's errand. I gave up on that virtue when I joined this piss-besotted 'free' company." He turned to Harden. "And you—do you not know what's being said about you behind your back? That you're addled with thoughts of revenge? While we're chasing your two wayward soldiers, we are not making *any* money. And that is the *only* thing an army of mercenaries cannot be cowed into suffering."

"Kill Keane, bring me Sarah," said Harden, his voice an unfriendly rasp, "and retrieve the wagebox. Without the wagebox, *no* one gets paid. I would have thought even you could get behind a plan like that."

Darkling hesitated. Eli had seen trapped animals with that same expression on their faces.

"Well enough. But that brings us back around to 'why me,' doesn't it?" Darkling said, though without his previous venom. "I freely admit that Captain Eli's men are better swordsmen. Why can't they do this?"

Harden leaned forward and gestured in the direction of Pippiton and its jail. "Because, Good Captain, this job does not require swordsmen. I need five soldiers to get arrested and put in a cell with Sarah and Keane. Once there, they will kill him and capture her. There will *be* no swords. I do not need master bladesmen—"

"You need brutes." Darkling finished Harden's thought. "And that *is* my specialty."

"And in particular—" began Harden.

"You need Burgen."

"Just so," said Harden.

A great ox of a man, Burgen towered half-a-head taller than the next biggest soldier in Wallace's Company. His limbs were so thickly muscled that Eli once watched him disarm a man who had stabbed him in the leg by flexing and twisting sideways. Most importantly though, Burgen was the only man in the company to have beaten Sarah in any kind of fight.

And he was utterly Darkling's creature.

"I will consider it," Darkling said, his composure changed from cornered animal to that of cunning bargainer, "for a double share in the next ten takes. Final offer."

Harden laughed. "Twenty-five-percent bonus in the next *three* takes. Take it or leave it."

As the two men haggled price, Eli contemplated the job. It seemed straightforward, but he couldn't help wondering if five would be enough. Keane was an excellent fighter, but Sarah—there were rumors that she had been *very* drunk and that Burgen had cheated the night he beat her unconscious with a pewter tankard. Sarah herself had never said either way which probably meant the rumors were false.

Probably.

"Very good, you skinflint bastard," Captain Darkling said. The smirk on his face said he thought he had gotten the better of the deal.

He almost certainly had not. "I'll send them immediately." He turned and left the tent.

"See that you do," Harden said to Darkling's backside, the accommodating openness on his own face fading away.

"Problem?" asked Eli.

"No," said Harden. "It's just... ah, hell. What's done is done."

"Aye," Eli said, befuddled by Harden's equivocation. "But you know, that cup o' piss were right about one thing."

"What is that?"

"Men're talking about why we's here. Now I ain't saying they's right—you know I'm with you till the end and all—but if'n this somehow goes sideways, we need to cut and run. Go find some more golden pastures, right?"

Harden was silent for a moment and then stood, moving as if weary beyond thought. "Make sure the company is ready to shift in the morning. We may have to go quickly."

"Aye, I will. But—"

"And, Eli," the Lord Marshal said, fixing his man with a dark-eyed stare, "If any other 'men' want to second-guess my orders, just send them to me so I can cut their throats myself. We're here for the wage-box, and that's that."

Eli stood rigid, looking Harden in the eye. The moment dragged as the two men sought to pull the intentions of the other out by force of will.

Eli looked away. "Aye, then." He stalked from the tent.

Some people were just damn hard to be friends with.

11

A PIG IN A POKEY

KEANE

Keane and Sarah were in the larger of Pippiton's two jail cells meant for small crowds of unruly prisoners. The other cell shared part of a barred wall with theirs and was just big enough to accommodate the drunk curled up in the middle of the floor. The rivan had taken the ironbound wagebox full of cash to her own home where it sat behind stone walls and under guard.

The smaller non-jail-cell portion of the stone block room housed a single table and chair, a cold fireplace, five or six lit candles, and four town guards in their brown cloaks and acorn caps who listened enraptured to Keane's tales of combat and mercenary derring-do. One of the guards sat cross-legged on the floor and absentmindedly stroked Gennie's belly while the piglet lay draped across his thigh, a recently emptied bowl of sow's milk to one side.

"This was, what... six years ago?" said Keane. "We hadn't been with Wallace's Company long back then, and Harden had the company in the field fighting some baron..."

"Tralgar," Sarah said, smiling and crossing her arms. She leaned back against the crumbling stone wall to listen to Keane's tale.

"That's right," Keane said, "Baron Tralgar. Big mystery who we were working for. Supposed to have been some wealthy merchant the baron cut out of his business dealings, but I think it was a noble from the west. Anyway, Tralgar lives in some worn-out wooden castle south of here. Old Oak? Something like that."

"Baron Tralgar lives in Castle Oak, at the south end of the town of Old Oak," offered the oldest of the four guards, a squinty-eyed codger whose red nose bent back and forth on his face like a zigzagging tree branch.

"His symbol is a big oak tree?" Keane asked. When the broken-nosed guard nodded, Keane continued, "So the company is engaging in the field, and Sarah and I get sent with a group of fifty or so mean-assed fuckers to sneak around the back. Disrupt supply lines, catch any messengers, that sort of thing."

"My first squad command," said Sarah.

"That it was," Keane said. They looked at each other, slight smiles on their faces, before Keane returned to his audience. "Anyway, what we found was a rear camp. Big tent, maybe a dozen infantry."

Sarah shook her head and grinned at the floor.

"We sent the men on ahead and went into the tent to scout it," Keane continued. "I figured if it was anything important, we'd go get 'em and bring 'em back. But, if not, maybe we'd snatch up anything valuable while no one was looking."

"What were you expecting to find?" asked the guard holding Gennie, a young man with yellow hair and freckles across his cheeks. Keane thought his name was George. The piglet, uninterested in the story, gave off tiny, squeaky snores.

"Maps, plans, communications, maybe some important person-nel," answered Keane. Behind him Sarah snorted, trying to stifle a laugh.

"What?" he asked.

"You knew what you were going to find in that tent," Sarah said with a chuckle. "That's why you sent the others away."

"I don't get it," said George. "What was in the tent?"

A pretend scowl stole across Keane's features as he regarded Sarah. He turned to the guards and nodded. "Baron Tralgar's wife."

Keane let the hoots and whistles die down a bit before he continued. "Sarah stayed outside in the brush to make sure no one else came in, and I snuck past Tralgar's soldiers and into the tent." He paused for effect, looking through the bars and into the eyes of each guard. "I tell you lads, you have never seen a more impressive-looking woman. Present company excepted."

Sarah rolled her eyes and waved him off.

"The Baroness Roselle Tralgar," Keane said, and his voice grew wistful. "She was tall and fearfully beautiful, with eyes that looked into your soul. I found myself besotted the instant I saw her."

"Didja' sex her up?" asked the broken-nosed guard.

"A gentleman never tells," Keane said with a prim smile. "But I will say we had a *very* special moment."

The guards laughed and slapped each other on the back, imagining the sordid encounter between a young mercenary and a vulnerable baroness.

"In the end," said Keane, "I was so occupied inside that I didn't realize the whole camp had got set off, and Sarah had fought and killed them all by herself. I walked out of the tent and there she was, wiping off her sword, surrounded by a dozen dead infantrymen. Piles of 'em."

"Wow," said George, his eyes wide.

Sarah shook her head and shrugged, sliding down against the stone wall to sit on a worn wooden bench. Keane sat beside her as the guards talked and laughed again.

"That story gets worse every time you tell it," she said, one eyebrow raised. "The baroness was a nice lady who was unhappy in her marriage. All you did was talk to her."

"True… but I did convince her to leave her husband and go live in the capital. That was *kind of* dastardly."

"And there were only six soldiers there, not twelve," Sarah said.

"Does that really matter?" Keane asked, his flat gaze on Sarah. "Six men or twelve, you're a ridiculous badass. Like, not the normal kind of badass. More hero-out-of-legend badass."

Sarah's brows pulled together, and she reached forward to pick a dried lump of clay from the edge of her boot. "I hate it when you say stuff like that."

Outside the bars, another burst of laughter erupted from the joking guardsmen. Gennie, very much awake and standing on George's boot, looked up as if wishing to join in the frivolity.

Moments later, a sour-faced guard opened the front door from the outside, interrupting the merriment and letting in the cool night breeze. He entered and stood aside for three more guards and five of the biggest and hardest-looking men south of the Greenshade River, dressed in the dirty and stained tabards of the King's Swords. The largest one stooped and turned his shoulders sideways just to fit in the door. All five were unarmed, their rumpled yellow tabards muddy and blood splashed. They all smiled—jarringly out of place with their situation.

Keane and Sarah, recognizing the thugs, exchanged a glance. Keane's hands went clammy.

"Picked these up makin' trouble at the Dapper Eel," said Sour Face. "Thought we might have some trouble, but they came along peaceable enough. They's King's Swords. Blowin' off steam, I guess."

"Hello, Burgen," Sarah said. She stood, relaxing just a few inches from the bars, and looked up into Burgen's eyes. If there was any nervousness about her, Keane couldn't see it.

"Hallo, Sarah," Burgen said, his voice sounding like a flour mill with rocks stuck in it. "Fancy a rematch? Seems like we've got us some time to kill."

"Haha," chuckled one of the other brutes, "Time ta kill. Mebbe some uvver fings, too."

There was general laughter and agreement among the brutes at that.

The guard from the floor, picking up Gennie and holding her in the crook of his arm, said, "Hang on then. If you lot are Swords, how d'you know Keane and Sarah here?"

Burgen stared at the guard holding the pig, his scarred and bearded face slack. He looked around at the other men who had been brought in with him and widened his eyes, hoping that another of his number might have a better answer than nothing.

They just mumbled and shrugged back at him.

"That *is* a stumper," Keane said, smiling his warmest smile. "If I might... George, right?"

George nodded.

"Extemporaneous speech has never been Burgen's strong suit. These men are bald-faced liars, George. They belong to Wallace's Company and have been sent here to do us harm. Their leader, a petty and grasping asshole of no moral character, is angry at us for stealing money from him that he stole from others. He believes you're going to put these apes in here with us so that they might murder us on your watch and make you look bad."

George didn't look happy, but he also appeared confused. "But...?"

"We ain't tossin' these ones back out on the street just because you're scared, boy," Sour Face said in his bitter grumble. "They busted up the Eel, and they gotta spend the night in jail for it. That's the law."

"Of course," Keane said with a small bow, "I would never suggest otherwise. Especially as they likely killed the previous owners of those tabards."

Burgen's mouth fell open at that, and Sour Face's countenance pulled together into a wrinkled frown, as threatening as the snarl of a wolf.

Smiling, Keane continued, "But if I may, a solution does offer itself. Why not simply accommodate these frost-cocked cows in the *smaller* cell?" He turned to indicate the tiny cell with the sleeping drunk. Taking longer to catch up to Keane's meaning, the other thugs' expressions of smug evil turned to disappointed helplessness.

"Them big bastards ain't gonna fit in there," Sour Face said.

"But wouldn't it be funny to try?" asked Keane.

In the end, all five of the burly mercenaries—and one terrified drunk—*did* fit in the tiny cell. One thug had to get stabbed a bit, and it took three guards to push the cell door closed. As it was, the feat could only be accomplished by pushing any arms or legs that would fit out between the cell bars, and there was still some stacking. Burgen insisted on being up against the wall shared by the two cells, and there he stood, glaring at Sarah and a smirking Keane.

"Come over 'ere an' smile like that," Burgen growled at Keane. "We'll see who's laffin' then."

"You mean here?" Keane asked, stepping well into what would have been Burgen's reach if he hadn't been pressed flat up against the bars or if his elbows bent backwards.

"Yeah," Burgen said. "There."

One of the men behind the giant shrieked as Burgen flexed and shifted, twisted his huge shoulders and—quick as a blink—caught Keane by the throat. "Gotcha," he said through gritted teeth.

Keane's face turned purple as wrenching pain engulfed his throat. The base of Burgen's thumb was a stone that tried to crush Keane's trachea and left him wanting to sob for lack of breath to cough.

But he could do neither.

He struck at the tattooed arm that lifted him off the floor as he himself might have lifted a much, much tinier man. It was similar to conducting a fistfight with an oak tree. Guards shouted and scrambled for keys, and somewhere in the background, a tiny pig squealed.

A hand took hold of Burgen's wrist and turned it, affording Keane a better view. Sarah didn't try to pry Burgen's hand open, which Keane decided he disapproved of. Spots danced in front of his eyes, and the edges of his world went dim. The oncoming darkness pulled around his pain, numbing him and offering comfort.

Instead of freeing Keane, she reached out with her other hand and gripped the thicker corner bar of their cell for leverage.

With a frown of concentration, Sarah *pulled*.

To his credit, Burgen's fist stayed closed around Keane's neck until after his elbow broke and his arm popped backwards at an alarming angle. The huge man released a wailing howl that lasted until Sarah jerked yet further back on the arm, separating the upper and lower bones entirely. Burgen's forearm hung from his elbow like a sack of heavily muscled cheese.

Keane sat and coughed on the floor of his cell while the other brutes squalled about being killed. Sarah, at George's insistence, raised her hands and backed away. Burgen slumped unconscious into the bars, supported by the crossbar under his armpits.

After a minute, the room settled down, and Keane sat unmoving from his spot. Though no longer coughing, he continued to spit on the floor, and he thought he might vomit just to reopen all the passages in his throat. He rubbed at his neck, still feeling that inhuman iron grip there. Keane closed his eyes and concentrated on not panicking at his inability to run away from the pain when he breathed.

George leaned over just outside the bars. "Hey, Keane."

"Yeah?" Keane managed to croak.

"You were right. That really *was* funny."

12

CATCH

KEANE

"Hello there, Princess."

Keane arose from the wooden bunk and rubbed his knuckles into his eyes. He gave his surroundings a bleary once-over while he tried to orient himself. *Right. Jail cell. Pippiton? Isn't Burgen...* He looked to his left and saw the stuffed cell full of stinking, snoring men. Keane chuckled.

"This funnier than I think it is?" That gruff voice again.

"Keane," came Sarah's voice, even and low, "we have a visitor."

The warrior woman paced back and forth in the cell. On the other side of the bars, a man in an unwashed yellow tabard with a green castle on the front and sergeant's bars on his shoulders tracked her movements with a small hand crossbow. In the light of the candle, Keane spotted George, crossbow bolt in his neck, slumped across the desk. Gennie slept on a pile of laundry on the floor beside him.

"Someone else wants to kill us?" Keane asked.

"Apparently," answered Sarah.

"That's typical. Do we get to know why?" Keane asked the crossbow-armed soldier. He was squat with short gray hair, a barrel chest, and looked tough as old leather. *Really mean old leather*, Keane thought.

"Can't see how that helps me none," the sergeant said. "Now if yer giant brute woman will just stop walkin' around, I'll shoot you both nice and proper so's I can find yer money and get outta here."

"Don't stop walking, Sarah," said Keane.

"Wasn't planning to," Sarah replied.

"Maybe I should guess why you're here," Keane said. "Given the dead George at the desk, it clearly isn't official business. And since you're here alone, I'd also guess that your moron boss doesn't know about your trip here either. My opinion is that you're simply a murdering thief who thought he'd steal a box full of money that the rivan took *and* that a nearby mercenary army is after... you're being not quite as smart as my less intelligent testicle. Too bad the money isn't here. Did you really think they'd keep it with the prisoners they took it from?"

"Keane, dear," Sarah said as she paced the floor, "please be nice to the murdering thief."

"Not like you mercs are any better," the sergeant said, spitting onto the floor. "But yer wrong. Lieutenant Falt knows what I'm about to do—or will—soon's I tell him." His scarred face split into a wide grin, showing several teeth. "Swift Shields're here collectin' a very important diplomatical asset from Tyrrane. Alla way from the Tyrranean capital city o' Dismon, right? Takin' it back to Treaty Hill. I reckon havin' you two here is a risk we don't need to take—given there's that whole mercenary army just past the trees waitin' to charge in here and take you from us. They seem pretty mad at the two o' you. As for yer money"—his grin widened further though no more teeth showed attendance in his mouth—"I reckon the rivan has it. I would if I was her. After here, I'll go pay the lady a visit and square up."

"So, you kill us," Keane summed up, "convince your Lieutenant Falt that you were acting in the best interests of the king back in Treaty Hill, neutralize a potential threat to your 'diplomatical' mission, *and* pocket our money for yourself. Very tidy. But how do you get away with chopping Rivan Kibbage to bits?"

"Simple," the sergeant said, "I just drag your body with me and leave it at her place, then throw your Pavi slit"—he indicated Sarah —"to the hogs. Who won't think you broke out and stole the box, an' she ran away with it?"

Keane gave the sergeant a long look up and down. "I gotta say, you are a *lot* smarter than you look. I mean a lot. You look pretty stupid, but..."

"I was gonna shoot the both of you anyway. Might as well do you first." With that, the sergeant turned away from Sarah and pulled the trigger.

Keane grimaced and flinched back for a strike that never hit him. Sarah leapt, her arm shooting out as she fell, hair spinning out behind her. She grunted where she hit the ground and then rolled backwards and up into a sitting position. Her mail hauberk scraped loudly against the floor stones.

Then she threw the bolt in her hand into the sergeant's barrel of a chest.

"What..." was all he said. He dropped the hand crossbow and looked down at the feathered missile protruding from the left side of his chest. His head wobbled up, eyebrows raised in confusion over hard little eyes, and dropped the candle. He toppled forward, knocking his gray-stubbled skull into the bars of their cell, released a single loud fart, and was still.

Sarah reached through the bars and pulled the sergeant's body closer, drawing a poniard from the belt.

Keane, his breath panicky, shot furtive glances around the darkened room. The mercenary thugs in the small cell were no longer snoring, but they weren't making any noise either.

"How did you..." Keane started, then stopped. He thought he was used to seeing Sarah do some pretty amazing things, but this was a different sort of incredible. "*Holy shit!* I didn't know you could do that," he said.

She handed him the sergeant's poniard. "Can you pick the lock with this?" Sarah asked. She glanced around the room. "I think we should go."

"I didn't know you could do that," Keane repeated. "Did *you* know you could do that?"

Sarah looked Keane in the eye, putting one large hand on either shoulder. "No, Keane, I didn't. I was walking back and forth hoping he'd come closer to get a better shot between the bars, and then I could grab him. When he shot you instead, I just sort of reacted. I'm glad you're not hurt."

"I'm not hurt," Keane said. "You didn't know you could do that? Normal people can't do things like that. I really should be killed right now."

"You still could be," Sarah said, brow furrowing over a half smile. "Now can you pick that lock or not?"

"Yeah, sure."

Most of the time she seemed normal-ish. Then things like this happened.

"Just so I'm not walking around waiting for you to catch fire or turn into a demon or something, can you tell me *how* you did it? I know that, whatever the case, you're still you, and I'm not gonna run away, but that was downright unnerving. Like going for a piss and finding a centipede wrapped around your cock."

"You mean a friendly cock centipede that saves your life at great risk to its own?" At Keane's expression, Sarah softened. "It's a little crossbow. It doesn't shoot a bolt that fast. I saw where it was headed, and I jumped. You could have caught it too if the angle was right."

"Hmph," said Keane, shaking his head.

"Anyway, I really never could have done it with a bigger crossbow. The bolts move too fast to see. Speaking of moving fast, maybe we could talk about this after we're gone?"

Keane looked at Sarah, then at the poniard in his hand. He looked back at Sarah, then at the lock. "Yeah, all right." He stood, moved to the lock, and reached around with the narrow blade.

"I *could* have been killed, you know."

13

THE PAIN OF LOSS... OF SOMEONE ELSE'S MONEY

SARAH

After saying goodbye to Gennie in a nearby farmer's pigpen, Keane and Sarah stole out of Pippiton in the night and headed north across the Greenshade River into Tyrrane. The overcast sky blotted out the whole world behind a gloomy black curtain. Sarah could see well enough. The starlight illuminated the cloud cover and cast a dim light over the land, but Keane ran off the path and into the bushes and long grass again and again.

She carried the difference, not him. She was the freakish one.

Most of the time, she didn't let it bother her, and she certainly would never let it show. But at times like this when that difference between herself and normal people was laid bare, it bothered her a little.

"Nobody will catch us," Keane said. "We can sneak out of town with a box of money just as easily as we can without one."

"I'm done risking my neck for Harden's coins," Sarah said as she marched ahead in the gloom. "You realize we never even opened it, don't you? For all we know, the thing was full of bronze fourthings. Besides, the damn thing was heavy, and we'd have been heard if we'd taken our horses. Did you want to carry it?"

"Not knowing what was in it makes me want it more," Keane groused, following the sound of her voice.

In truth, it did bother her as much as him to leave Robert and Brownie behind. Those horses had been with them for years. When all of this died down, they would be back for them.

He returned to the wagebox. "It had to be worth a lot. Harden brought the whole company after us."

"All the more reason to leave it," Sarah said. "Maybe if we let him get everyone's wages back, he'll forgive the Amadeo thing and let us be."

"Are we forgetting Harden had me in a prison cart with the intention of killing me *before* we killed Amadeo?"

"I talked him out of it."

"That time you did. Was him just *wanting* to kill me not reason enough to leave? What happens when he changes his mind and you're not around?"

"No, you're right." Sarah heard the tiredness in her own voice. "You two were obviously never going to get along."

"So it's my responsibility to get along with the toad-fucking shit weasel who wants to murder me?" As he ranted, Keane failed to make a turn in the path, and she guided him back. "What's his goddamn problem, anyway? I'm not that hard to get along with."

Sarah's laughter filled the dark.

"Thank you. That makes me feel a lot better." A night breeze stirred dust, and he coughed into his fist. "Fine. I'm an asshole, and everyone who knows me more than fifteen minutes wants to cut my throat."

"I don't want to cut your throat," Sarah answered.

She really didn't.

"We should have trusted Simon instead," Keane said. "Simon's a good kid."

Though he could not see it, Sarah could not help rolling her eyes.

"If we go back for that box now—" he began.

"We have no idea what the layout of the rivan's place is," Sarah interrupted, "how many guards there are, what other defenses there might be... we don't even know which house is hers."

Keane looked three feet in front of Sarah and pointed his finger at the distant sky.

"You know, we'd really be doing Kibbage a favor. What if Harden decides to attack the town to recover his property?"

"That tough old bird is the one person in all of this I am *not* concerned about," Sarah said. "She's one to watch out for. Who are you pointing at? There's no one flying above the road in front of us for you to yell at."

Keane lowered his arms and walked in silence for a time. Every so often, he would raise his arms and open his mouth as if to offer some new rebuttal or argument, only to deflate and continue stumbling along in a sullen quiet.

Sarah wouldn't have minded having the money, but there was a chance that if he recovered it, Harden might be able to walk away with enough dignity intact to forget about her and Keane. Leaving the box behind was a roll of the dice she was more than willing to make.

There was no price on not being dead.

"I can't believe that pig," Keane said at length. "Like I never existed. Just ran off to some fancy sow's bosom without even saying goodbye. And after I gave her my *name*."

Gennie had grunted and squirmed in excitement when Keane and Sarah neared the pig-keeper's farm. The instant her tiny hooves touched the ground, she lit off, leaping in and burying herself among a litter of piglets gorging on their mother's milk. The big sow raised her head to acknowledge the new addition, then relaxed.

It seemed a painless adoption.

"Better luck next time," Sarah said.

"Pork is a fickle mistress," answered Keane. They walked in silence for another few minutes.

"I just really *wanted* all of that money," he said at length.

"And I wanted it for you," Sarah answered, just a bit sarcastic. "Maybe we'll have better luck in Tyrrane."

The two of them traveled for several hours in the dark, talking about anything other than the lost box of coins. After stumbling several times, Keane tried walking behind Sarah with the hem of her cloak in his hand. He said that his grief over the money must have affected his night vision.

But Sarah found her patience vanished and temper raring to be let free after the third time he tripped and yanked on the cloak, choking her. She grabbed his hand and pulled him up alongside her like a mother and child at the market.

His dignity was *not* too large a sacrifice to keep her from murdering him.

"I feel bad about George," Keane said, once he and Sarah made cold camp beside the road.

"Who?" asked Sarah. She tilted her head back and finished the bottle of whiskey they had found among the guards' possessions. It wasn't good, but it didn't need to be.

"George, the dead guard."

"Oh yeah. He was good looking." A little weedy maybe, and could've used a bath, but like the whiskey, he would have been good enough.

Slago's eyeteeth, the boy was *dead*. This was not a very respectful line of imaginings.

Keane rolled over and propped himself up on his elbows. Watery light from the beginnings of dawn lit the sky as well as Keane's mischievous grin. When Sarah was drunk, she liked to find a pretty man to carry off and enjoy until the sun came up. It left her feeling light and happy and in control of her life. Despite all of the hardships her chosen manner of living might present, her ability to choose her own bedfellows still struck her as worth the sacrifice of every possible convenience and comfort of a husband's ownership. She loved her independence and was determined to enjoy it.

That set her at odds with an Andosh nation that thought boobs came with ownership papers and the only fit decision for a woman was what to make for supper. Most of the time she didn't care. They couldn't touch her. Not really. Not where she lived. She knew she was better than that.

But Keane just *loved* to tease her about it.

"You know, men have value beyond what you might do to them naked," he said to her. He chuckled. Keane had entered the phase of tiredness where he thought everything he said was the funniest thing he'd ever heard. While he liked to needle her when affected this way, he was even easier to poke back.

"If you say so," Sarah answered. "Though you couldn't prove it by me."

"Well, you still hang out with me, and I'm *never* going to have sex with you." This time he giggled.

"Yeah, why is that?" Sarah asked.

"What?" Keane asked. He stopped laughing and his eyes went wide. "Because that's gross. You're like, my sister or something."

"No, idiot," she said. "I know that. I meant, why do you suppose I still hang out with you?"

"Oh, that's easy," he answered, calming back down. "You hang out with me because I'm the only one not afraid of a giant crazy-assed she-demon like you."

"Keep talking. I'm gonna rub one out, and I'm pretending your voice is George's."

"You make me *so* uncomfortable when you drink."

Sarah just laughed and rolled over. She was asleep in seconds, leaving Keane awake with his unease.

14

NEVER PUNCH A LADY

KEANE

After hiding in the high brush throughout the day, they ate as the sun set and took once more to the road. The cloud cover held and if possible, made this night darker than the previous.

Although frustrated by stubbing his toes against rocks, tripping into bushes, and walking into Sarah's back, Keane could not deny the utility of the nighttime travel. They had encountered literally no one on the road north.

If no one saw them get away, and Keane thought no one had, they could be home free.

As they walked, Keane considered the way in which they had escaped the Pippiton jail. "Sarah," he said, his voice low, "you've always been a goddamn amazing fighter, and there is no one in the whole world I trust more than you. But"—Keane paused, searching for the right words—"recently it seems like you've been getting a lot... more... amazinger."

There was silence for a few minutes, and then Sarah replied, "Does that bother you?"

"Does it bother me when you humiliate Burgen and then break the jackass's arm while he's trying to kill me and *then* shove a bolt through Sergeant Toothless's uniform while *he's* trying to kill me? No. It doesn't bother me. Maybe it scares the piss out of me—a little—but I'm always good with not getting killed."

"Maybe you wouldn't have to be scared so much if you were nicer," Sarah said. "You know, made fewer people want to kill you."

"That's a fair point," Keane conceded. "It's just, I worry about you, Sarah. I don't want anything to happen to you."

She stopped walking. "What would happen to me?"

"I don't know," Keane said. "Villagers with torches and pitchforks? Hunted by the crown? Whatever the hell happens to people who stand out and are better than everyone else?"

"You're very sweet," Sarah said, patting Keane on the hand she held and beginning to walk again, "but I'm not better than anyone."

"I think you need to take another look," said Keane.

"I can't be," said Sarah. "I'm still friends with you, and all the decent people I know want you dead."

"What decent people do you know?"

"Well, decent by comparison," she replied.

Keane let the matter drop, and the pair crept up the road, silent except for the occasional telltale jingle of Sarah's mail hauberk.

"Do you see lights ahead?" she asked. "Maybe a mile off."

"I can't even see *you*, and you're right"—Keane waved his arms about, touching nothing—"somewhere."

"Looks like torches. Some kind of camp. We'll have to be quiet."

"Sure. Can't see you, and now I won't be able to hear you. What could go wrong?"

"Take my hand and shut up." Sarah reached out and grabbed Keane's hand.

"Oh yeah, I knew that."

After a few hundred feet, they crested a small rise, and Keane could finally see the camp torches Sarah mentioned. They were set up in rows, squaring off a flat area to the east of the road. Between each torch post were three or four small white tents, all surrounding a larger, better-lit pavilion in the center made of a deep red canvas.

"Tyrannean military camp," Keane said, smiling to himself. "We can work with that."

As soon as they were close enough to be heard, Keane shouted a greeting to the longbow-armed soldiers watching the road.

"Hello there! Pair of travelers here. No harm to anyone, and certainly no need to shoot us with arrows."

The men, wearing the black-on-gray tabards and shiny black helmets of the Ebon Host, the Royal Army of Tyrrane, raised their bows and shouted back. "Come forward into the light. Show us yer palms now. Very good... Whoah! She's a biggun."

Keane smiled at the four soldiers, who lowered their bows and quivered their arrows. "That she is, boys. And mean, too, in case you're getting any ideas." He approached the closest soldier and stuck out a hand. "So, anyone around here know how to play cards?"

~

SITTING at a tiny table on the grass with three soldiers, Keane dealt himself another handmaid from the bottom of the deck, using both the dim torchlight and the noise of the fight behind him to his fullest advantage. In an impromptu gladiatorial pit, surrounded by dozens of yelling and drinking soldiers, Sarah pounded her third challenger into the dirt. The other card players at Keane's little table craned their necks to watch her instead of watching his deal. He didn't blame them. She looked impressive enough just leaning against a tree. Watching her fight was something else altogether.

Both the card table and the fighting ring butted up against the red central pavilion of the big military camp. Smaller tents went out from it in straight rows, lit by the intermittent torch poles. These tents were not like the small and filthy single-occupant tents of Wallace's Company. They were tall as a man, wide enough for a pair of cots, and close to white. The Ebon Host of Tyranne held themselves to higher standards than the mercenaries Keane was used to. But it didn't matter. In all the ways that counted, soldiers were the same everywhere.

"Family of tarts, boys. I'm sad to say this round is mine as well."

The Tyranneans around the table groaned as Keane laid down his cards. The soldier to his left collected everyone's hands and shuffled.

Sarah stopped for another flagon of ale between bouts. Alcohol didn't really change the warrior woman's personality all that much, but she did get more intense and less inhibited. That always livened the evening up toward the dangerous end.

Keane took a moment to examine the tabard of the soldier across the little table. The royal device of Tyrrane, a black fist gripping a peculiar, short-bladed dagger, covered the center of the gray tabard. Keane wondered what it meant but decided not to mark himself as an outsider by asking. He wouldn't be surprised if every infant in Tyrrane got a dagger at birth for hunting trolls or some other crazy evil crap like that. They would have to be careful traveling through this place. The country was not safe.

Even their babies hunted trolls.

A collective intake of breath sounded from behind followed by a wild whooping. A sweat-stinking body bowled Keane forward into the table, and silver coins and pasteboard cards flew in all directions. The dirt-crusted and shirtless man Sarah had thrown out of the makeshift fighting pit rolled and then limped to his feet. He bellowed an inarticulate cry of rage.

"I understand your pain. I really do," Keane muttered as he stood and assessed himself for damage.

The previously flying man reached behind his back, produced a short-bladed dagger, and ran back toward the pit and the intoxicated Sarah. Without thinking, Keane balled a fist and clubbed the half-dressed soldier in the face, which caused the man's feet to fly out ahead of him and brought him down on his back.

Keane paused a moment to glance at the knife the soldier dropped when he fell. It looked similar to the one decorating the Host's tabards. In person, the short, thick blade looked perfect for punching through a coat of mail.

"Oh," he said, "That makes more sense." Stabbing an armored

assailant in the armpit would come up more often than sending your evil babies off to hunt trolls—in an army situation, at any rate.

Silence descended as all eyes turned to Keane. Even Sarah, her bare arms gleaming with sweat and her dark hair a disheveled mane, seemed surprised, though she was the only one looking happy.

"Cheat!" yelled one of the card players. The man was on the ground, collecting coins in one fist and pointing the other at him. "He helped her in the pit. He cheats!"

Keane felt an instant of relief when he realized the man wasn't yelling about cheating at cards. A pair of soldiers grabbed him by the arms and jerked him away from the table. He considered that this might not be any better.

From his vantage, he saw a Tyrannean soldier threatening Sarah with a sword. She snatched the weapon away by the blade and swung the pommel into the man's head with a loud crack. An instant later, bowmen of the Ebon Host converged on the pit and drew, half a dozen taught bowstrings waiting for the order to release.

Keane had been wrong when he thought that the Tyrannean soldiers were the same as the mercenaries he used to live with. Real army soldiers were so much more uptight.

"Drop the sword! It's over! Oldam's foreskin, Sarah! Listen to me... *it's over!*"

The shouting crowd drowned him out. Keane watched, terrified, as she transferred the weapon to her other hand and menaced the soldiers with the pointy end. Keane struggled against the men holding him back all the harder but to no avail.

More bowmen arrived, and Keane screamed himself hoarse. He watched Sarah, who smiled and swayed, waving them on in challenge.

It was time to change tactics.

Keane stomped the foot of the man to his left and reared back, biting the ear of the man to his right. He kicked up and behind and managed at last to break free. He ran into the pit and faced his friend.

"Sarah, please. Just drop the goddamn sword."

If Sarah heard him, she gave no sign. She grabbed Keane by the shoulder and swung him easily around behind her. Ten bowmen trained razor-honed arrowheads at her heart.

A horn blast sounded and caused everyone present to stop and look toward the central pavilion. A man in a fancy gray uniform with dark silver-shot hair, who looked more intoxicated than Sarah, stood in the pavilion doorway and shouted. "Who are that? What? Bring those... here." He waved in Keane and Sarah's basic direction, turned, and tottered back into his huge tent.

A more senior-looking soldier, probably an officer of some type—Keane didn't know Tyrranean insignia—grabbed both of them by the upper arm and led them away from the angry crowd.

"Hey!" said Sarah, wriggling in the officer's grip. "Are we getting arrested again? We aren't even *wanted* in Tyrrane yet." She pulled free of his grip, but he simply used the hand to shove her in the back.

"Major Talon," the officer said to the tent flap, "your prisoners." He pushed both Keane and the off-balance Sarah through the flap, and into the dark red pavilion.

15

MEETING THE PRINCE

KEANE

Keane straightened and looked around. The very drunk man, whom he took to be Major Talon, stood off to the left, while opposite a long table and chairs, three other officers scowled in a conspiratorial huddle. Several patterned rugs covered the floor, and a wooden candelabra hung from a short beam jutting off the center post. An unmade bed peeked out through another flap in the back.

"That's good," the major said as he approached Keane and clapped him on both shoulders. He grabbed Keane by the cheeks and shook them, looking as if he might weep. "Very... good!"

"Um, do we know one another?" Keane wanted to jerk away or shove the wobbly major, but his near brush with the bowmen outside muted his reflexes. The guy creeped him out though.

The major's unkempt hair and wine-laden breath stood at odds with his otherwise neat appearance.

"I think he fancies you," said Sarah and snorted laughter.

With a start, Major Talon turned on the other men in the room. "Out! Geddouttahere!" he shouted, waving his arms. Alternating between outrage and surprise, the three officers quit the tent.

"They are not to be trusted," Talon said to the front flap. When he turned and smiled, Keane registered a healthy dose of desperation beneath the alcohol.

"You're gonna help me."

"Yeah, I hate those prissy little marching clowns, too," Keane said, beginning to feel a measure of control creep over the situation. "Sarah, why don't you go lie down through there"—he pointed to the bed in the next room—"and I'll chat with our new best friend here."

Desperate was good. Desperate could be manipulated.

"Mm, good idea," Sarah said, a lopsided smile on her face. As she walked past, she leaned over and slapped Major Talon on the butt. "I'll be in the bed," she said, giving him an exaggerated wink.

Keane massaged his forehead while Talon watched Sarah walk into the back room of the tent. Her hips swayed and one finger played with a long, curling strand of hair.

"I'm sure she didn't mean anything," Keane said to Talon. "She's um... She's drunk."

"She hit me," Talon said, rubbing his rump. "Hard." He stared after her. "She's so big."

"Don't let it throw you," Keane said. "She's also a really bad singer. It evens out."

"Hey," Sarah called from the bedroom, "who's the dead guy?" She laughed. "Get it, Keane? Remember in Dahnt? *Who's the dead guy?*"

"How can you remember anything from Dahnt?" Keane asked. "You were twice as dusted as the rest of us."

Talon blinked twice and then jumped. He ran to the back, all the while making loud shushing noises. Keane followed and crowded into the tiny room behind the major. On the far side of the bed, in a gray uniform of the Ebon Host, though with ornate stitching and covered in black and silver chasing and ornamentation, lay a young man. He stretched out maybe six feet, with brown Pavinn skin and dark, longish brown hair. Most noticeably, his neck twisted around and backwards at a sharp angle that made Keane uncomfortable to think about.

"That is Prince Despin Swifthart of Tyrrane," Talon answered, looking at Keane, his mouth turned down. "Think his clothes'll fit you?"

This time it was Keane who stood there blinking. He looked from the despairing and sweating Major Talon to the prince and then up to Sarah, who lounged on the bed beside the corpse and threw smoldering glances at the major. He considered the front flap of the musty red pavilion, outside of which waited hundreds of angry Tyrranean soldiers.

"This is what I get for a life of wickedness and depravity," said Keane. "Yeah, I think they'll fit."

Keane stripped the prince while Major Talon explained his predicament. Sarah—at Keane's insistence—brewed a pot of the major's coffee.

"How is the prince of Tyrrane a Pavi?" Keane asked. "Was someone fooling around with the help?"

"Yes," Talon answered.

"Oh. I didn't... So, how'd he get dead?"

"We were riding in the... uh, the carriage," Talon said. He stared at dead Despin's brown face. "The royal carriage—all the royals have one—and drinking. The prince can drink—could drink. He had good stuff too." Talon sat down on the bed while Keane pulled off Prince Despin's shirt. "I told him a joke. You ever hear the one about the dog who thinks he's a limner?"

"Yeah," Keane said, removing a thick gold neck chain. *"I would, but I can't understand a thing you're saying."* Both men repeated the punchline, and Talon laughed briefly before becoming glum again.

"Prince Despin thinks it's funny, so he punches me on the arm. I'm laughing too, so I punch *him* on the arm. Only he goes back against the door of the carriage, and it isn't shut proper. Falls out backwards, lands right on his head. Crack."

Keane pulled on a wide steel armband above the prince's right biceps. "Talk about not being able to take a joke. Can you help me get this off?"

Talon looked down. "Don't bother with that," he said. "No one will see it under your shirtsleeve anyway." He blinked and held his head. "Ow. My head really hurts."

"So, you shove Prince Fancyfuck of evil, black-hearted Tyrrane out of the carriage and kill him," Keane said, pulling at the dead man's boots. "That still doesn't explain why I'm changing clothes with him." Sniffing, he said, "Well there's a goddamn miracle. At least he didn't shit himself."

"He's not *the* prince. Just *a* prince," Talon replied. "Is that coffee ready?"

"Almost," called Sarah from the main room.

"I feel like I'm dying here," Major Talon said as he ran his fingernails up and down his scalp. He twisted his silver hair into angles, giving him a crazed appearance. "Right. You're changing clothes with the prince because I have been charged to deliver him to Greenshade where he will marry their Princess Megan Rance and secure peace between Tyrrane and Greenshade." He said all of this with a kind of sliding mumble as if the words were greased, and he couldn't properly bite down on them.

Several thoughts clicked together in Keane's mind, adding up to an irritating and problematic whole. "Are you supposed to pass this dead guy off to a Lieutenant... um... Falt?"—*Was that the name?* —"Lieutenant Falt in Pippiton?" he asked, thinking about the murderous sergeant's 'diplomatical' package.

"Falt. Yes. That's the one. In Pippiton. Just over the river. Only it's not supposed to be a dead guy. Not a dead prince, I mean."

"Right," Keane said as Sarah brought in coffee for the two of them. "And you want me to pretend to be Prince Fancyfuck here so you don't get, what? Kicked out of the Host?"

"Executed," the major replied.

"This is well and truly the *stupidest* thing I have ever heard," Keane said. He stood and wiped his hands on his pants legs. "Even if I did want to do this, which I do *not*, I don't look a damn thing like that man. Who's going to be stupid enough that they believe I'm him?"

"Do what now?" Sarah asked, returning with a fresh cup of coffee and blowing across its surface.

"No one outside Tyrrane has ever seen the prince," Talon said as his voice rose. "Barely anyone outside of the capital city of Dismon has. The royals are paranoid about their security and never go anywhere."

"They *should* have been more concerned with their sodding door latches," Keane said. "Can you believe this shit?" he asked Sarah.

"What shit?" she asked back, glancing up from her cup. She no longer moved much like a drunk person. Alcohol traveled through her fast.

"You can ride in the carriage the whole way there," said Talon. Fresh sweat broke out over his face in the chill tent. "Once you're to Treaty Hill, you can escape. No one will stop you—who's going to say no to a prince? Maybe you can even take away a few keepsakes?"

Keane's angry retort died on his tongue. Sure, it was a stupid idea, but even the stupidest ideas had *some* merit. Traveling to the capital of Greenshade and ripping off the king, being invited right in through the front door of his castle to do it—now *that* was Keane's kind of stupid.

"Oh no," Sarah said, shaking her head, brows knitted together. "There is *no way* this is happening. You can forget it right now."

Keane pulled the prince's silk shirt on over his bare skin. It felt amazing. "We're in," he said.

Major Talon, his eyes glassy but excited, lit up.

"We're out," Sarah responded. "Sorry Keane, but this is just crazy. Even for us."

Talon's face fell once again.

"Look, Major, we're not royals. We don't know how to act. The very first person who has even *met* a royal would have us out in a heartbeat. There's just no way this could work. And as soon as they figured us out, you know who'd they come looking for." Sarah's face turned a forbidding shade of stern.

"Me," Talon said, a queasy pale green color creeping up his neck. "Oldam help me—what was I thinking?"

"Not so fast," Keane said. His mind was buzzing through plans and fantasies of rich treasures. He shoved the prince's money purse and a small gold-inlayed box half-filled with tiny black biscuits into a nondescript canvas sack. "We don't *have* to know how to act. We're going to be in the carriage the whole way there, and when we arrive, we beg off tired from the road. Anyone doesn't like it, we threaten to set 'em on fire or some horseshit. That's what a real prince would do. And you'll be my bodyguard"—he patted a frowning Sarah on the shoulder—"so *you* won't have to talk anyway. Then, in the middle of the night, we grab what we can, slip out of Forest Castle, and walk ourselves right out of Treaty Hill. From there we toddle off to Fish Hill and catch a ship away from Greenshade altogether. It's brilliant!"

"It's stupid," Sarah said. She looked around the big outer room. "Do you have someplace in here to piss?"

"Yes," said Major Talon, pointing to a large ceramic pot with a heavy lid. He returned his attention to Keane.

"That would work. And if you ran away as soon as you got there, no one would ever know you weren't really Prince Despin. They'd just assume he'd taken off again, and I could never get blamed. Nnn... more coffee please."

"Get it yourself," Sarah said, squatting over the pot. "I'm busy." Her normally smooth brown features looked a little pale and blotchy. It was as close as she ever got to an actual hangover. "I have an idiot to try and keep from committing suicide." She looked around. "Is that water?" Talon nodded, and Sarah stood, fastened her breeches, replaced the pot lid, and walked to the water urn where she filled her cup with sweet, cool water.

She took a sip and wrinkled her nose. "Ugh. Water." Sarah stuck out her tongue and then finished the cup.

"Think about it, Keane," Sarah said. "Look at that boy. You're at least five years older than he is. Even if no one has seen him, they're bound to know how old he's supposed to be."

"I didn't think of that," said Talon, hand over his mouth. "They'll know as soon as they see you! Oh, this is *never* going to work."

"I have a *very* youthful face," Keane said, casting a black look at Sarah. "Everybody says. They usually guess me six or seven years younger than I really am." He leaned toward the candle, letting the light illuminate his features.

"What about the rivan," Sarah asked. "She isn't likely to have forgotten us in the last two days."

"We'll be in the carriage the whole way, remember?" Keane lifted both hands, palms up.

"I don't know..." Talon said, examining Keane with a frown.

"It's *very youthful*," repeated Keane, his voice dropping lower.

"This is ridiculous," Sarah said. "Major, what did you mean when you said people would assume Prince Despin had run off *again*?"

The major answered, staring off into the pavilion's deep-red wall. Mold stained the canvas in a blotchy black shape, like a billowing cloud. "He's the youngest of five sons. He's not that important. His mother's not even Andosh. She was a Pavinn maid." Talon's stare wandered to the corpse. "I guess no one ever really bothered with him much. He's a—*was* a—bit of a... a cad, I guess. Not responsible. Runs off and leaves people hanging." Talon turned to look at Sarah. "I was supposed to be keeping a sharp watch on him. Make sure he didn't run off and shirk his duty. He *really* didn't want to get married." He paused. "Oh. Maybe they might try to stop you escaping at that."

Keane pulled on one of Prince Despin's boots and rapped a knuckle on the corpse's shin. "A cad, huh? I'm liking this kid better all the time."

Sarah crossed her arms and frowned at Keane, mouth set in a firm line. She already looked healthier. Keane sort of hated her for those fast recoveries. It wasn't fair.

"What? Why are you looking at me like that?" he asked.

"Were you not listening? The prince is a scoundrel. He's going to be under constant supervision so that he doesn't flee. *Exactly the way we want to.*"

Talon moaned.

"Nah," Keane said, waving the notion away. "He's a prince, not a professional. There's no way that the people watching for this brat to escape are going to be able to stop us."

"You think so?" Talon asked. He looked up at Keane, eyes wide.

Sweat soaked through his fancy uniform, adding to the musty smell inside the big tent.

"Sure I do," Keane answered Talon. "But that's not really the best reason to do this."

Sarah's frown turned into a scowl.

"No, Major Talon, sir, the best reason to continue is that you're already in the soup. You get caught, you're a dead man. You have literally nothing left to lose. But if we succeed, you just might come out of this with a whole skin, and retirement in, what, a couple years?"

"Three months," Talon answered.

"Three months," repeated Keane with a shake of his head. "Wow. I'd hate to see a whole career that close to payoff go off the cliff."

"Well, I'd hate to see us dead even more," Sarah said with a frown. "The major's career aside, we leave now, and we get away without being hung for impersonating a royal, or murder, or stealing a prince's clothes... you look pretty good, by the way."

"Thank you," Keane replied.

"Or whatever else they'd want to hang us for. It only takes one reason to make us dead, and we'll be giving them plenty."

"Well, I, of course, agree with you, Sarah," said Keane.

"You do?" Sarah asked, one brow going up.

"Of course," Keane answered. "Sadly though, we no longer have a choice."

"You don't?" asked Major Talon.

"Not a bit," Keane said, gripping Talon firmly by the shoulder. "You see, Sarah, now that the major here has finally grasped that our complaints are irrelevant, he will undoubtedly order his men outside to cut us down where we stand should we refuse the task."

"I will?" asked Talon.

"Stop interrupting," said Keane. He leaned an elbow on the major's shoulder. "He may look like a bowl of drunken oatmeal and piss, but Major Talon is really quite canny and utterly ruthless."

Talon began to reply, but Keane raised a finger up to his lips and said, "Shh."

Sarah cast around, head shaking and arms raised, as if looking for the answer to their dilemma somewhere in the major's tent. After a brief moment, she closed her eyes and relaxed. "You really are impossible," she said to Keane.

"Don't look at me." He pushed off of the major's shoulder and pointed at him with both hands.

"I'm going to need a uniform," Sarah said. "What rank would a prince's bodyguard be?"

"Uh," Talon said, looking from Keane to Sarah, "sergeant ought to do. One of my men is almost your size. Look in... that chest over there." He rubbed his eyes. "I have to dispose of the prince's ah... body. I need your help," Talon said to Keane.

"Hey, that's why I'm here," said Keane with a smile. "Let's grab one of those rugs from the other room."

After adding a royal Tyrranean sergeant's gray tabard and black cloak to Sarah's mail hauberk and breeches, they wrapped the prince in a long rug. With the hoods of their cloaks raised, the trio carried the body through the now-sleeping camp, dumping it in a shallow bog well off the road.

"Good night, used-to-be-a-prince," said Keane. "And don't let the bedbugs bite."

"The prince is dead, long live the prince," replied Sarah. She was not able to suppress a grim chuckle.

Talon lowered his head, his face a study in misery. "I am going to die," he said.

The three of them returned with the rug and replaced it in the officer's pavilion. Major Talon, scouting ahead, managed to get Sarah and Keane to the prince's carriage without being spotted by the soldiers on watch.

"Lock yourselves in here," he said, rubbing his right hand against his temple. "There's at least one more hour of dark, so try and get a little sleep. We'll be moving out at dawn. See the metal screen on the inside of the window? You can talk to people outside without them getting a good look at you as long as they aren't too close. Best try not to talk to anyone, though. If you can help it."

"That sounds like a smart plan," Keane said. "You've got a real head for criminality, Talon."

Talon grimaced. His hangover was only beginning. "We'll hand you off to the King's Swords just north of the border. Then you'll go right through Pippiton and on to Treaty Hill."

"Perfect." Keane nodded at Sarah. "We'll be safely ensconced in the carriage, which will be surrounded by King's Swords. Even if Harden knew we were not the prince and his bodyguard—which he will *not*—he wouldn't dare approach us. The captains would turn on him in a second if he tried. This couldn't be a better plan if I'd come up with it on my own."

"I agree with that much, anyway," said Sarah. The carriage tipped to one side as she climbed up into it.

The major watched her backside as she went through the doorway.

Keane grinned at him.

"Missed your chance there, soldier. She's a bit shy when she's sober."

Major Talon glanced away from Sarah and stood looking at Keane. He stared blankly for a few seconds and said, "Good luck."

He turned and walked away.

Keane watched Talon lurch back to his oversized tent. This really was a dumb idea, but it would be *so* incredible if they could pull it off. How could he say no? *Of course, if we get caught...*

He pushed the notion out of his head and thought of how much fun it would be to fence the crown of the king of all Greenshade. Smiling, he turned and climbed up opposite Sarah.

"What did he say?" she asked as he closed and fastened the door, leaving them both in the dark.

"He said your ass looked fat."

"No, I meant what did he say about *your* ass."

"Oh," answered Keane. "He said *my* ass looked fabulous."

16

DON'T FORGET TO PEE BEFORE YOU LEAVE

KEANE

After far too short a time, the sounds of breaking camp rang out around the carriage. Soon thereafter, the coach began to move. The infantrymen limited the pace and enforced a placid ride along the well-maintained road. As the sun rose, the interior of the carriage began to heat up. A breeze through the screened side and back windows kept them from getting too warm.

"I think I could get used to this kind of shit," Keane said as he ran a hand over the purple satin upholstery. "If this is how the useless son lives, can you imagine what the important ones get?"

"Pillows made from the breasts of angels?" Sarah shifted, put up her feet on Keane's side of the coach, and crossed her legs. "I could use a few titty-pillows."

Keane smiled. "Honestly, from what I've heard of the Tyrranean royal family, I expected the seats to be cushioned with nails and the headrests to be hooked spikes. But this is..." he trailed off. "I wonder how much a carriage like this is worth?"

"Probably a snapped neck at the end of a rope if you try to sell it anywhere in the Andosh kingdoms," Sarah answered, "and the Darrish wouldn't be caught dead in anything that wasn't 'empire built.' You might sell it in Sedrios though. You could definitely sell it in the Paradisals."

"You can sell anything in the Paradisals, from what I hear," Keane said. "Not always the best prices though."

"I wonder what old Walder would have to say about all this," Sarah said, leaning into a corner of the carriage and smiling. "He'd probably have loved it."

Keane chuckled. Back when he and Sarah had been children on the streets, Walder had taken them in and made them part of his "gang" of children in Levale, a largish city in Northern Greenshade famous for horse breeding. They were the Roaches, and they ran a rundown ghetto of Levale called Slap-Town.

"I know what he would have said." Keane puffed himself up. "Hmph. Do it again."

Sarah joined in. "And don't stop till you get it right!"

Walder had been a father to his little gang of miscreants, though not a good one. He taught the boys and girls equally to fight, to steal, and to stay out of sight when the watch came around—which wasn't often in Slap-Town. The one decent thing he did instill in his Roaches was a sense of discipline. He drilled them in their lessons with yelling, starving, and the old standby—a good cuff to the side of the head. At the time, they had loved him dearly and would have done anything to please him. Now...

They both laughed and then were silent, each lost in their own thoughts and memories. There seemed to be something contemplative in the lilt of the carriage, and the soft clopping of the horses' hooves on the hard-packed dirt outside. Quietly, Sarah undid the braids in her hair and set the leather sleeve on the seat behind her. With her fingers, she brushed the tangles out of the long dark curls.

Keane sat and thought about the time when they first met, before Walder and the Roaches, when they were just two little kids on the street trying to steal enough to eat—and keep out of reach of the bigger kids. Sarah always accused him of romanticizing the time, but you couldn't argue that their goals had been simpler then.

"What do you think ever happened to Walder?" asked Sarah.

"Wasted away drinking spirit milk, most likely," Keane replied.

"I always hoped he'd find a woman worth quitting that stuff for," Sarah said.

"He had a few women," said Keane, "but he could never keep them long. He *was* a hardheaded jackass. I expect that's why he kept going back to the drugs."

Sarah thought about that a few moments and said, "Do you ever wonder what happened to the kids who didn't go to Wallace's Company with us? The rest of the Roaches?"

"Is this about Amadeo?" Keane asked. "Because he was the last of us?"

"Maybe," Sarah replied. "I guess I just wonder how many connections we have left out there."

"We were all street kids. Criminals. They probably graduated to bigger gangs or maybe took off on their own." Keane picked at the dark cherry trim of the carriage's interior and wondered how many of his old crowd were still even alive.

Sarah nodded, keeping her thoughts to herself.

They'd seen a lot of their friends get pinched or killed. Lunei was grabbed one night by the watch and never heard from again. Cass was trapped in a suspicious house fire. *Damn.* Keane hadn't thought about this in a long time. *Sarah used to have a thing for Cass, didn't she?*

As if reading Keane's thoughts, Sarah asked, "What if the kids we knew are dead now? What do you think that means for us?"

Keane broke out into a grin. "Less competition?"

"I'm serious," Sarah said. "They could all be gone. Every single one. We'd never know."

"Then *no* competition."

Sarah leaned over and knuckle-punched Keane on the shoulder, forcing a howl of pain from him.

"Is everything all right in there, Your Grace?" came a call from outside the carriage.

"Everything's goddamn daisies in here!" shouted Keane, rubbing at his shoulder and glaring at Sarah who sat back in her seat looking smug. "Don't know why you'd ask."

"I thought I heard a shout..." said the soldier.

"Can't a man have sex with his own bodyguard without the whole army getting involved in it?" Keane yelled back.

"Ah... sorry, sir. I, ah... forgive me," came the stumbling reply. "Please go on with, uh... whatever."

Sarah's jaw dropped open, and then it was Keane's turn to look smug.

It didn't last though. In an eye blink, Sarah grabbed Keane's wrist and pushed him sideways, twisting his arm up behind his back so that he was certain it was about to come off.

"That was a joke!" he yelled, his voice straining. "No sex in here!" Sarah bent down and whispered something in Keane's ear which he then repeated. "And my bodyguard, who belongs to no man, is totally available to be called upon by respectful gentlemen. Now let me go! Oldam's drooping nipple rings, woman!"

"Ah, all right, sir. I'll, uh... tell the men?"

Sarah let Keane go, and they both retreated to their seats. Sarah brushed her hair out of her face and smoothed her sergeant's tabard.

"After all," she said, "I am a lady."

The two managed to keep quiet until the instant they overheard the driver mutter "royals" under his breath. They both burst into laughter that brought tears to their eyes.

17

ARE WE THERE YET?

KEANE

M ost of a day later, the carriage slowed and stopped in the road. From atop it, the driver announced, "We are arrived just north of the Greenshade River from Pippiton, Your Grace. We have sent men to announce our presence to the King's Swords. Would you like to come out and stretch your legs a bit?"

"What? Ah, no. No thanks," Keane said. He exchanged glances with Sarah. "We're all stretched out in here, you know. Lots of room."

"Very good, sir. I'll inform you when the King's Swords approach."

"Yep," Keane said, shrugging at Sarah. He looked around, and said, "You know, this thing really is roomy. You can sit up straight, and the benches are wide enough to lay down on. Everything is sculpted wood and upholstery... there's even a little glass window in the front. I might just keep it."

"It suits you," Sarah said. "In a sort of I'm-a-fake-prince-in-a-stolen-carriage way."

"You're making it sound so tawdry."

"That's what I meant by 'it suits you.'"

"Your Grace," the driver said, leaning over to speak through the side screen, "the Swords must have had lookouts. They are almost here now."

"Whatever," said Keane, "just tell them we're asleep or something. They can wake us when we get to Treaty Hill."

"I believe their Lieutenant Falt will wish to speak to you during the transfer, sir. Face to face."

Keane turned to Sarah, mouthing the words, "Lieutenant Falt? Did we ever actually *meet* that guy?"

"I don't think so," Sarah whispered back. She leaned up and peered out of a metal screen.

"You don't *think* so? What the stone ballsack does that even mean?"

"No," Sarah whispered, nodding her head. "We absolutely did not meet Lieutenant Falt when we came through Pippiton last." She smiled nervously at him, then returned her attention to the screen. "I am nearly positive," she muttered.

"That's fine," Keane said to the driver. "Just him and Major Talon, though. Too many commoners looking at me at once gives me gas."

There was a pause, and the driver said, "As you request, sir."

"We didn't meet him, right? No, we didn't meet him," said Sarah.

"Well," said Keane, "I guess we'll find out in a minute."

"He's not the guy with the beard, was he?" Sarah asked, fretting. "Because I met that guy."

Moments later there was a knock on the side of the carriage. "Prince Despin Swifthart, Earl of Badiron, Hero of the Paras Plain, and... what does that say?" The reedy voice paused while a mumbled discussion took place. Keane recognized Major Talon's voice. "Liba-tion? That doesn't make any sense. Oh, *liberator*. Yes, of course— ahem—*Liberator* of the Red River Pass. I, Lieutenant Renee Falt of the Swift Shields Unit, King's Swords of Greenshade, do officially welcome you into our nation, and thank you for... what do you mean the door is supposed to be open first? What...? Seriously...? But he didn't open it. All right, hang on."

Another pause, and then Major Talon's voice, "Prince Despin, may we please open the door?"

"Yes?" Keane said. "If you're sure it's, you know, *safe*."

Keane unlatched the ornate padded door from the inside, and Talon opened it. Watery light from an overcast sky settled on a field beside the road, where peasants and travelers walked in order to circumvent the two contingents of military men. A third or so wore the acorn caps of Greenshade, and the others wore floppy brown hats, which Keane guessed must be a Tyrranean thing since Prince Despin's shapeless black velvet hat sat on the seat beside him.

Closer to hand, the clean-shaven Major Talon in his fresh-pressed uniform could not have contrasted more with the chinless and haggard-looking Lieutenant Falt.

The skinny lieutenant held a small stack of fluttering papers in his hands, and the knob in his stubbly throat was clearly visible, bobbing up and down as he gulped air. Keane guessed the man was in his mid-twenties and never served a command post before in his life. Falt tried in vain to straighten the wrinkles in his pale-yellow and green tabard and began again.

"Prince Despin Swifthart, Earl of Badiron, Hero of the Paras Plain, and Liberator of the Red River Pass..."

Keane let him run through the entire speech again, as much to enjoy the lieutenant's obvious discomfiture as to familiarize himself with Prince Despin's titles. When he was finished, Falt took a step back, and said, "If you would be so kind, Your Grace, we have the carriage from Forest Castle just up the road waiting to take you to our capital. I will have your luggage transferred immediately." At that, Falt stepped back and waved a gangly arm for someone to come and get the prince's bags, nearly overbalancing himself and falling backward.

Sarah grasped Keane's arm and gave him a wide-eyed look of alarm. The two of them had interacted with several dozen soldiers of the Ebon Host the night before. If they got out of the carriage and any of those men called them out, the jig was up.

"Nope!" said Keane, with as much authority as he could muster. Although Keane never had a command of his own, he was a studied observer of the men above him and a practiced imitator as well. Very little got more laughs than his impersonation of Captain Eli taking a shit after a big battle.

It was Eli's voice that Keane used now, which threatened to break Sarah's composure and tilt their gambit from its track.

His arm ached where Sarah gripped it.

Lieutenant Falt froze.

Keane said, "We're not getting out, so you can shove a rope up your ass and"—Sarah poked Keane in the ribs, not entirely suppressing her giggle—"uh... that will not be necessary. We're keeping this carriage. I like it."

"But"—Falt riffled through his papers—"that's not... You see, I have to follow the procedure. Everything has already been agreed to. Diplomats, and everything."

Keane's hand was turning white and cold, and the pain from Sarah's grip was inhibiting his breathing. "You are crushing my arm."

She glanced down and released Keane. "Sorry. Just eager to see how everything is going to turn out." She gave him a wide nervous grin and shrugged.

Flexing life back into his fingers, Keane returned his attention to the lieutenant. "Can't switch carriages. I've had this one since I was a little shit, see? Ow... A baby, I mean. The King of Norrik gave it to me as a present on a dun-fishing expedition."

"But—" Falt said.

Keane leaned forward, lowering his voice, "I lost my virginity in this carriage, right? My grandmother died in that very seat."

Lieutenant Falt's mouth fell open.

"The two incidents are unrelated," Keane added.

Sarah tapped Keane on the shoulder and whispered, "I think you might be overexplaining."

Shifting to face her, he whispered back, "Well excuse me for being nervous, sitting here between *two frost-cocked armies*."

She nodded. "You're right. Don't worry about it. You're doing fine."

Keane turned back to Falt, who was glancing back and forth between him and Sarah.

"I think..."

The rest of what the jittery lieutenant thought was lost on Keane, as one of the peasants walking through the field stopped and leered at him. The man loomed head and shoulders above the crowd, one huge arm bound in a sling, and a gray-green acorn cap on his head.

"Burgen," Keane said.

"What?" said Falt. He spun about to follow Keane's gaze, but the giant mercenary had already hunched over and slunk away, losing himself in the crowd. Sarah leaned forward in her seat and scanned the multitude.

"Lieutenant Falt, it is time to go. Now," Keane said. "If it will make things easier on you, you may consider that a royal decree. Or command. Whatever is more appropriate in your strange country."

Falt dropped his gaze to the papers once more, shrugged, and saluted Keane.

"Yes, sir," he said and strode off. He shouted orders to the Swords in his halting voice.

Major Talon stood silently in the doorway.

Keane frowned at him. "If you want this to work, I need a favor. There is a huge guy who just walked by out in that throng. He has a beard and one of those dumb mushroom caps the Greenshaders wear, and his right arm is in a sling. He's nasty as a starving bonewheel but dumb as a sausage. Make him dead."

Talon's eyes narrowed. "It is fortunate for us both then that we are on the Tyrranean side of the river." He gave a tight-lipped smile and held out his hand. "Merry ships and red waves."

Shaking Talon's hand, Keane returned the smile and said, "Happy retirement, Major." With that, he closed and latched the door, then sat back in his seat, giving a worried sigh.

"You saw Burgen out there?" Sarah asked.

"I certainly did," answered Keane.

"Did he see you?"

"Most definitely."

"Think he'll alert the soldiers?"

Keane considered it but shook his head. "I wouldn't put it past him, but no. I don't think so. I imagine he'll be running back to his momma, Captain Darkling, with this kind of news... maybe even Harden." He looked up at Sarah, "Unless we get *really* lucky and Talon's men are able to find and kill the giant bastard."

"That'd be nice," said Sarah.

18

TOO MANY SWORDS SPOILS THE EVERYTHING

ELI

T he early morning sun had not yet crested the Middle Peaks east of Pippiton when Captain Eli entered town alongside Lord Marshal Harden, the three other captains, and a dozen more free fighting men. Rivan Kibbage and two of her guards stood in a half-grown field of emmer next to a mule and cart waiting for them. The crop was tall and golden, near to harvest time, and came up to the men's chests. Kibbage was lost to sight in it. The King's Swords were a day gone, and Wallace's Company were now the only fighting men anywhere nearby.

Eli did not care for Harden's decision to bring the others. Too many soldiers invited violent solutions to everyday problems, and he trusted the other captains about as far as he could shit all three of them with his pants on. The old man just wanted them to be there to see it when he got the wagebox back.

"Good morning, Rivan," said Harden, opening an arm wide to take in the burgeoning day around them. "It's wonderful to meet with friends on such a glorious day as today."

"I'm happy to hear you say that, Harden," Kibbage replied. Her thin lips pulled back in a smile, spreading pleasing wrinkles over her weathered face—though her eyes stayed narrow and observant. The rivan pulled out a long-handled wooden pipe and a leather pouch and stuffed the bowl with damp leaves. The smokeweed smelled like roses and sassafras left too long in the dark. It was the kind of thing you puffed on to hurry strangers away from your door.

Nevertheless, to Eli's ear, it sounded as if the old woman was happy. Having been around for all of Harden's interactions with the rivan of Pippiton, Eli doubted that either of them considered the other a friend, but Kibbage jumped a bit in Eli's estimation for faking it so well.

"Any news from the world?" Kibbage asked as if she were discussing the weather with any farmer in the field.

From behind, Captain Darkling sighed, expressing his impatience. Eli whirled and cast him a black glance. Darkling pulled at the sleeves of his ridiculous blue coat and looked off into the sky.

"Verran and Egren are still at each other trying to decide which country's royals get to be the rulers of the next Darrish Empire," said Harden, smiling.

"Alir help us if they ever reach a decision," replied Kibbage.

Eli glanced north toward the distant mountains where the Alir were supposed to live. The old Andosh gods had never been much use to him, but even he still said an occasional prayer to Hagrim the Dwarf.

"Tyrrane and Coldspine continue to waste good men over the Paras Plain," Harden continued. All of this chat was irrelevant, of course, but Eli thought it proper that the forms were observed. Not like the other captains would ever have done it.

This time it was Captain Lowger who coughed, letting everyone know he'd had enough chit-chat. Eli ignored the tall Darrishman. The conversation was coming to a close anyway.

Eli missed Rivan Kibbage's opinion about the Paras Plain. One of her guards pulled the wagebox out of the cart with obvious effort and shuffled toward Harden with it.

"All here," Kibbage said about the battered wood and iron cash box. "We never even opened it, just heard it jingle. Whatever was inside when they came into town is still in it now."

"I am pleased you were able to keep my belongings safe," said Harden. "I more than half expected the Swords to take everything—especially with the way that sergeant was talking."

"I did too," Kibbage replied. "But they let out of here yesterday morning without even a goodbye, and no one mentioned the box to me. I figured that meant it was yours." Her face grew even less expressive than normal. "And apparently that sergeant had an accident. They're taking him back in a box."

"Can't say that's bad news." Harden's grin widened. "You've earned some goodwill here today, Rivan. And that is no lie. If the day continues as it has so far, I may not kill anyone at all." He winked at her underneath the wide brim of his hat. "That's a joke. We're all friends here."

Harden stepped around the struggling guard and looked in the cart. "What's in the saddlebags?"

"They had those bags with them when they showed up. Looked like money and some keepsakes from raids and such. I figured they were yours too."

"Good enough," Harden said, turning to look down at the rivan. "Now tell me," he said, becoming serious, "what happened to Keane and Sarah? Why are they not here along with my box and my saddlebags?"

Eli thought Kibbage must be nervous, but she hid it well.

"I really don't know," Rivan Kibbage said, spreading her hands, "though I have suspicions. The morning after they were taken prisoner, one of my guards was dead in the jail, as well as that sergeant you mentioned. I imagine this had something to do with his accident. Both my guard and the sergeant had crossbow bolts in them. Your two were gone, and the others in the next cell all claimed not to have seen a thing. They'd lied about being Swords instead of your men, but the Swords were about to leave, and I figured you might take it as a kindness if I cut 'em loose. You should ask them what happened."

Harden *had* asked them, Eli knew. Except only three of them had made it back, and the story they told matched what Kibbage was saying. As soon as word came in that Sarah and Keane escaped,

Harden had sent runners out in every direction and put guards at every point in or out of town, all of it fruitless.

Captain Lowger slid off his horse and stepped forward. He was six-and-a-half feet of ropy muscle, fast as a wildcat, and far less predictable. Eli thought he must be from Egren, judging by his superior behavior. Of all the Darrish nations, Egren was by far the most arrogant.

But then they *had* almost taken over the whole damn world.

"Lord Marshal," Lowger said, his voice a rumbling bass, "we have the wagebox. We do not require the traitors."

"Oh? Are you Lord Marshal now?" Harden asked, his smile full of menace and blood.

"We ever follow where you lead, Lord Marshal Grayspring," Captain Vancess, last of the captains, joined in from his horse. His bright armor glittered as the first morning rays topped the mountains. Unlike Lowger, Vancess did not leave the relative safety of the dozen soldiers around him. "But we have the welfare of the men to consider above all. They wait to be paid, not wreak bloody vengeance. I sympathize with your plight, truly I do, but we must set our prows toward gain. Perhaps an easy target, currently within striking distance, to sate the men's appetites and fill their pockets?" Vancess gestured toward Pippiton and twirled his mustache.

Rivan Kibbage's pale blue eyes grew hard.

Eli rested a hand on the pommel of his short sword. Harden's years of command had built a reputation around Wallace's Company. When the army came to town, people paid them to leave. Simple as that. The arrangement not only saved the lives of a lot of townsfolk and villagers, it also saved the lives of mercenaries as well. Central to that reputation was the assurance that the company would leave when whatever deal at hand was struck. Vancess's suggestion threatened their ability to do business.

"I see," said Harden. "So now not only do our promises of cooperation mean nothing"—he swept an arm in Kibbage's direction—"but the justice of our own code is meaningless as well." He jabbed the forefinger of his other hand at his heart. "Keane steals from the freemen of Wallace's Company, the very teat from which you *all* suck, and that carries no weight? No consequence? Should we lay down our swords and become farmers and craftsmen? Become the very prey on whom we live? He stole from *you*. Our law, the freeman's law, demands he pay for it."

At the last, Captain Darkling stepped forward. Dressed in bright blue finery one would never expect to find out-of-doors, much less on a battlefield, he looked the utter embodiment of calm discretion and reasonableness.

Eli hated him most.

"We are hardly ready to become farmers, Lord Marshal. Our hearts yearn for justice, and we are all lessened by the unrequited contempt we feel for those two bitter souls who both took our dignity, and who wounded you so grievously. But the simple truth is, we no longer know where to look. They are gone—snowflakes in the ocean. If we but knew where they were, in which direction they headed, I would personally follow them to the ends of the world to capture them for your pleasure. But we do not. It saddens me to admit, but it is time we moved on."

Eli watched Harden. His old friend stood staring at Darkling, saying nothing. Eli figured Harden knew he had been outmaneuvered, and that a reckoning could not be far behind.

Harden opened his mouth to speak.

"I know where they are!" Burgen shouted, running across the field from the north, one beefy arm waving in the air, the other tied tight across his middle. His face and arms were covered in scratches and other small wounds, but his eyes were fever bright. "I saw them. I know where they's going!"

Harden turned to look at Darkling, a wide, toothy grin on his face. It was the captain's turn to be a stone.

Darkling's left eye twitched.

"Well good on ya," Eli said as he clapped Darkling on the back and gripped him by the arm. "Let's ask your boy Burgen and find out which end of the world you'll be off to, then."

As Burgen came huffing and blowing into the circle of mercenaries, Eli noticed Rivan Kibbage and her men slink back to town. He chuckled and shook his head. Kibbage always knew exactly when to make her exit.

"Catch yer breath, lad," Eli said to Burgen, "and tell us where you spied our wayward soldiers."

"They was on a carriage," he said, breathing like a bellows. "All dressed up like nobles or whatnot. The Ebon Host was escortin' 'em, an' passed 'em off to the King's Swords. They's headed to Treaty Hill!"

"Impersonating nobles?" Harden asked. Burgen nodded his head in answer. "Son of a bitch. We watched that Tyrranean carriage roll right through here yesterday with the Swords in tow. That explains how they got past us, at any rate."

Darkling sighed, and Eli spotted Lowger running his fingers across the pommel of his scimitar. Vancess looked from face to face, as if not certain what just transpired, searching for clues. If Vancess's men loved him any less than they did, he would be useless. Somehow his fever transferred to them, and they followed him anywhere, no matter the danger.

"The Swords left yesterday," Eli said to Burgen. "Why are we just hearing about this now? Mighta been we coulda done something about it if'n you'd gotten here more timely-like."

"Swords took off, but the Host is still out there," Burgen said. "It was Keane and Sarah's fault. They set them Tyrranean fuckers on me. They been after me since yesterday, and I been hidin' all night long. They're probably still out there lookin'.'"

"Everyone, back to camp," commanded Harden. "Eli, disburse the men's wages. I need to think on this for a while."

The freemen all grinned and laughed, bragging to each other about the ways in which they would waste their money. In front of them, their captains exchanged dark stares, their intentions murkier. Eli did not display the satisfaction he felt at Harden's victory over the evil bastards.

Harden Grayspring had commanded Wallace's Company for over twenty years now, with Eli walking beside him every step of the way. History bound the two men together. History of blood, violence, and terrible, terrible deeds. Against all odds, the two of them yet survived. Eli watched many different types of men serve the Company as captains, but eventually, all of them that made it through the fighting part turned out the same. They all thought that they deserved to be in charge and live in the big tent. But whether they were hard-assed, crazy, or just plain evil, Harden eventually bested them all.

Eli didn't reckon that would change anytime soon.

19

PLANNING OTHER PEOPLE'S CRIMES

ELI

As the group rode back to the encampment, Eli and Harden moved apart from the rest.

"You were pretty quiet back there," Harden said. The horses picked their way through a line of beets. "Until Burgen showed up, anyway. Something on your mind?"

Eli considered, choosing his words. "Well, o'course you know I'll back whatever play you got, but truth to tell, I just don't see the profit in it." He thought for a moment more and pressed on. "The cap'ns ain't happy because they ain't earning, and while the three of 'em together would lose a game of castles to a cat, I ain't sure they're wrong. Chasing them kids ain't gonna fill no bellies, and we both know what that does to men like ours."

"Sarah and Keane aren't kids anymore," Harden replied. "They haven't been for quite a while."

"A'right, that's true," said Eli, "but it ain't the point. Hell, Darkling..."

"When Captain Darkling becomes the lord marshal, then he can decide what this company will do." Harden's tone was the kind of calm that Eli knew better than to argue with.

They left their horses with the corral master and continued on foot. Eli hefted the wagebox and maneuvered one end to Harden. Together they carried it toward the lord marshal's tent.

Eli tried a different tack. "Good enough, good enough. No one is trying to overthrow you. Yet, anyways. But... can you just tell me *why* we're doing this? You didn't get this outta joint when Marbles ran off, and that bastard took two o' your favorite women... *and* your hat."

Harden's hand went to his dust-colored leather hat, and he ran a finger along the wide brim. He'd pinched it as a replacement, but he often said that he never did like it quite as much as the one Marbles stole.

The weight of the box between them threw the pair off-balance. They moved slow and awkward through the tents in the dusty field.

"If we ever find out where Marbles is living," Harden said, "I feel certain that Captain Darkling will want to pursue him to the end of the world as well."

Eli tilted his head. "That ain't an answer."

The two old mercenaries entered Harden's tent. Eli took the other end of the box from Harden and set it on the map table with a loud thump. Blue morning light shone in through the canvas walls of the tent.

Harden sighed, staring at the grassy floor. "Keane tried to kill me. He snuck in here while I was asleep and tried to cut my throat."

"Sarah with him?"

"Of course Sarah wasn't with him," Harden answered. "I'm alive, aren't I? I don't think she knows anything about it."

Eli puffed out his cheeks and leaned back against the table. "So, whyn't we kill him then?" He had a feeling that this was less about hearing the reason for chasing Keane than it was foolproofing the one that Harden was creating on the spot. Wouldn't be the first time.

"I was half asleep, wasn't I?" Harden replied. "Couldn't be sure it was him. Not until after I found that... thing that he always wears on my floor. That thing that came off in the struggle."

"I'll go through the shit we took off him 'fore we threw him in the wagon," said Eli. "I'm fair sure that thing he always wears is a dagger."

"That's right." Harden snapped his fingers. "It *was* a dagger. I only just found it and connected the pieces."

Eli scratched at his shiny pate. "That gives you reason to want him dead, but it ain't good enough to push the whole company after one man when there's no profit in it."

"Did you notice that Keane got half the coin out of the wagebox before we recaptured it?" asked Harden. "Poor Sarah's carrying it thinking it's money rightfully stolen from the rivan of Pippiton, and she has no idea it's really ours."

If anything, the damn box felt heavier now. But Keane stealing half their wages might motivate some of the company to want to go find him.

"So... Sarah's an innocent babe in alla this?" Eli did not know why Harden kept trying to kill one thieving traitor and protect the other thieving traitor.

Probably best not to think about that now. He might not want to know.

Harden clapped his hands. "Just so. Keane is probably planning on selling her as a soldier slave in Egren. Regardless, he is definitely planning to hire his own mercenaries in an attempt to come back here and destroy the company—and myself—for good."

If only.

"I don't think anyone'll buy Sarah getting sold anywhere she don't wanna," Eli said, shaking his head. "Might wanna back offa that part. Rest is good, though."

"Too bad," answered Harden. "She's popular. The men would've liked the idea of riding off to rescue her."

In Eli's estimation, it was Harden who would've liked the idea of rescuing the big she-ox.

"Either way," Eli said, his expression neutral, "sorry to hear about your near brush with death and all."

"Always sleep with one eye open," Harden said. He rubbed his hands together. "So, once we pay the wages we're behind, how much will we have left?"

Eli pushed himself off the map table, turned, and then opened the wagebox with the key he kept around his neck. He pushed aside the hard leather bags of coin and dug in the loose silver to uncover a woodbound ledger wrapped in a dark leather strap. He unwrapped it, opened it, and flipped forward to the halfway point.

"Minus what the traitor Keane just stole, quite a lot. There's almost eight thousand silver—mixed Arlean, Rousland, and Green-shade—and there's still the four hundred in Tyrranean gold we got as half pay for sacking Gullhome." King Brannok of Tyrrane had stiffed them on the remainder of the job and became the reason Harden no longer worked for royals. The subject continued to stick in Eli's craw.

"I *still* get the shivers when I think about that place. I don't know how them nutters live in that kinda cold. That purple wizardfire their demon made would kill a man fast enough, but it didn't heat for shit."

Of course, it got just as frigid in Coldspine, where Eli had come from, which might have been the reason forty-five years had passed since he last saw home.

"That ought to be enough," Harden said.

"We doing some shopping?" Eli asked.

"That we are, my friend. We are headed to Vastard."

"*What?*" Eli's eyes widened in disbelief. He could not believe what he was hearing. "That is *not* a good idea, Keane story be damned. Harden, the other cap'ns—"

"Hang the other captains," Harden said, a faraway gleam in his eye. "This isn't about them."

"It'll start being about them right quick when they string you up by your innards," Eli said. He wasn't getting through. "You expect me to keep a lid on those bastards while you're gone? Hell, they're more like to string me up than—"

"No, I'll need you with me," Harden said. "There'll be more than enough for you to look after as it is."

Eli bit his lip, thinking hard. "You can't leave the three of them," he said.

"We'll take Lowger, then," Harden said. "He's a big, glowery sort of fellow. That could come in handy."

"No," said Eli. "We gotta take Darkling."

"Really? Why is that?"

"Either of the other two would listen to him, and by the time we got back, Wallace's Company would be his—all sewn up with a bloody red bow. But Vancess and Lowger hate each other. They'll never cooperate, and they'll make such a mess that by the time you get back, everyone'll be pleased as kittens to see you."

Harden grinned at his friend. "And they say I'm the smart one."

Eli's mouth fell open as one grizzled brow shot up. "Huh? Who said that?"

The two of them sat silent for a moment, and Harden took his steel and gold whiskey flask out of his belt. It was dented and the gilt had mostly rubbed off, but other than Eli, it was the oldest thing in the camp. He took a swig and offered it to his friend.

"Hagrim's bitter backside, yes," Eli said. He reached for the flask like a man floating in the ocean reaching for a jug of ice-cooled water —carried by a dozen, beautiful, naked women. He drank deep. "For what you're planning to do," he told Harden, "we're gonna need all the whiskey we can carry."

20

PREEMPTIVE SKULLDUGGERY

ELI

Two days had passed, and a group of twenty mercenaries camped just off the road beside a log-built roadhouse. This lay halfway between Pippiton and the city of Levale, where travelers would be sure to need it, on Greenshade's eastern border with Tyrrane. Their small dirty tents faded into the wooded foothills of the Brighthorn Mountains as the sun fell past the world.

The roadhouse was one of the many that dotted the highways, each about a day's travel from the last. Composed of four or five rooms, a common area big enough for six to eight people to eat and drink, as well as the means to feed them, most were pretty much the same.

Eli and Darkling brought ten freemen each, and these pitched tents and built fires, getting ready for the night. The two groups stayed separate and watched each other with distrustful glances and dark scowls.

The windows of the roadhouse glowed a cheery gold against the twilight woodlands. Smells of cooking meat rolled out of its chimney and worsened the moods of the mercenaries eating cabbage and hard tack outside.

Harden and his two captains quartered in the roadhouse. Only one other patron was kicked out to make room, and he had been happy to leave as soon as he understood the nature of those doing the kicking.

Eli walked down the dark and low-ceilinged hallway to Harden's room with Burgen in tow. There was no question of whether skull-duggery might erupt from Darkling's corner, only how bad it might be. Harden agreed with Eli's notion that the only way to stop the troublesome captain's scheming would be to preempt him with a vile plot of their own. Burgen was Darkling's right-hand man and, being both stupid and selfish, the perfect lever to pull.

A few moments earlier, Eli had discovered Burgen throttling the poor man who had been booted from the inn to make room for the captains. Out of professional courtesy, he waited until the traveler was dead and his pockets thoroughly looted before he cleared his throat and made himself known.

Burgen had looked surprised, embarrassed, and angry, like a boy caught with a corpse and his pants down. The thought caused Eli to reflect—not for the first time—that he had been a mercenary for longer, and seen far more than anyone should ever have to.

Now, in front of Harden's door, Eli knocked. At the lord marshal's response, he and Burgen entered.

Eli moved to the side of the room and sat on a sturdy wooden stool beside a small table. Harden sat up on the edge of the straw-tick bed, looking calm and carefree. Burgen stood in the middle of the little boarded room, fidgeting with the sling that held his injured arm. His head brushed the ceiling.

"Would you mind closing the door?" Harden asked the giant man. "This is going to be a private conversation. Just us friends."

Burgen turned about, trying not to bump into anything, and closed the door. Lighter than expected, it slammed shut. The big man jumped and knocked his head on the wooden slats above him. His elbow pushed a candle off a wall sconce. It bounced on the floor and guttered.

Harden waited for Burgen to replace the candle and spoke. "You look kinda worried, Burgen. Everything all right?"

"Oh, um... yeah. Sure." Burgen looked at Harden and down at his own feet. Harden let the silence stretch. "Everything's... fine. Y'know. Just the usual stuff."

The big freeman's rumbly voice wavered, uncertain.

"The usual stuff?" asked Harden, crossing his legs and reaching over to the table for his teacup.

"Um..." Burgen's fidgeting was spreading to the rest of his body. He started shuffling his right foot, sliding it back and forth against the floorboards. "Cap'n Darklin's wonderin' what we're doin' out here, I guess. I guess we all are."

Once again Harden said nothing. The longer the quiet went on, the more the big man twitched.

"Darklin's not happy, for sure," Burgen said, sweat breaking out across his forehead. "He says..." Burgen looked pained like he was adding long rows of numbers in his head, and his brain was cracking under the stress.

"I've been noticing you, Burgen. You stand out around the other men." Harden took a sip of whiskey-laced tea.

"I'm big," Burgen replied.

Eli couldn't repress a chuckle at the obviousness of the statement, and Harden threw him a dark glance. Burgen dragged a foot and pulled out beard hairs, dropping them on the floor.

"That's not what I meant," Harden said, blowing past the interruption. "You have your own crew, do you not? Four or five of the biggest men in Wallace's Company? The men that your captain sent in after Sarah and Keane."

"Yessir," said Burgen, wincing.

"See, Eli, that's what I was talking about. Initiative. Men with drive. That's what our company lacks."

"Right as always, sir," Eli said.

Given that their biggest problem was almost always folk overreaching themselves, Eli found it bloody unlikely that they needed any more ambitious ball hangers in their midst, but this was Harden's show.

Burgen stopped picking at his sling and looked almost hopeful at the turn the conversation had taken.

"You're a leader, Burgen, whether you realize it or not. You shouldn't be taking orders—you should be giving them." Harden said this matter-of-factly, as if it were the most obvious thing in the world.

"Am I gonna be a captain?" Burgen asked.

"Maybe," said Harden, "maybe. But that's not really the main reason you're here. Eli? Did you happen to mention to Burgen the real reason he was here?"

"Musta slipped my mind, sir," Eli said.

"That's all right," Harden said. "I'm happy to tell him. You see, Burgen, I am afraid that Captain Darkling is planning to betray me."

Burgen's face froze, confirming what Eli and Harden already knew. His eyes darted around the room. *Looking for another way out?* Eli thought.

The big fella seemed to master himself, and said, "I don't know nuthin' 'bout it."

"Of *course*, you don't," Harden said, his easy smile seemed wolflike to Eli. "But I'm willing to bet that you will."

"Huh?"

"Captain Darkling is going to ask you to kill me, Burgen. He'll probably give you a dagger and tell you to come at me in the night or when I'm off taking a piss. I know this because you are his best man and because you are utterly trustworthy. That's why you are his only choice."

This was a strange dance Harden was engaged in. He flitted from accusation to flattery and then back again. It seemed to mesmerize poor, brutish Burgen. Eli had seen Harden do this before, and he always found it fascinating.

"I... what?" Burgen said.

"Now, of course, a man like you wouldn't strike against his commander in such a cowardly fashion—we both know that. But a man who would *let me know* that such an order had been given by a traitorous captain... well, that man could find himself in a promotable position. Especially if he were a natural leader. With *initiative*."

Eli watched the puzzle pieces turning in Burgen's head. With ponderous slowness, the giant's expression of confusion changed back to his more familiar evil leer.

"Aye, sir," he said at length. "I know *just* what to do."

"Good, good," said Harden, clapping his hands and rubbing them together in a gesture more familiar to Eli than his own voice. "Now, let's see. We're going to need an excuse for you to be here talking to me."

"We will?" asked Burgen.

"We will indeed," said Harden. "Captain Darkling will undoubtedly find out about our little chat and ask you what it was all about. It would be better if you ran to him straightaway and gave him a different story."

"Oh. Uh, all right."

"Tell your captain that I questioned you mercilessly about whether or not he'd made contact with a tinker in a wagon with a red-painted roof. Tell him I tried to hide it, but that you thought I looked scared. Terrified."

"I can do that," Burgen said.

"Wonderful," Harden said, standing and extending a hand. "I believe you and I are going to have a very long, very *profitable* career together, Burgen. I truly look forward to our next visit."

"Aye," Burgen said, his leer that of a demented executioner. "Can't imagine it'll be long now." He shook Harden's hand, giving it the appearance of a child's.

There was a pause. Harden said, "Off you go."

Burgen turned and let himself out, knocking over the candle again. After the door closed, Eli listened to the huge steps plodding down the hall and stairs.

"You know," Eli said, still staring at the door, "I don't believe he intends to wait for Darkling to actually give him that order before he turns the evil ponce in."

"Never occurred to me he would," said Harden. "Hell, I'd be

surprised if Darkling had the stones to do it at all, out here on the road. Everyone would know it was him. He certainly couldn't blame *you*."

Eli looked over at Harden and shook his head, smiling. "You, Harden Grayspring—and I say this with alla love and respect in the world—are the biggest fucking bastard I have ever met."

"You're a sweetheart," Harden said.

"You know Darkling'll never buy all that crap about a tinker with a red-roof wagon. He's a rotted piece of shit, but he ain't actually stupid."

"I know," Harden said, sitting back down on the bed. "But he won't be able to stop himself from sending men all over the country-side looking for one anyway, and that'll keep him distracted—which is less time spent plotting against me."

"Why'd you ever make that backstabber a captain anyway?" Eli asked. He already knew the answer, but he thought that perhaps pointing it out might offer a little perspective.

"He reminded me of myself," Harden answered. "Besides, I had just asked him to kill *his* captain, and there was an opening."

21

MOVING ON UP

KEANE

Keane sat forward on the purple upholstered seat, his face pressed up against the screened window. After eight days of travel, the interior of the carriage smelled of old feet and sweat.

"I suddenly feel vastly underprepared for this," Keane said. Outside the window of the carriage, he saw the city of Treaty Hill and Forest Castle, where the royal family of Greenshade lived, looming over the skyline. The greenish-gray castle sat atop a smooth-sloped hill with one wall that encircled the castle keep and another that ran all the way round the base of the hill. Most of the city lay outside this outer wall, but Keane observed a great many large buildings within, with an unusual variety of architecture.

Both Keane and Sarah had been to Treaty Hill before, multiple times in fact. But neither of them had ever ventured into the walls surrounding Forest Castle. Today, they would not only go through those gates but into the keep itself.

He wiped his clammy hands on Prince Despin's borrowed tabard.

"You were completely ready to sally forth and plunder a week ago when I was trying to talk you out of all this," Sarah said, inspecting the uniform in her lap for lint. She had been restless most of the trip, stretching and twisting and all but pacing the tiny interior of the cabin. She was not built for sitting still.

"What if I put the stupid crown on backwards, or eat my soup with the wrong fork, and they know I'm not a royal and they execute us?"

"Unlikely," said Sarah. She put a stray thread between her teeth and bit it off. "You eat soup with a spoon, and you don't have a crown."

Keane looked at her as if her brains had just fallen out the back of her head. "*It's not about the goddamn crown!*" he said between clenched teeth. "We need to get out of here. Right now."

"Too late," Sarah said, regarding Keane with forced calmness. She slid the tabard over her head and pulled back her hair, getting arranged for their debut at Forest Castle. "You'll be fine. Just tell them you're tired and you need some sleep. You look horrible. They'll believe it, easy. Hold this."

"Easy..." Keane repeated, holding the end of one of Sarah's braids.

"Sure," Sarah went on. As she spoke, she pulled the main part of her hair back and held it in place with one braid from each temple. "And as soon as everybody is asleep, we go right out the window. By the time they know we aren't there, we'll already be on our way to Sedrios. Or Rousland. Did we ever decide?" She pulled the braids together in the leather sleeve behind her head and pushed a wooden pin through it.

"Yeah. Sure. Sedrios." Keane sat upright, clutching Sarah's knee. "Oldam's merry stone prostate! You're right. Where's my crown?"

From outside the carriage, Lieutenant Falt spoke up. "We are entering Treaty Hill now, Your Grace. If you would like, I can describe the city as we pass by, and give you a flavor of your new home."

"I've already been—ow!" Keane said, rubbing his ribs where Sarah poked him.

Sarah glanced between Keene and the metal screen in the carriage door, brow furrowed. "You may have been here before," she whispered, "but Prince Despin hasn't, remember?"

Grimacing, Keane coughed and called out through the grate, "That would be very good, Lieutenant. Please do."

Falt cleared his throat and began his narration of the remaining leg of their journey. "As you can see from here, Forest Castle sits atop a large hill, which gives the city part of its name. Most of Treaty Hill slopes a bit, all the way out to the farmland here at the edge of Three Sister's Wood. The crops are primarily..."

"You think they'll want to give me any gifts when we show up?" Keane asked Sarah. He was standing on one leg, his other knee on the seat, with his nose pressed against the screen. Sarah sat on the other seat against the opposite wall, her powerful legs stretched out in front of her.

"What, like for showing up?" she said.

"I don't know. Isn't that something rich people do whenever they visit each other? Bring bugs made out of gold or fancy shoes or crumpets and chicken?"

"Are you wanting a pair of fancy shoes?" Sarah asked, a slow smile creeping up one side of her face.

Keane turned and looked at her. "Are *we* supposed to be bringing gifts?" he asked, eyes widening.

Sarah's face shifted from smile to stern mock scowl. "How is it that when *I* am the one preaching caution," she said, "*you* want to charge ahead like a Norrikman toward a pasture of unwed sheep. But the very instant that it is too late, and we are completely committed to *your* plan, all you can do is worry and stress."

He shrugged. "I'm a very complex person."

They rode for a while, listening to Falt drone on about merchant guilds, his favorite places to eat, the pros and cons of military life in a big city, and, for some reason, an extended digression about the care and feeding of cats. The carriage slowed, and Keane and Sarah moved to peer out of a side screen. They had reached the Country Gate, the entrance through the outer wall of Forest Castle, where neither of them had ever been.

"Inside the outer wall," continued the lieutenant, unaware that he only now had an attentive audience, "lies the Quarters, also known as

'Little Everywhere.' As I am sure you know, one quarter is given to the embassies of the Andosh peoples, one to the Pavinn, and one to the Darrish. These three and the final quarter, which is reserved for the thirteen international markets of Andos and some important government buildings, ring the castle itself, now in front of us. If you look to the right as we pass the embassy halls of Norrik, you can spot the delegation house of Tyrrane. It's that big black building with the wall around it. I'm sure they'll be happy to drop in and pay their respects."

Keane felt as though he was going to throw up. He hadn't even considered diplomats dropping in to say hi. This whole adventure could be over before it started. He felt Sarah's firm hand on his shoulder and drew strength from it.

"The short white wall is the grand courtyard of the Rousland embassy," Falt said, indicating a twenty-foot-high wall made of marble blocks. It was short only in comparison to the eighty-foot-high walls of the castle and outer ring. "You will likely see it often, as the embassy lends it for all kinds of festivities and pronouncements."

The Rousland embassy looked brighter and friendlier than the other state buildings here. Its white walls were not even gated, always open to all comers. Keane thought it must be a place of celebrations and friendships—the results of nations who put away their swords in favor of trust.

It sat directly across from the Tyrranean embassy, its own dark gated walls opposite in every possible way.

The sky went dark for the second time as the carriage passed beneath the interior castle gate. They were inside Forest Castle itself now. Keane swallowed, though his mouth had gone dry and his hands were clammy.

"They're going to greet us at the door," Keane said. "What if the guys from the embassy are there too?"

"I honestly don't know," Sarah replied. "Try our hands at escaping the dungeon? Didn't one of Vancess's men claim to have escaped from here?" She looked calm, but Keane could hear the anxiety in her voice.

"Yeah," Keane said. "That was Zeffer. He also said he got swallowed by a giant bonewheel and lived for three days in its stomach by eating its eggs. Remember the conversation about birds not being hollow, feathered sacks?"

Sarah was silent a moment as the hope drained out of her face. "Oh. Yes. I suppose I do remember that. As I recall, he also thought that Pavinn women could fly if they went outside naked."

"I think he may have just been trying to see you naked with that one," Keane said, a bitter smile on his face. He turned back to the screen and Lieutenant Falt.

"The four primary towers of the castle, the Crows Tower, Stone Tower, Night Tower, and Monarchs Tower," Falt went on, "are accessible from the palace, of course, and are also interconnected by the famous 'flying halls.' These are a source of amazement to all our visitors."

Craning his neck, Keane could see the four towers, each a different width and height, as well as the wide hallways that spanned the otherwise empty spaces between them. These halls were over a hundred feet in the air, supported by strong-looking arched buttresses against the greenish stone towers. Except for the wide gray one called the Stone Tower, everything seemed to be constructed of the same green-tinted granite.

The flying halls were more than high enough to toss an imposter to his death from.

"Are those... trees?" asked Keane.

"Yes, Your Grace," answered Lieutenant Falt. He pointed up to the half-opened rooftop of the gray Stone Tower. "That is the Tall Garden. A small forest *inside* Forest Castle. I'm told it is a very contemplative place to withdraw. There are foxes, I understand."

Sarah shook her head and looked back at Keane, one brow raised and a smirk on her lips. "Rich people build giant stone houses to get in out of the woods and then find themselves so separated from the outside world that they have to build the woods inside their houses." She did an almost perfect job of masking her nerves. No one but Keane would ever have noticed.

"We have to assume that there will be Tyrraneans there when we open the door," Keane said, thinking as he spoke. "If they are just some political appointees, it's *possible* they might never have met the prince."

"Or that they met him only as a child," Sarah said. "Who knows how long they will have been here?"

"Even if they did recognize me as not being Despin," Keane said, nervously picking at the corner of the screen, "they might assume I am some kind of ruse by King Brannok. That could buy us enough time to..." The carriage lurched to a halt.

"Shit. We're here. Shitshitshitshit..."

Sarah took Keane's hand and pulled him to the seat beside her. "Whatever happens," she said quietly, "we face it together. Just like we always have."

Her quiet strength flowed into his arm and settled him. Then he noticed her leg bouncing up and down, and his anxiety returned.

Keane looked back up through the grate. The carriage was on a wide curved cobblestone drive of light-colored bricks that ran straight to the front steps of the castle keep. From this close, the keep stretched away into the sky, and the almost friendly-appearing structure made a decidedly military turn. Big picture windows rose far above, but closer to the ground, soldiers looked out through arrow slits and steel doorways, and the whole projected a sense of thick, inviolate strength.

At the foot of the tall stairway stood a row of people Keane could not make out very well. They were surrounded by guards, and behind them stood an ordered column of gold-and-green-liveried servants.

"How screwed are we?" asked Sarah, fidgeting behind Keane.

He shrugged. "Dunno."

Lieutenant Falt's voice, strident and high, jolted from just outside the carriage, causing both of them to jump. "Announcing Prince Despin Swifthart, Earl of Badiron, Hero of the Paras Plain, and, ah, Liberator of the Red River Pass!" The carriage door handle turned but failed to open. "Uh..." Falt's voice came.

"We can't go out there," Keane said, looking out the screen. Keane held the unlatched door handle shut in a white-knuckle grip, pulling it fast against Lieutenant Falt's efforts. "What if I said I was sick?"

"We have to face it like everything is normal," Sarah said, her face set and grim. "Now."

Sarah pushed Keane to his feet with one hand and opened the carriage door with the other. She shoved him out. He stumbled but managed not to go tumbling onto the cobbles.

Keane stood up straight, his most winning smile pasted to his face. Seabirds called overhead, and from his right, the hooting cry of some unfamiliar animal drifted over the wall. The air was sweet and fresh after the confines of the carriage, but it only made Keane feel more exposed.

Looking ahead, Keane concentrated on his peripheral vision. He could make out no one dressed in either black or gray, the typical Tyrranean colors. No one but an actual Tyrranean should recognize that he wasn't Prince Despin of Tyrrane. Could they be safe here?

Lieutenant Falt shook Keane's hand, grinning, and then jumped away with a look of horror on his face. "Your Grace, I... I... I'm sorry. That is, I didn't mean to..."

Keane looked back at Sarah, who shrugged at him as she clambered out of the carriage. Not understanding why the lieutenant was upset, Keane decided the best thing to do was forgive him generically and hope for the best. He stepped over to the cringing Falt, pulled up his hand, and shook it firmly.

"Lieutenant Falt. Thank you for a most excellent journey. You were... really great at... uh... journeying."

The change in Falt was immediate and earnest. He grinned ear to ear, though he seemed at a loss with Keane's familiarity. His hand went limp in Keane's. "Thank *you*, sir! The honor was all—"

Before Lieutenant Falt could finish assigning the honor of their trek, a green-and-yellow-liveried servant cleared his throat with a noise that commanded silence. The thin gray-haired chamberlain stood behind and to the right of a row of five impressively dressed men and women with a longer row of servants at their backs. A jolt ran up his spine when he saw a crown on a tall fat man and jeweled circlets on a pair of women.

He didn't even think of stealing them.

"Prince Despin Swifthart," the servant said in a booming voice, "please greet the King of Greenshade, Eggan Rance the Fourth!"

Keane stepped up to the king, who was an improbably large man. Nearly as tall as Burgen, the king wielded a tremendous paunch that he used to both hold Keane at bay and, at the same time, make himself intimidatingly close. His white hair which he kept long and folded back up over the top of his head, perhaps to compensate for its thinness, was held down by a gold circlet set with flashing emeralds.

Obviously, the king was not a Tyrranean. Keane was safe for another few seconds. But the royals only accounted for three of the six people out here.

Keane held out his hand and said, "Your Majesty," but the king ignored it, his lip crawling up in an expression of distaste. Or maybe he could just smell Keane.

"Prince Swifthart, would you..." King Rance stood a moment, looking down on Keane with beady red eyes. "Would you like a bath? Secreed, see that the prince is bathed and made presentable."

The servant nodded, made a mark on his notepad, and shouted, "Prince Despin Swifthart, please greet the Queen of Greenshade, Loffa Rance!" Keane sidestepped to the queen who appeared to be a third the age of the king. She was a statuesque woman—large brown eyes, pointed chin, and pulled-back blonde tresses. She looked more like some genius artist's porcelain creation than what a real woman might hope to be. But Keane immediately perceived something off about the way she stood. Or maybe it was the way she looked at him.

"A pleasure to meet you, Queen Loffa," Keane said.

"Do you fish, Prince Despin?" the queen asked him.

"Uh... no." Keane answered. The question caught him off guard.

"You'll have to try Cook's fried bread then," the queen said. "You can dip it in honey. That's prudent."

The queen was possibly simpleminded but also not a Tyrranean. Still safe, but four more to go.

As Keane stepped sideways to move to the next important personage in the line, he looked into the widening eyes of the queen's handmaiden standing behind and left of her. Short and attractively plump, she dressed in bright and dark green, her red and white hair held back in a bun with a matching hat on top. This was the woman he spent an evening with in a tent those many years ago talking about her husband and her marriage. This was the woman who ultimately decided, with Keane's advice, that she should leave her husband, the baron's drafty little wooden castle, and come... here.

Not a Tyrranean, but literally the only noble in the Thirteen Kingdoms who actually knew him by name.

"I..." Lady Roselle got out before the expression on her round face turned from surprise to alarm as Keane leapt across the space between them and engulfed her in a hug. She did not return his hug, and Keane looked for Sarah for help. She looked back at him, eyes wide, every bit as panicked as he was. A mailed hand grabbed him by the shoulder and yanked.

Lady Roselle's hat fell to the floor.

"Stop, I'm fine. Return to your posts," Lady Roselle said to the King's Guardsmen. In addition to the one pulling on Keane, two more approached with halberds raised.

"I said, shoo."

They retreated to their posts.

"Please don't tell them who I am," he breathed into her ear. "I only want to get out of here, I swear it." There was no time for anything else.

Keane held Lady Roselle out at arm's length to look into her face. She had aged well, and even flustered and taken by surprise, she commanded her space. She looked up at Keane with canny blue eyes.

"It is so very good to see you again, Prince Despin," she said. "Too much time has passed since the baron and I visited Dismon."

The sense of relief might have taken Keane's legs out from beneath him had he not been gripping the baroness's sturdy shoulders. With a sigh, Keane leaned over and picked up the fanciful arrangement of silk, flowers, and pins he knocked off of Lady Roselle's head.

"Your hat," he said.

"We must speak again, soon," she replied, replacing the hat over her red hair which was streaked here and there with white. "After your bath." Her brows came together, and her lips pursed. "Move along," she whispered. "You've got three more, and don't slight the royals."

Acknowledging the end of his conversation with Lady Roselle, Keane straightened and sidestepped again. "Prince Despin Swifthart, please greet the Royal Secretary of Greenshade, Duke of the Western Marches, Collin Hubrane!" This man he knew even though they had never met. Duke Hubrane had an unsavory reputation in parts of Greenshade and had even hired the freemen of Wallace's Company on more than one occasion for one form underhandedness or another.

The duke bowed at the waist, though not much. He was Keane's height with a thick shock of brilliant white hair and flashing dark eyes that made Keane feel naked. He was thin, dressed like a golden priest, and radiated authority.

Hating him on the spot, Keane bowed back, making certain to lean just a bit less than the duke had. Hubrane's scowl threatened to blister Keane's face, but neither he nor the man next to him were Tyrraneans. Keane and Sarah might survive long enough to grab a few choice baubles and flee the castle yet.

"Prince Despin Swifthart, please greet the Royal Chancellor of Greenshade, Omah Finnagel!" Chancellor Finnagel contrasted with Hubrane in every conceivable way. He was shorter than the duke with a square build that belied his obvious Darrish heritage. His longish hair and well-kept beard were black with a bit of gray, and his skin was only slightly lighter. He had a warm smile that seemed to suggest hidden and amusing secrets.

Finnagel held out his hand to Keane.

"Glad to finally meet you. The castle's all abuzz."

Keane took the man's hand and shook. If Finnagel noticed the anxious dampness of Keane's hand, he was too polite to acknowledge it.

"Thanks," Keane said.

"Prince Despin Swifthart, please greet your betrothed, the Princess of Greenshade, Megan Rance!" Keane stepped again, relieved that this seemed to be the end of the line. He had somehow forgotten the tiny princess at the end, even shorter than the chancellor and tucked out of sight. He looked up and... the rest of the world floated serenely away.

He saw only a beautiful scowling girl with pale skin, her throat a sculptor's masterpiece. Dark curls fell from her head so as to perfectly capture the afternoon sun and return it in golden glints that pierced his heart. Had he the presence of mind, he would have realized he had stopped breathing. As it was, he stood before her making arrested gulping noises.

"What?" Princess Megan said. She looked over at Finnagel. "Is this guy alright?"

"Was when I had him," Finnagel answered. "Did you break something?"

"Hi," said Keane, a slow smile spreading over his face. His chest swelled, and his heartbeat pounded in his ears, but he was unaware of any of it. Unbidden, his attention focused on one person. One face. The rest of the world blurred away and unraveled to inconsequence. Delirious happiness crashed through him, and his thoughts slowed to a warm golden halt.

The princess rolled her eyes heavenward, frowning. "Don't be an ass," she muttered, just loud enough for Keane to hear. "I am very aware of your reputation with women."

When Keane failed to rouse, Princess Megan leaned back and gave him a critical once-over. "No," she said aloud. "I don't believe that I am going to like you much at all."

With that, she spun about and stalked back into the castle. After she passed into darkness, Keane stirred. The king made an impatient noise and stormed away after her. Without looking at Keane at all, the queen followed with Lady Roselle on her heels.

Sarah approached Keane and put her hands on his shoulders, turning him around. "Well, that went *far* better than expected," she said with a smile. Her face held none of the tension she carried mere moments before.

Finnagel looked up at her. "You the bodyguard?" he asked.

"Yes," Sarah answered, glancing down. Her smile disappeared. "*Sergeant* bodyguard."

"Good," he said, and turned away, walking after the others. "That's very good."

Sarah watched him go, then returned her attention to Keane. They were still surrounded by at least a dozen royal guards as well as the elder servant. Behind them, the congregated staff from the keep filed back up the steps.

"We good here?" she asked.

"Yeah," Keane answered. "We're great."

The gray-haired servant swept over. He stood tall, his serious face rigid. "Please hand your weapons to the guard before entering the castle." At Sarah's raised eyebrow, he added, "Until the marriage takes place and the treaty is signed with Tyrrane, you are to be considered hostiles. You will be closely guarded at all times. Have no fear, the King's Guard is the most fearsome in the Thirteen Kingdoms. You will not need your weapons."

"Wonderful," Sarah said, unbuckling her sword belt. "If I get killed, I'm blaming you."

22

SARAH AND KEANE DO NOT JUMP OUT A WINDOW

KEANE

S arah looked out the window of Keane's bedroom at the city surrounding them. With Forest Castle atop the central mound, the city of Treaty Hill spread out in a wide swath. The streets were interspersed with tall oaks and small copses of chestnut trees. A sinking sun cast everything in a deep golden light and gave the city a feeling of warm coziness. Bizarre noises from animals all over the continent of Andos, sent as diplomatic presents, floated through the air from a wide, mostly flat building attached to the outside of the castle wall, where the diverse creatures were housed as a public menagerie.

The prince's room looked south and east past the flying hallways. Beyond those, the twin canals known as the Cattle Streets flowed from Treaty Hill to Fish Hill on the coast. Easily visible from the castle, the fishing and dock town of Fish Hill was where the two of them would need to go in order to find a ship to carry them away when they made their escape. As the shipping arm of Treaty Hill, the much smaller community also housed much of the city's less decorous forms of entertainment, such as would be visited by sailors and the like. It was therefore also the place that Keane and Sarah were most familiar with from their occasional visits to the capital.

Keane lay, clean and scrubbed, on his back in the center of the most massive bed either of them had ever seen and watched Sarah work a white and blue towel through her hair at the window. Both of them wore the white linen robes they found in the bath hall.

Outside, the cobblestone walkway dropped a vertiginous eighty feet below their room.

Sarah sighed. "I think the window's out—for an escape, that is."

"Guards are still in the hall too," Keane answered without moving. "We may need to stay long enough to build up a little trust."

"That's dangerous," Sarah said, biting her lip. "Maybe we can try sneaking out, disable any guards we come across, take their uniforms and—"

"That way leads to certain doom," Keane said, turning his head to look at her. "You can't leave disabled bodies behind in a place like this without raising every alarm in town. And you're forgetting the loot. There's enough gold in this *room* to set us up for years. All we have to do is bide our time. Wait for the right moment. Of course, it may be a while, given what that butler or whatever said. We may not be able to go until, y'know, *after* the wedding."

"After the..." Sarah rolled her eyes. "Please don't tell me I'm risking my life just so you can bag a nineteen-year-old princess. Did you forget that there are Tyrraneans in this city who will know what the real Despin looks like? I swear these people won't get the chance to execute you before I murder you myself." She bit at her thumbnail. "I still don't understand why no one from the Tyrranean embassy has stopped in to pay their respects. That doesn't make any sense to me. We're not that lucky."

"She's a princess." Keane sat upright. He decided to ignore Sarah's less-important concerns about the Tyrraneans for now. "And did you *see* her? She is *amazing*."

The pair of them were spared having to find out if Sarah would, in fact, murder Keane herself, by the door to the bedchamber flinging open. King Rance, shadowed by Secretary Hubrane, came storming in. The yellow-liveried guards outside the door remained immobile.

Keane jumped off the bed, and Sarah circled around.

"Remove this she-ox, Hubrane. I need to have a talk with my future son-in-law." A big man to begin with, the broad ermine mantle he wore over his shoulders, as well as the wide red surcoat and outsized golden sleeves of his shirt, made the king appear just as wide as he was tall. The overall effect was intimidating.

"At once, sire," Hubrane said and snapped his fingers at Sarah.

She paused to pull on boots over her bare feet, earning an impatient snort from the duke.

Keane knew she probably wanted to kill everyone in the room, himself included, and then go find a barstool to keep warm, but instead she just walked out into the hall and waited for the secretary. His own face indifferent, Hubrane followed her out and shut the door behind them.

Returning his attention to the king, Keane discovered the man was now pointing a dirk at him. Rance poked it into Keane's chest, forcing him back into a sitting position against the bed.

Keane forced a smile. "So, what did you want to talk about?"

23

SARAH ADMIRES THE TAPESTRIES

SARAH

Hubrane strode the stone corridors of Forest Castle at speed with Sarah on his heels. His white and gold robes flapped behind him in the wind of his passing. Servants and guards alike flattened themselves against the walls as he passed.

Sarah thought the brittle old man moved like a force of supreme will, pushing everything out of his path, rather than an octogenarian civil servant. He wore imperiousness like armor, and his lack of regard for the people jumping out of his way raised the hairs on Sarah's neck.

Her own clothing left a little to be desired. As she stalked behind the duke, she fastened the wooden toggles as far up, and down, as they would go on the front of her bathrobe.

"The Hubranes—*my* family—were kings in Greenshade," the secretary said, "until recently." Sarah was almost certain he was speaking to her, though she spent most of her concentration keeping up with his retreating back. "The grandfather of the current king, Volker Rance the Third, returned the throne to the Rances after nearly a century of Hubrane rule. It is important for you to know this in order to understand what you must now be shown, Sergeant, and it is important for you to *be* shown in order to serve in this castle."

Sarah had no idea what Hubrane was on about, but she was certainly intrigued. She knew of Collin Hubrane because of his dealings with Wallace's Company. Working for a duke was worthy of note, and his insidious tactics had garnered praise from Harden and the captains. But she had never met the man before today. She didn't think she had ever met anyone like him, either, now that she had.

She concluded that they were not going to get along.

"As part of the arrangement, and in order to prevent a civil war, the Hubranes were granted a dukedom and a permanent position on his majesty's staff. That is the position I now fill." Hubrane stalked up corridors and down staircases. They turned, spun, and bore ahead, until they reached a portion of the castle where servants no longer hustled to and fro and dust collected in the corners.

Hubrane came to a halt outside a broad oaken iron-reinforced door with a small grilled window at face height. The hallway here was tall and wide as if intended for throngs, all the more eerie for its dead emptiness.

Anyone could be hiding in a place like this.

She wondered how Keane was getting on with the king. Getting his own earful of 'I'm the boss' most like. She hated being pulled away from him, but was she supposed to have ignored a direct order from the king? This was silly. She didn't need to worry. Keane could take care of himself.

It wasn't as if the *king* was going to attack him.

"This is part of the old castle," Hubrane said, pulling out a heavy keychain and looking for the proper key. "Built before the outer walls were raised to encompass the upper hill and thereby create the entire diplomatic circle of Treaty Hill. Embassies from every one of the Thirteen Kingdoms are within those walls—Andosh, Pavinn, and Darrish peoples. It is the only place in all of Andos they will get along. This nation survives on an intricate and finely balanced network of treaties spread over the entirety of Andos. They come to us to avoid war in their own lands, but every one of those treaties benefits Greenshade in other ways. Combined, they turn us into what is effectively an empire."

He unlocked the door and turned to glare at Sarah. She resisted the urge to flinch away.

"Your master is an idiot," he said.

"I know," Sarah replied.

Hubrane raised a bushy white eyebrow and continued as he opened the door, "Only an idiot with his brains in his cock would make a woman his bodyguard. I do not mean offense, but you and I must remedy this situation before the prince marries into the most powerful throne on Andos." Hubrane stepped aside. "Ladies first."

The slight didn't bother Sarah. She was no lady, but she "accidentally" stepped on Hubrane's foot anyway as she entered the barely lit room, prompting a gasp of pain from him. "Sorry," she said with a shrug.

She appeared to be in a small ballroom—small for a ballroom at any rate—with walls covered by tapestries featuring life-sized figures of dancing nobles and servants carrying plates of ornate foods. A pair of dim candles in a fixture far over her head lit the room. At the same time that Sarah realized three of the figures stitched into the tapestry were actually real people hiding against it—and carrying swords at that—the door slammed shut behind her.

Sarah's lip curled up in a half smile as she tried to bury her anger at herself. Of *course*, Hubrane led her into a trap. She knew better. Why didn't she listen to herself? Now she *was* worried about what the king might be doing with Keane.

The little grilled window within the larger door slid open, and Hubrane put his face up to it.

"Given that the prince is an idiot, he must be controlled by persons who are not," Hubrane said as the masked swordsmen began circling the room. "I have determined that this type of control is better exerted over an individual who feels entirely cut off and alone. I am therefore terminating your contract."

Sarah's eyes adjusted to the darkness, and she tracked her attackers' movements. At least the bathrobe wouldn't hinder her.

The secretary paused a moment and said, "I must admit,

Sergeant, that I had expected you to have some clever rejoinder to hurl at me in the instant before my men cut you down."

"Would that make you feel better?" asked Sarah.

"I rather think it would," replied Hubrane.

"Then no, I don't have anything to say."

24

A LESSON IN DIPLOMACY

KEANE

K ing Eggan Rance the Fourth possessed the reputation for being the most successful diplomatic negotiator in the history of the Thirteen Kingdoms. To Keane, that conjured up visions of an intelligent, patient, and, above all else, *compassionate* man, who put his opponents at ease, listened to their problems, and then created solutions that benefitted everyone.

Nothing could have been further from the truth. In the last thirty seconds, Keane realized that the king was a brutal bully who used any kind of force at his disposal to pressure people into giving him what he wanted.

Keane might have been more at home here than he'd thought had his life not been in such immediate danger.

"Just who do you think you're dealing with?" the massive king, red-faced with anger, asked. The point of his dagger stayed an inch from Keane's eye. "I have made the best system of treaties in the world. All of Andos owes its peace to me. *Me!* I am the smartest person you will ever meet, and I can tell what's in a person's heart the instant I meet them. And, sure as the Undergates open for whores and lawyers, I know what's in yours."

Keane wasn't sure what he'd done to slip up already, but it was obvious that the scam wasn't working out. Immediate escape had become the new priority.

"You know what's in my heart? Can you tell what I had for dinner last night too?" Keane asked. As was typical in these situations, his mouth flew well ahead of his brains. Less typical was not having Sarah around to yank his ass out of the fire.

Somewhere in Keane's mind, it occurred to him that maybe it wasn't good that he *had* a "typical" reaction to being in situations like this.

Running through a variety of ways to take the dirk from the inexplicably homicidal king and stab him someplace non-vital, Keane selected the one he thought would be the easiest and least likely to get him hunted down for regicide. He kept stumbling, though, on how he would get out alive after that. And he could hardly leave without Sarah.

"Is it possible that this isn't the best time for you?" Keane asked. "You seem... distracted. And kinda angry."

By way of answer, King Rance spun the dagger in his hand and jabbed downward, impaling Keane through the lower thigh just outside of the bone. Air rushed in through his open mouth, and Keane howled in pain.

"FUCKTHEFUCK!"

"I am talking," the king yelled.

Rance's hand stayed gripped round the pommel of the dirk, and Keane sat as still as he could on the bed. His every hitching breath brought fresh agony.

He settled down, his face white and clammy. His thoughts bent away from trying to decipher the motivations of the royal madman and toward survival. Forcing a stark grin, Keane said, "You were saying, sire?"

"I was saying that I know who you are, boy. You have peaked at twenty-four by becoming a political pawn. I asked Brannok for a suitable husband for my only babe, and he sent me his most useless brat. A simpering man-child who thinks he can bed anything in a skirt without consequence." Rance smiled, a horrible sight under the circumstances. "You're not going to die, stupid little prince. At least not today. You're hardly the first asshole kid I've 'explained' things to with a knife in the leg. You won't be the last. I just find it's easier for me and clearer for you if we start at blood and pain. What do you think?"

So, King Rance really did *not* know who Keane was. He was simply trying to assert his dominance over the new male in the house, albeit in a psychopathic, murderously crazy way. The man was a blunt instrument. A blunt instrument who favored pointy instruments.

25

DANCING IN THE DARK

SARAH

No more time for doubts and guilt. These men were here to kill her. She needed to kill them first and get back to Keane before anything awful happened.

In the murk of the tapestry-laden ballroom, Sarah danced away to the left and crossed two of the swordsmen behind a third. That third assassin came in alone and high, counting on his weight to drive his sword point through Sarah's shoulder and into her vitals. She twirled to the right and gave him an elbow to the back of the neck. Her other hand reached up and over to grasp his sword hand behind her own back. As he fell, she continued her spin, now with his sword in *her* fist. The leather of the grip, broken in by another hand, felt strange. She slid the blade of the second attacker aside and kicked that man hard in the crotch.

Sarah already saw better in the dim light of the ballroom than her attackers, and on an even field, none of them could have kept up with her.

Also, she was clearly the more irritated.

Sarah leaned back as the third man attempted to run his sword through her neck and grabbed his wrist in her empty hand. She lifted the wrist and drove the pommel of the first man's blade into his elbow. There was a loud cracking noise, and the end of a shattered humerus punched through his upper arm. Sarah muffled his scream with a hand over his mouth in case Hubrane or more guards were in hearing distance outside the room and lowered him to the ground. She walked to the first assassin, now unconscious, and returned his sword to him, then went to the door she entered through.

She wanted to keep the assassin's blade as a show of what happened to would-be killers in the dark. But Secreed's warning about her and Keane carrying weapons left her sure that the sword would only provide the castle guard with a reason to attack them both.

Colin Hubrane, by her judgement, was not a stellar host.

She stepped back from the door, counted to ten, and kicked...

26

HOW TO TALK TO A DUKE

KEANE

Oldam's rocky right butt cheek, that dirk hurt. Keane was used to battlefield injuries and fought people with swords for a living. This did not even qualify as his third-worst stabbing.

Maybe the fifth.

But typically, no one was holding a blade in his leg just to impress him. It made a difference.

A long, groaning howl followed by a series of forlorn honks wafted in on the breeze from the menagerie below. They sounded so sad.

Keane knew how they felt.

He squinted toward King Rance, who sat next to him on the bed. When had the bed chamber become so *bright*? The door opened, and a white-haired man in white and gold robes entered. His eyes were as dark as everything else was light.

Secretary Hubrane closed the door behind himself and straightened, his hands clasped behind his back.

"Your Majesty," he said, something that would have read as concern on another person passing across his face, "the boy is losing quite a bit of blood. You may have struck something important in his leg. I doubt we will get much of a peace treaty with Tyrrane if we kill Brannok's son. Even this one."

"He's fine, trust me," said the king. "I know what I'm doing. You take care of his whore?"

"It is done, sire. I will send a servant I trust to clean up her mess and dispose of the body. She followed me to her slaughter as a sow to her slops."

King Rance chuckled.

Keane couldn't figure out what was funny, but something in the back of his brain was screaming, and he didn't think that whatever it was these two were discussing would be funny to him. Keane reached up and put a hand on top of his head to try and keep it from swaying about.

"Sarah," he managed to say. "Where's Sarah?"

"Your bodyguard is dead," King Rance said, his eyes taut and his meaty brow rumpled. "Now it's just you and us. You're all alone. And I think you understand now that we *will* have your obedience. You can trust me on that." The king patted Keane on the leg just above the protruding blade. "Sorry for the theatrics, but you need to know when serious people are serious. And I'm the most serious person you've ever met."

"Sarah... dead?" Keane asked, trying to focus on the oversized tomato of the king's face.

"Honestly, I don't get it," said the king. "Pretty face, big tits, sure. But she's the size of a horse. You'd need a saddle to bed that one." He turned to his secretary.

"Get it, Hubrane? I'm saying the kid needs a saddle to have sex with that woman."

Hubrane pulled his lips back in an imitation of a smile. No other part of his face moved.

"I swear," King Rance said, "I am the only one in this whole castle with a sense of humor. Everybody says." The king heaved himself to his feet and strode to the center of the room.

"She's dead?" Keane whispered, his mind tried to understand

what was being told him, but the concepts fell away like water from a sheet of glass.

"Yes, boy," shouted Hubrane, running a hand over his thick white hair. He stepped closer and leaned in over Keane. "Your strumpet is dead. I killed her myself..." The secretary looked up at King Rance. "Sire, I really think we should get him to the surgeon. He has... AHH!"

Keane came off the bed like a striking rabbit snake, connecting a solid punch to the royal secretary's nose and bringing them both to the ground. Keane's screams joined Hubrane's outraged cries of pain when the stone floor drove the king's dirk even further into his leg.

All at once, Keane felt himself being lifted from the ground as a baby might be.

"Sarah?" he said, looking into her eyes. "Am I dead too?" He dropped his head and hung there, breathing into the white linen robe, with a wooden toggle pressed into one cheek. No, he wasn't dead. He gripped her stonelike shoulder to prove to himself that she was alive.

Alive and angry.

Sarah turned to leave and clutched Keane to her, but the king already stood in the doorway to block her with his considerable bulk. Her face hardened into a frightening scowl.

"I don't know how you're still alive, woman, but you need to know this," he said. "If you or your simpleton master stick a single toe out of line, a single toe, you will be killed in ways *nobody* ever dreamed of. Believe me. This is *my* house, and you are *not* safe here. You get that?"

"That seems pretty obvious," Sarah replied. The cords of her neck stood out and her wide shoulders twitched. Her face, on the other hand, revealed nothing.

As he stared into her features, Rance's confident sneer slipped.

The king gave a derisive snort and stood aside. "Guard!" he yelled. "Take these two to the surgeon."

Silent, Sarah took a slow look around her at the fat and angry king and the disheveled and blood-spattered Secretary Hubrane.

"I got stabbed inna leg," Keane said, his head rocking backward.

"And the duke killed you, but I broke his nose, so now you're alive again."

Sarah rolled her eyes and returned her attention to King Rance.

"Get out of my way," she said.

Rance stepped aside, and one of the two guards in the hall reached out to help her carry her friend.

Keane's head lolled to one side as they left the room. His mouth hung open in a lopsided grin, and he gave a boneless sort of wave.

"Bye," he said to the king.

27

THE MERCENARIES TAKE A CRUISE

ELI

F ish Hill smelled exactly as the name suggested in Eli's estimation, like a small mountain of rotting fish. It was kind of funny because it seemed to be almost all these poor sots ate out here. Eli thought living with *that* kind of reek would likely put him off fish forever.

He and Harden, with Captain Darkling and fifteen more wicked cutthroats following, were walking out the length of Fish Hill's "Great Dock" where, at least, the air was cleaner. The dock seemed less great than it did old and rickety, but it was more than twice the length of the others. The further they walked, the shabbier the ships were that they passed. A close dock cost more money, while any old scow could tie up out here in the middle of the damn ocean.

Though Eli and Darkling left Wallace's Company with ten freemen each, last night five of Captain Darkling's men rode off in five different directions. Eli's spy said that they rode in search of a tinker's wagon with a red roof.

The news left Eli chuckling the rest of the night.

Further out to sea and not connected to land at all, were the infamous ship houses of Fish Hill. While the capital city just inland boasted the largest trading hub in the world, it was here in the houses where the *real* money exchanged hands.

Each of the four open ship houses, two to either side of the port proper and facing parallel to the shore, were gigantic. They were big enough to house a pair of large ships with sails furled—which was the point. Those ships would tie onto a strip of dock that ran the length of the house, right down the middle. Two or more ships could enter one of the houses, swap cargo fast and unseen, and be gone with no one the wiser. The only records kept were the numbers of barrels and crates moved, which were assessed a fee by the government of Greenshade. It was a system deliberately made for corruption.

At the far end of the Great Dock rested *The Floater*, a wide-bellied merchant brig made mostly out of patchwork. Double masted and maybe thirty-five yards long, it was as nondescript as it was possible for a ship to be. There were dirty and much-stitched white sails bound to the yards and no other distinguishing features at all.

"Well, that's perfect," Harden said as soon as he saw the rented ship. "Good job, Eli. Good job indeed. No one will ever look twice at us in that."

Voice lowered so the sixteen mercenaries coming up behind couldn't hear, Eli responded, "I have some news before we board. I just heard from my man in what's left of Darkling's squad. That bastard Burgen spilled his guts, and now Darkling's got him to say that *you're* stealing the wagebox, and using the coin to try and pay Burgen his own self to kill all the captains *and* anyone loyal to them."

"Do we know when this is happening?" Harden asked.

"Aye, we do. Soon's the ship leaves sight of land. No hope of interference."

"Thank you, Eli," Harden said with a grin. "That works out just fine."

Eli made a face. "Well and good, sir, but are you sure you still want to do this? We ain't in the water yet, and we don't *have* to go."

Harden turned and frowned at Eli. "Where is this coming from? You have always been happy to support me in the past and against far greater danger than a little insurrection in the ranks. It isn't as if you are on some grand crusade to preserve the freemen of Wallace's Company. I know you really hate the lot of them."

Eli's brows went up in surprise. While true, he had never told anyone.

"Oh, don't bother trying to hide it," Harden went on. "I've known for years. Your secret's safe with me. I just wish you'd do me the same favor and let mine lie."

Reeling, Eli attempted to keep the conversation on track, even though he found he now had a thousand questions. "That's... that's not the same, sir."

"Oh?"

"No, sir." Eli struggled for words. "See, that's just it, ain't it? You know my secret. Devil take me if I know how, but you do."

"You're not that hard a read," Harden said with a wink.

"Be that as it may, sir, you already know why I make the choices I do. If I run some Pavi through, it's because that Pavi deserved it, not because he reminds me of some other Pavi my sister was with once who treated her shitty. That'd be a surprise to you, right? Cause you don't know what other Pavis my sister been with." Eli was pretty sure he'd made a hash of that, but talk wasn't his best quality.

"So you're saying that if I, Lord Marshal Grayspring, explain myself to you, my distant, servile underling, you'll deign to follow my orders?"

"No, sir," Eli said. "That ain't it at all. I'll follow you no matter what. Always." He paused to take a breath and consider. "What I'm saying is that if I understood *why* what we're doing is important then I could shove the trying to understand and get on with the doing. Maybe it'd be important to me too, instead of just confusing"—another pause—"and maybe it'd be of help to you to say something to *someone*."

Harden glanced over at Eli. They were getting close to *The Floater* now, and Eli knew this conversation was about to be over for good, one way or the other. There was little sound this far out on the dock except for the cries of gulls and the jingle of Eli's mail. The wind blew salted and cool.

"We are mercenaries, Eli. Soldiers." He inhaled the salt air deeply, puffing out his chest. "We don't talk about... about *things*." Harden swallowed.

Eli, alarmed, turned to him. Harden gripped his arm and pushed him forward—his eyes were beginning to redden. Distracted with panic at getting the answer he had just asked for, Eli tripped on a weather-raised board on the dock. If Harden hadn't been clutching his arm, he would have gone sprawling. As it was, he could only look back over his shoulder at the following band of freemen to make certain none of them were listening.

"I guess I just love her, Eli. I love that girl like she was my own kid. And it hurts." Harden was still walking as if nothing was at all amiss, even as—surreal as it seemed to Eli—he bared this piece of his soul. Harden's grip pained his captain mightily, but no force in the Thirteen Kingdoms could have persuaded Eli to mention it.

"It hurts because..." Harden stopped speaking as the pair reached the merchant vessel. Just like that his softness vanished, replaced by cold gray competence.

Eli had no concept of how to approach this, so he did the only thing he could think to and ignored it. "Well, here we are! Permission to stomp aboard, Cap'n?"

A small man, short and thin with a torn and faded long coat and no shirt or shoes but wearing the biggest hat on the ship, swung around one of the stays and grinned wide as he looked the two mercenaries up and down.

"Greetings! Master Eli, you would all be the twenty-three passengers you mentioned? Very good. Most excellent. Pleased to make your hellos."

"Eighteen now," Eli said. "I'll be adjusting the fee to match."

Up close, Eli noticed again the little captain had but half the normal complement of teeth and was wall-eyed and scarred as well. Eli was familiar with the marks of a doubtlessly violent and brutal life.

The captain leaned over the wale and stuck out his hand. "Pahvo Sharkheart, killer o' men, thief o' brides, scourge o' the Beacon Sea, and captain o' the merchant ship *The Floater* at yer servings."

"Sharkheart? Really?" Harden asked, his melancholy replaced with fresh amusement.

The ship's captain lost his grin by degrees, though he kept his hand extended.

"People don't honestly call you that, do they?" Harden said, pulling himself up past the small man and onto the main deck. "Everyone up! Collect the anchors and do the sails! Man the paddles! Let's go!"

Sharkheart watched as the mercenaries climbed past him, laughing and whispering. His outstretched hand fell to his side, and his happy expression fell from his face.

"We waiting for something?" Harden asked, leaning down over Sharkheart's shoulder.

Up next to the captain, Eli noticed with no small amount of amusement that while the captain's weather-beaten red felt hat was taller than Harden's, the mercenary's faded leather one was much wider. It almost took his mind off of the violence he knew was to ensue.

"Shove off!" the little captain yelled to his crew. He walked away from Harden and stomped up the steps to the quarterdeck. As the sailors pushed off with long poles and the big tub inched away from the creaking docks, Harden turned and addressed his men.

"Freemen of Wallace's Company, swords out!" He and the rest of the men raised their blades into the air. Only Eli, who stood off to one side, and Darkling, who wore no sword, did not.

"Burgen, of Darkling Squad, step forward!" Burgen, broadsword in his left hand, right arm in a sling, and fear on his face, came forward. Harden stepped up to him and reached up to place his free hand on the giant's shoulder. He turned the big man around to face his fellows.

"Gentlemen, Burgen here has come forward with most distressing news. It seems that Captain Darkling is plotting not only my death but the deaths of Captain Eli *and* all of his men here in order to steal the leadership of Wallace's Company for himself. What say you to that?" There was a roar of disapproval from Eli's ten swordsmen while Darkling's five looked confused and uncomfortable. The sailors worked the rigging like madmen, doing their best to stay uninvolved. Eli spotted Sharkheart dashing aft, holding up a large sea chart between himself and the mercenaries.

On the dock, less than two feet away, a pair of sailors coiling line looked up in alarm.

Burgen's eyes grew big as saucers, and Captain Darkling stammered. What became obvious to everyone though, with all the men standing on the deck, their weapons drawn, was that with Darkling having sent half of his men out searching for a tinker's wagon with a red roof, he only had five soldiers present to Eli's ten. And while both Eli and Harden were excellent swordsmen, Darkling himself was no fighter at all.

Eli's men chanted, "Justice! Justice!" and in very short order, Darkling's men, Burgen included, were chanting along as well.

With *The Floater* now just under three feet from the dock they stood on, the two sailors turned and ran toward land.

Captain Darkling glowered at Lord Marshal Harden Grayspring. He had lost, and he must have known it. Taking the only path Eli reckoned might save the frilly ponce's life, Darkling shouted, "I renounce my position. Take my men. Take my treasure. I will leave you now, never to return." With that, the well-heeled captain moved to step past Harden and make the short hop to the dock, his gaze staying on Harden's drawn cutlass.

Harden stepped aside, and while he kept Darkling's attention focused on the cutlass, he pulled his knife and thrust it into the man's neck. Harden leaned over and whispered, "Fuck you," into his former captain's ear and shoved him overboard. Darkling's head whacked the edge of the dock before his body fell, unconscious and spurting blood, into the water below.

Far up the dock, the two sailors continued to run.

The man who lives is the man who's right, Eli thought, watching the body fade beneath the waves. And Darkling was wrong as could be if he thought he was the equal of Lord Marshal Harden Grayspring.

"Captain Sharkheart," Harden yelled, trying to spot the little man among the aghast sailors, the rigging, and all the sails hanging about.

"Aye!" yelled Sharkheart as he ran up. The blood ran out of the little captain's face and left him pale and jittery. "Whatever it is you want to do here," he said, "it's no business o' mine, nor my crew. We saw nothing. Sort of a collective blindness, as you will."

"Sharkheart... no. No, sorry, I just can't do it. I *cannot* call you that." Harden made a show of pondering for a moment. "I know, we will simply shorten it. From this moment, you will be Captain Shart. Now Captain Shart, I suggest you get us out of here before the dock watch—or whatever form of interfering constabulary you fishy-types have on the ass-ends of skinny docks—arrive and throw the lot of us in prison. What do you think of that, Captain Shart?"

The captain winced and looked around to see if any of his sailors had heard his new nickname. From a glance, Eli guessed they all had. Shart looked down at the splatter of Darkling left on his deck and began shouting orders to his crew. "Tie off and raise the main. Get us the blazing hells out of here!"

Eli stepped up and smiled at Harden. "Still making new friends wherever you go," he said.

28

KEANE WEARS SOME DINNER, AND SARAH IS NORMAL

KEANE

Keane awoke in a comfortable bed in a long vaulted room full of empty beds. Sunlight streamed through a row of tall arched windows along the east wall.

Sarah sat in a chair beside him, resting her booted feet on his shin, and snored softly. In her sleep, there was no hint of the hardened warrior who had claimed so many lives on the battlefield. She simply looked pretty. Beautiful, really, although Keane rarely considered it.

Sarah once more wore the black-on-gray uniform and armor of a Tyrranean sergeant. Keane noted the lack of a weapon in her scabbard. He started to shove her boots off of his bed, but the pain in his thigh when he moved made him gasp.

"Oh, right. Forgot about that," he said, teeth clenched.

Sarah smiled as she came to, removing her feet from the bed and stretching her arms high. Her mail jingled with the movement. "How ya feel?" she asked.

"Like I shouldn't have had to get stabbed in the sodding leg just to get some rest," Keane answered. "Am I making stuff up, or did I punch the Duke of the Western Marches in the nose yesterday?"

A grin broke out on Sarah's face. "It was the day before yesterday, but yeah," she said.

"I slept for two days? It was just a little light stabbing."

"You lost all your blood," Sarah said. "We had to replace it with herbed chicken broth. It took your body a while to acclimate, but at least you're delicious now."

They both laughed, but it was short-lived.

Sarah's brows came together. Not a frown, just deep in thought. She waved to a young woman in a nurse's uniform, and said, "Would you fetch the baroness? She asked to be informed the instant the prince awoke."

"Oldam's balls," breathed Keane. "Sarah, Baroness Roselle is here. *She knows me!* Why are you calling for her?"

"She and I have spoken at length," Sarah replied. "She knows pretty much everything now. I don't understand why, but she seems quite well disposed toward you. I guess you weren't a complete cad when you met her in her tent."

"You know what happened in that tent," Keane said, "Sure, I may have spread *rumors* about seducing a baroness, but that's all they were."

Sarah grinned again at that. "True, but apparently those rumors got around. Lady Roselle seems to enjoy a lot of influence in the castle based on her ability to juggle some powerful consorts. According to her, that all came from her notoriety as the woman who beguiled a murderous mercenary with her female charms and convinced him to kill the rest of his evil band."

Keane's mouth hung open. He was used to exaggerating his own exploits. Having someone else blow up his story was new territory for him. Sarah laughed.

"Sarah," he said, becoming serious, "you were right. Before. This was a really bad idea. I am *so* sorry I brought us—you—into this. I don't know how you can stand to still be my friend."

"You were not entirely wrong at the Ebon Host camp, Keane. While this is a preposterous situation, had we not accepted it, we would likely have been killed by that Major Talon and his contingent."

"Maybe, but that's not all of it," Keane said. "This whole thing was my fault from the beginning. If it hadn't been for me..."

"Stop that right now," Sarah said, leaning over and grabbing Keane's hand. "No one deserves to get treated the way Harden treated you. It wasn't punishment. It was vindictiveness. And it wasn't about you anyway. Somehow that son of a bitch thought that if he—"

"Not interrupting, am I?" A dark-skinned Darrishman in his early forties wearing a loose-fitted, gold-colored kaftan that displayed his well-developed forearms, stood in the doorway, leaning against the green-gray stone. A bit of gray showed around his temples and was sprinkled in his beard.

"No, ah... Chancellor Finnagel?" Sarah said.

"Just Finnagel is fine," he said, smiling. Unlike Hubrane or the king, Keane noticed that Finnagel smiled with his whole face, eyes crinkling at the corners. His ebony skin conspired with his features to make him seem even more warm and open, unlike the other Darrish that Keane knew who seemed distant and superior. Captain Lowger was like that.

"What can we do for you, Finnagel?" Keane asked.

"I honestly just came to see the warrior who felled Collin Hubrane," Finnagel said, his smile widening into a grin, "and, of course, his stalwart bodyguard who fended off three armed men with her bare hands."

"What?" Keane asked. "When did... oh."

"It wasn't a big deal," she said.

"And who threw Jabbash Ro, the infamous assassin of Banah-Sek, from the roof of this very castle just last night."

Keane turned to look at Sarah. She shrugged.

"I guess Duke Hubrane and the king haven't given up," she said.

"Nor are they likely to," said Finnagel.

Keane turned to him next, expression hard. "And just what part have you played in these attempts on my bodyguard's life?"

"None whatsoever," Finnagel said, raising his hands. "I merely observe your exploits with amusement and enthusiasm."

"Do you?" Keane said. "Sergeant, is it your opinion that anyone else at all knows about the failed assassins?"

Sarah rounded on Finnagel and narrowed her gaze. "No, it is not."

Finnagel rolled his eyes and sighed. "You are wise to question, but I am the king's intelligence, His master spy, if you will. I observe—it is what I do. I daresay that nothing happens in this castle that I do not know."

"Did you know I have to pee?" asked Keane.

"You have been in that bed for the past thirty-two hours," Finnagel responded. "You have to urinate, you are thirsty, and you are half-starved to boot."

"This guy is good," Keane said to Sarah.

"When I heard you were awake, I took the liberty of ordering you some supper," Finnagel said.

"But I just woke up!" exclaimed Keane.

Finnagel only smiled in answer.

"Thanks."

The Darrishman turned back to Sarah. "Forgive me for saying, but these heroics of yours, well, most would consider them beyond the capabilities of a normal human woman."

"Well, I *am* a normal human woman," Sarah said. She didn't look as irritated by the comment as Keane felt, though. Was she liking this guy?

"I meant no offense," Finnagel said. "You certainly *are* a woman." He walked to the end of the bed and directed a stern gaze at Sarah. "Avoid Secretary Hubrane whenever possible. He is an incredibly busy man, and it is feasible that he may forget to send assassins after you for a while *if* you are not underfoot." Finnagel glanced between Keane and Sarah. "Try never to be outside of one another's company, even in the privy. Their goal is to kill you, Sergeant, and thereby make the prince more pliant. I should consider that a genuine shame."

"Me too," said Sarah with a short nod.

"Uh-huh," agreed Keane.

"Just before you arrived," Finnagel said, returning to Keane, "the ambassador from Tyrrane and several of his senior staff took a sudden turn and died. No one even knew they were sick. I suppose some people might consider this a fortunate turn of events."

Keane and Sarah exchanged a nervous glance. "I... guess so," Keane said. That explained the lack of Tyrranean ambassadors at their arrival in a terrifying kind of way.

"I know that it is difficult to trust right now, but I am your friend here in the castle. My door"—his gaze lingered on Sarah—"is always open."

There was a knock at the front of the room.

"It looks as if your meal has arrived, Prince Despin," Finnagel said. "I shall leave you to it. Good health, young man... though perhaps not quite so young as we were led to believe, hm?" With a wink, he turned to leave.

Oldam's sweet sandy release in a bucket, thought Keane, *did that crusty son of a bitch just call me old?*

Finnagel and a redheaded serving girl carrying a tray full of silver cloches passed each other, and she set the tray down on the table beside Keane's bed. She removed the cloches one by one, and Keane's stomach gave a loud gurgle.

"Excuse me," he said as he stuffed sausage pastries into his face.

After the girl left, Sarah whispered to Keane. "What do you think of Finnagel?"

"I think he's a stone-creepy old fuck," Keane answered through a mouthful of cheese and bacon torte. "Why are you whispering?"

"Spies," she said, pointing toward the ceiling.

"Let 'em listen," Keane said. "Hey spies, I'm scratching my balls now." With his other hand, he picked another tart from the tray.

"I trust him," Sarah said. "And besides, I think we need all the allies we can get. We can't afford to be picky."

"No, but we *can* afford not to get stupid just because you think some old guy is cute... shit!" Keane chewed as fast as he could and pulled himself up straighter in the bed. As he adjusted, another lance of pain shot through his leg, causing him to cry out. He barked a series of loud coughs that sent bits of pastry across his blanket.

Alarmed, Sarah pushed him forward and pounded on his back.

From behind Sarah, a young woman said, "Will he live?"

Sarah hopped sideways, arms wide, but relaxed when she saw Princess Megan standing there, the obvious cause of Keane's distress.

"Oh, him? Yes, I believe so."

"This has not been a happy home for the past few years. When my mother died..." the princess trailed off and met Sarah's gaze. "I have not been happy. If you have any influence at all over this shambles of a human being, please utilize it to curtail his predilections. It is humiliating enough to be married off to a scoundrel without all the maids turning up pregnant. I would consider this a personal favor."

Keane finally stopped hacking and looked up at the princess. His eyes streamed tears, red blotches stood out on his face, and mint and cherry tart ran down his chin. He gave her his best smile.

The princess's eyes widened. She nodded once, spun, and strode from the room.

Sarah, still watching the slim figure retreating down the hall outside the sick room, shook her head and said, "I can't quite decide if she wants you dead or not."

Keane swallowed and cleared his throat. "Don't be daft." His voice came out a croak. "Can't you tell true love when you see it?"

"Is he awake?" Lady Roselle asked as she hurried into the room. Today she was dressed in a fitted green satin dress with a short coat made of black lace and dotted with pearls. A tall matching hat was pinned to her red and white hair. At first, Keane thought she looked like someone's mom, but the authoritative way she moved and the firmness of her curves, well, he could see the attraction. Maybe she really was the player Sarah described her as.

"Awake and delusional as ever," Sarah said, smiling at Lady Roselle. To Keane's surprise, the women embraced before the baroness turned to him. Just two days and it seemed this pair were already close friends. *That's what happened when women kept secrets together.*

"I am still alive, thanks to you," Keane said. "If not for your discretion..."

Lady Roselle moved to Keane's side and put a hand on his chest. "Think nothing of it. I already know you'd do the same for me."

"I understand you know all about the two of us," Keane said, directing a glance at Sarah, "but how did you get here? What have you been doing?"

"That's a bit of a tale," Lady Roselle said, sitting on the corner of Keane's bed and patting his foot. "After my conversation with you in the tent that day—about being unhappy and letting miserable people make us miserable—I left Horace's rear camp and returned home. I think I said something about a stomach illness or some such. But when I got there, I didn't know what to do. My family held all the money, so that wasn't a problem, but leaving the baron felt like failure." Her face became wistful.

She nodded and continued, staring down at the blanket tented over Keane's right foot. "Despite our talk, I decided to stay with him and make the best of it—do my duty and all that. But a simple decision on my part did little to address our real problems. He still blamed me for what happened to our son." She trailed off, contemplative and sad. "Horace returned two weeks later in a horrible fury."

Keane remembered something about the son from that night. The boy fell in love with a Pavi girl from Sedrios. The baron objected because the girl's family held no wealth to speak of and hired some men from town to scare her away. They thought that rape and murder would be scary. When Roselle and Baron Tralgar's son found out who paid for his would-be-wife's death, he ran from home, never to be seen again.

"Apparently, someone had been spreading word that a mercenary from Wallace's Company had crept into my tent and spent several hours enjoying my bed. Horace ordered me out of Castle Oak on the spot. Because of my assumed infidelity, by the laws of the kingdom, I had little more than the clothes I was wearing. Horace kept everything. I should have taken your advice and left him after our chat."

Keane looked away, coughing into his fist. He could *feel* Sarah's gaze boring into him.

"If you don't tell her, I will," Sarah said, her voice low and threatening.

"Tell me what, dear?" asked Lady Roselle.

"I started the rumor," answered Keane. "About us having sex in your tent. I said... that... you couldn't keep your hands off me."

Instead of the expected rebuke, Lady Roselle raised one brow and smiled. "Really..."

"And so then you came here?" Keane asked, trying to steer the conversation back into the road.

"Indirectly, yes." Lady Roselle answered, still smiling disarmingly at Keane. "First, I spent some time with Lady Lucrenza at Fenrath Hall. She was very good to me. People think she's stern, and I suppose she is, but that's just her public face. She's also quite generous.

"The king and queen came to visit while I was there. Queen Loffa had recently lost her attendant, and the two of us got along well enough. So, when King Rance told me I was to be the new royal companion to the queen, I humbly accepted. It was a step up, and I had nothing better to do."

"King Rance hasn't tried to stab you, then?" Sarah asked.

"Not as he did you, no," Lady Roselle said.

"What about the queen?" asked Keane. "What's her deal? She get hit in the head or something?"

Lady Roselle smiled. She seemed more alluring now than ever. The wisps of white in her hair and the crinkles at the edges of her eyes and mouth all spoke of experience and kindness.

"The queen is as she was made to be. But for everything she has witnessed and been through, she remains an innocent. Perhaps there is something wrong in that, yet I find I am jealous."

Keane was about to ask what the hell that meant when Sarah interrupted.

"What do you make of the deaths in the Tyrranean embassy, milady? Keane and I were worried once we realized that there were people in town who might know what Despin really looked like. Not to damn the nets, but that seems really convenient."

The smile faded from Lady Roselle's face to be replaced with a worried frown. "The situation is stranger than that," she said. "At the same time that the diplomatic personnel from the Tyrranean capital of Dismon died, six members of the house staff here in the castle died too."

"That is strange," Keane said. "Is there any—"

"Also, three councilmen from the Grand Council, twenty-three highly placed officers of the King's Swords, at least fourteen well-connected merchants, and over eighty attendants and servants including most of the Tyrranean embassy staff—messengers, teamsters, and one barber. And a few assorted criminals."

Keane's mouth fell open. Sarah's expression grew hard.

She leaned forward, and when she spoke, her voice was a rough whisper. "Why?"

"At first no one was certain," Lady Roselle said. "It all seemed so random. But as the list expanded, the connection eventually became obvious. Everyone who died had either been *from* Dismon or had visited there. Maybe they met with one of the Tyrranean royals, or they just stood in the background while their masters did. By glad coincidence for *you*, that meant anyone who might have known what the real Prince Despin looked like is dead."

"We've got to get the happy hell up and out of here," Keane said, trying again to sit up. "We're being set up. Someone is cleaning house and killing all those extra people to make it look like our fault. If we don't run, we'll be blamed, sure as Oldam's giant stone prostate."

Sarah slid from the bed and glanced at the door. Her frame was taut, ready for trouble.

"Just a moment, dear," Lady Roselle said, looking up at Sarah. "If you were in danger, I certainly shouldn't have nattered on for all this time. Sit down."

Sarah turned to look at Lady Roselle but said nothing. Her brow was creased with worry, her mouth a grim line.

"Have it your way," Lady Roselle said after a brief moment.

"Chancellor Finnagel has apparently captured one of the culprits, and after spending a night with the king's torturer, he revealed that he had been sent by King Brannok in Tyrrane in response to a rumored plot on Prince Despin's life. All that was known was that the plot originated in Dismon and that time was short."

"So they just murdered everybody," said Keane. "That's... I mean, I've seen people do some shitty stuff, but that's just... Do they think there's some kind of prize for the world's most evil son of a goat-raping—"

"Keane," Sarah said, rolling her eyes. "Lady Roselle *is* a baroness."

"It's alright," Lady Roselle said with a slight grin. "After all, he's a prince, right? He outranks me."

"Do you think there really is a plot to kill Despin, and now they want to kill me?" asked Keane. Damn. He really *did* need to pee. "Why did you just say I was safe?"

"Because I don't buy the story," answered Lady Roselle. "As you said, it's too convenient. But I only know that because I already knew who Keane actually was." She reached up and lifted her green-and-black hat off her head. Pearls dotted the black crown as if it were a tiny hat-shaped piece of night sky. She reached up, pulled several pins out of the tight bun of hair that had crouched beneath the hat, and let it loose. Waves of rich red hair, with small curls of white roiling like sea foam, spilled over her shoulders.

Keane sat up a bit more and bloused the sheet out over his groin.

"That's better," she said. "That thing was pulling on my brain. I don't mind uncomfortable shoes or corsets or even plucking the hairs from my face, but I have never learned to love screwing my hair up until my eyes don't close."

"What about the man Chancellor Finnagel caught?" Sarah asked. She settled back in her chair. "The tortured one?"

"Hired by the chancellor, is my assumption," said Lady Roselle. "Paid to take a night's beatings and then reveal a nonexistent plot. My guess is the man disappears before he faces punishment."

"He already has," said Sarah. At Lady Roselle's arched eyebrow,

Sarah explained, "I heard the nurses discussing it an hour ago. I just didn't know who they were talking about."

"Hmm," the baroness said, looking irritated. "I'll have a word with Secreed about keeping me better informed. At any rate, there's your proof."

"Um... of what now?" Keane asked. Were they getting killed or not? And was Lady Roselle having an affair with someone named Secreed? The thought would have made Keane smile if he hadn't been so worried about dying.

"For whatever reason, it appears that Chancellor Finnagel has chosen to be your ally and patron," Lady Roselle said. She tapped her chin with an immaculately manicured fingertip. "So much so that he was willing to murder over a hundred people just to ensure your safety."

"He was nice to me earlier," Sarah said. Keane and Lady Roselle turned to look at her. "Not *that* nice," she said, eyes widened. "I never got the impression he was on a killing spree for me or anything. He was just... polite."

"The problem is," said Lady Roselle, "that we don't know *why* he's doing it. And that's dangerous."

"Can we talk about this later?" Keane asked, his voice strained. "If I don't fill that bucket *right dammit now*, I am going to piss over all three of us."

Sarah grinned and handed the bucket from the floor to Keane and walked out of the big hall with Lady Roselle. As he relieved himself, Keane considered that infiltrating a royal castle as an imitation prince was a lot more bother than he'd first thought it would be.

"I guess that's why everyone isn't doing it," he muttered aloud.

29

SARAH AND KEANE PLAN A TRIP TO THE ZOO

KEANE

A salty-fresh morning breeze lifted the gauzy curtains in Prince Despin's bedroom, while the sunlight set them aglow. The effect looked to Keane like an upside-down lantern flame.

"This is not a good plan."

Keane, in Despin's gray doublet and black hose, lay on his back on Despin's bed. It had turned into the place where he did all his best plotting.

He ran a brown finger over the stitched emblem of Tyrrane and traced the short-bladed, brutal dagger.

Sarah put on her dark green cloak over her sergeant's tabard. "Then help me make it better. You're the expert on this sort of thing."

For their first official outing together, Princess Megan and Prince Despin were to be chaperoned on a trip through the menagerie just after lunch. Sarah reasoned that while they typically had a pair of castle guards following them around, on the street between the keep and the menagerie, those guards would not be backed up by a hundred and fifty of their best friends.

Sarah had just finished lunch, and her plate sat on a tray against the inner wall. Keane's uneaten meal lay beside it. He thought clearer on an empty stomach.

"I'm not saying it's a bad start," said Keane, "only that we might want something more than 'then we run away.' What can we work up as a diversion?"

"I could punch a guard unconscious," Sarah said, smacking a fist into her hand. Her dark hair, braided at the temples and free down her back, rolled across her rounded shoulders with the motion.

Keane sat up. "So, the idea of a diversion is to keep attention focused elsewhere while we do something we're not supposed to be doing—not to focus attention *on* us and all the bad things we don't want anyone to see."

"Then I should punch *you* unconscious?"

"Let's do Bag of Coins," Keane replied. "I've got about two hundred crowns so far. What have you got?"

"Two hundred?" Sarah's brows shot up. "I've only got fifteen. Have we both been stealing from the same people?"

In preparation for their departure, Keane and Sarah had been fleecing the courtiers that flitted hither and yon in Forest Castle. No one too important and no one who would be listened to if they noticed. He kept his money in a slit he cut in the underside of his mattress toward the middle—the women who changed his sheets never noticed it.

"I suppose that'll do." Keane didn't like Bag of Coins as a distraction ploy. Too expensive. But it *always* worked. "Maybe I can trade some gold for silver somewhere."

"No time," Sarah said. "We're due pretty much now."

Keane hopped off the bed and slid underneath it on his back. After a week of recovery, his leg didn't complain too much. He pushed his hand into the small slit he made behind the rope mattress support and removed four linen bags of gold coins. He stopped to push the feathers that fell from the mattress back in and slid himself out from underneath it.

"One of these oughtta take care of it." He tossed Sarah one of the bags and placed the others into a leather satchel he slung over his shoulder.

"Let's go."

They had been led to the safety of the castle by fleeing Lord Marshal Harden and his company of nasty mercenaries, and now they were fleeing the castle to get away from being revealed to the people they intended to keep them safe. It all gave Keane a headache to think about.

The two of them left the room and met their retinue in the hallway. A green-and-yellow-liveried page led them, and a pair of castle guards marched behind.

"Fine day for a walk about the city, eh boy?" Keane asked the page, a shortish youth with light brown skin and amber eyes. His black hair marked him as at least part Darrish.

"Yes, Your Grace," the boy replied. "But we's only going to the menagerie. It's attached at the outer wall. It's only just outside. We won't be going on no walks around the city, sir."

"My mistake," Keane said and threw a wink to Sarah.

"If it's your first time, sir, you're in for a treat. There's beasts from all over the world. King Rance gets 'em as presents and lets us all look."

"For free?"

"Well, nossir." The boy tugged at his collar. "The king charges a fourthing a head. But you can pay with a dog or a cat to feed the animals if you can't afford it. There's plenty of 'em on the streets if you're fast."

"And are you fast?" Keane asked.

"Oh, yessir," the page said with a broad smile. "I never paid coin to get in. I can always catch me something to cover my way. I go loads."

"I'll just bet you do." Keane would need to shift his plans for this. A fleet-on-his-feet kid running after them when they made their move could cause problems.

At some point Keane could not determine, they left the huge Monarchs Tower and entered the Welcome Hall. The walls of the whole castle consisted of the same greenish granite blocks, other than the Stone Tower where the walls were gray. Finnagel said the green was because of copper in the stone or something.

Keane's leg ached a bit, but it was nothing he couldn't stand.

The Welcome Hall itself was a play on words. It provided space for the welcoming of visiting dignitaries and was the "face" of the keep. But in the event of an invasion, the Welcome Hall took on a more sinister cast. Those granite walls hunched twelve feet thick at the base, and hundreds of arrow loops adorned the hall's front. Upper stories held wider loops behind which ballistae on half-moon tracks rested, easily capable of firing over the inner wall and into the Quarters.

An invading force would find themselves facing an altogether different sort of welcome.

As the group stepped into the gigantic foyer, Keane rolled his eyes at the twenty-five-foot statue of King Rance looking young, fit, and muscular. The statue was one of a dozen lined up along the north and south walls of the foyer, each a king of Greenshade. Keane didn't know who any of them were except for the current king and the very first king of Greenshade. That one was King Eggan Rance the First who'd hacked the land out of the hands of Tyrrane some two hundred and fifty years ago and walked away with a Tyrranean princess in the bargain.

"Guess that makes me the princess," Keane whispered to himself.

To the north side of the tall door leading to the courtyard, the real Princess Megan stood with another pair of castle guards. Her scowl deepened when she noticed Keane coming.

Sarah shoved him from behind when Keane unconsciously slowed as he always did whenever Megan was within sight. A lopsided grin appeared on his face, and his hands felt too big. The princess glowed in the sliver of sunlight that found her through the tall door as if the sun naturally sought the allure of her cheek. Her pale blue dress clung to her youthful shape and sent Keane's brain dribbling out of his ears.

Unable to meet her direct gaze, he stared at her feet.

"Good morning, my grace," Keane said with a wavering bow. Baroness Roselle drilled him relentlessly on the proper etiquette to use among royalty. *My* grace was reserved for when addressing a prince, princess, queen or duke of your own country. Those from other countries were Your Grace. Keane hoped to display his devotion and commitment by using the more familiar term.

"Your Grace," Megan replied.

Ouch.

"Uh, ready to go?"

"I will go with you because I must, Prince Despin, but I would like to make one thing entirely clear between us." Megan's cheeks flushed red as she spoke. Her words were fast and low, for Keane's ears only. "My life is full of idiotic men who believe they know better than I do by virtue of their pricks. I don't need another one. I know what Tyrrane is like, and I know what kind of reputation you have. If I have to marry you to keep the peace between Greenshade and Tyrrane, I will. I will be the dutiful queen, and the throne will have its heir. But that's as far as this goes. We are not friends, and I will never enjoy your company. I will endure you for the sake of Greenshade but nothing more."

Keane stood looking at her a moment, unsure how to respond.

"Great," he said. "So, you're ready then?"

30

KEANE, SARAH, AND MEGAN RUN AWAY

KEANE

Keane, the princess, Sarah, one page, and four guards made their way down the grand stair in front of the keep. Well-heeled nobles and merchants alike paused to stare as they passed. Around them lay the primary courtyard of Forest Castle, secure behind eighty-foot green-gray walls and the massive castle gate. A steady stream of colorful people walked in and out along the cobbled walkway with grass to either side. The walkway also served as the western end of the lengthy Coach Street that led east all the way out of town.

Passing beneath the enormous gate, they entered the Quarters. To their left, the Andosh embassies stood tall and proud—the white marbled Rousland walls, the longhouses of Norrik, Mirrik, and Coldspine, and the menacing militarism of the black stone embassy of Tyrrane. Interspersed among these were dozens of shops and homes.

"Homesick already?" asked the princess. "I'm astonished you haven't spent any time there among your own kind. No one would mind."

"We, ah, we don't all get on well." Keane stared at the Tyrranean embassy, wondering how many people Finnagel had left alive in there and if any more were coming. "I'm not really their favorite." He winced as he stepped on the side of a cobblestone and slipped off. That leg still hurt.

"I suppose that's one thing to recommend you," Princess Megan said.

To their right on the south side of the street sprawled the Thirteen Markets in a colorful, haphazard, and energetic celebration of mercantilism. Every nation of Andos represented themselves here with items both exotic and mundane and with every type of food imaginable.

Because he skipped lunch for escape planning, hunger now pulled at Keane's nose. He made a mental note to return here and try every kind of traveler's roll the market offered. Though present in most countries, each of them made the filled bread rolls differently, and he never met one he didn't like.

Sarah flicked him on the side of his head, out of sight of the guards. Right. Love of his life now. Time for rolls later. His attention wandered because he found himself too nervous to converse like a normal person. What did he have in common with a princess?

"I don't look too old to you, do I?" Keane asked Megan. His head filled with the scent of flowers from her hair.

"Too old for what?"

"To marry you?"

"Don't be preposterous," the princess answered. "You're a man. All you need is a pulse. I suppose I should be grateful you don't look like my father's grandfather."

"I'm twenty-four," Keane blurted out. He couldn't stop himself. "But people say I look younger." In truth, Keane was not certain how old he was, but twenty-four seemed like a good guess.

"I thought you were seventeen. I'm supposed to be two years your senior."

"I told them to say that." Keane invented the lie as he spoke. "I wanted you to feel confident. More experienced. But now that I know you better, I see that you don't need any of that."

Princess Megan's eyes narrowed. "So, revealing that you are a liar is intended to make me feel more confidence in you?"

"Um..."

He was making himself look like an ass. Why was he even talking?

"Why are you talking?" the princess asked. She sighed and moved to the front of the group next to the page who tried to keep his face straight ahead, though he could not help throwing shy smiles her way.

"You have an amazing way with younger women," Sarah whispered into Keane's ear.

"I'm thinking of writing a book," he answered her.

Instead of heading beneath the Country Gate and into the city proper of Treaty Hill, they turned north and took a smaller path behind the white walls of the Rousland Embassy. Princess Megan led from the front while Keane watched her behind. Without her attention focused on him, he thought of all sorts of brilliant conversation. *How old is the castle? Who is your favorite king or queen in Andos? Tell me about your mother. Can I touch your breasts?*

Well, maybe not that last one. Imaginary conversations were difficult to keep on topic.

Sarah cleared her throat.

In this walkway between white embassy and green castle walls, pedestrians pressed closer together. A gaggle of washerwomen competed for space ahead of them with about a dozen stable boys, none of them realizing they were about to encounter royals.

Keane nodded to Sarah who hefted the linen coin-bag, its mouth pulled wide open.

The first of the castle guards raised his arm in preparation for fending off the oncoming citizenry. A subtle *twang* sounded from somewhere behind, and the guard pitched forward into the cobblestones, a thick feathered shaft lodged in his spine. The second had just enough time to shout, "Halt!" before he reached around to clutch at the arrow protruding from his lower back, and his legs gave out beneath him.

"Bowman on the wall!" Sarah shouted. "*Run!*"

Sarah and Keane broke into a run toward the washerwomen and stable boys, both of whom began to scream.

Keane banked hard right and headed for the princess. He couldn't leave her here. Violence and danger were his world, not hers.

"Ow!" shouted Megan when Keane grabbed her up as he ran past. He broke out of the crowd on the other side, and Sarah ran past him, the shouting page over her shoulder.

"The menagerie," Keane yelled. "It's already cleared out for our visit."

Whoever was attacking them would have to do so without shooting from the building tops. That was one advantage down.

Keane and Sarah's lack of any weapons was a different issue. He should have grabbed one of the guards' swords.

Too late now.

They ran for the long, low building that hugged the castle wall. Keane's leg burned wet fire with every step. A pair of huge wooden open-framed domes covered in netting protruded from the roof at this end of the menagerie, the cries of birds ringing from them. The open doorway was wide enough for ten people to enter side by side, making it easy for the two mercenaries to dodge the lone guardsman standing beside an elderly attendant.

"Summon the guard," Princess Megan yelled to him as she bounced past over Keane's shoulder. "The princess is attacked!"

The guard blew a fast trio of shrill tones on his whistle into the streets for more guardsmen and planted his halberd beside him. The last Keane saw of the guardsman was when he fell over backward, clutching at an arrow in his throat.

"Put me down," Megan ordered. "We'll move faster."

Already limping hard, Keane did so. He was still a little surprised at himself for having picked her up in the first place. He hadn't thought, just acted.

"We need to hide. Where do we go?"

"Follow me," Meagan said and ran deeper into the building with the young page in tow.

Keane and Sarah exchanged a quick look. He shrugged, she grinned, and they both ran after the slight, young princess.

They ran past the first aviary too fast for Keane to make out much more than some trees and flashes of feathered color. The covered stone walkways in the menagerie meandered around the exhibits. Some of the displays, like the aviaries, had nets instead of roofs, while others nestled deep in the walls. Very few corners existed here. Most of the joinings and edges were rounded and smooth.

Leather boots skidded and slipped as Keane came around a wide double-trunked tree that twisted upward through a hole in the ceiling. He came face to face with a golden-fringed bear twice his height. His injured leg went out from under him before he registered the two sets of iron bars separating him from the animal. He fell to the ground and rolled up against the bars. His fingers clutched at his now-bleeding leg as he tried to regain control of his breath.

As soon as he did, he screamed.

Something sharp poked him in the back. Sarah grabbed him by the arm and slung him away from the bars. The bear, foreleg as far out as it could manage, looked at Keane with large brown eyes.

"I think... it wants a treat," Keane said, his breathing harsh.

They both heard running footsteps behind them. Sarah lifted Keane to one foot and pulled his arm around her shoulders.

"I hear one coming," Sarah said as she and Keane loped after the princess.

They ran past broad, milky tanks full of green and blue glowing fish, through a netted corridor surrounded by half-foot-long hornets that buzzed with a sound like purring cats, and over a narrow bridge beneath which a pool full of furry red crabs watched tiny fish floating just inches above the water.

The pursuing footsteps drew closer.

"Down here," whispered Megan. A wide curving hall sloped down into blackness with the princess and the page just visible at the turn.

Sarah guided Keane down after the pair. His major concern at this point was that their pursuer might simply see them long enough to sight and shoot one of them. Megan could not have picked a better path than the curving spiral tunnel to keep that from happening, though.

With a gasp of pain at every step, Keane followed the rest down the twisting stone and into the safety of the dark.

"That's unfortunate," Sarah said as she neared the bottom.

At the base of the walkway, a columned room a hundred feet long and thirty feet wide waited for them, stuffed with night-animal exhibits and carved to appear as a vaulted natural cavern. On either side of the entryway rose hollow glass pillars shaped like extended hourglasses and filled with hundreds of emberflies. Another pair of these columns appeared every twenty feet, filling the room with dim orange light. The dark would offer them no cover here.

The smell of moss and dirt from fenced enclosures hung heavy in the air, mixed with excrement and animal musk. Murky creatures paced their displays or crouched still as dead things, observing the newcomers.

The page stood in the middle of the hall, his eyes round with fright.

"Get him," Keane told Sarah and pushed her at the boy. He hobbled left to get around a wide circular pool of slinks. The wooden fence and tall rocky island in the middle might hide him until he could figure out something better—as long as the damn things stayed quiet. Their song put animals and people to sleep so the otter-like animals could deliver their paralytic bite and eat them. In a cage like this, a family of slinks was little more than a novelty—unless a murderer was chasing you, and your injured leg kept you from running any further.

With the page in hand, Sarah ran deeper into the room and vanished.

All Keane had to do was stay quiet and let the killer go by. When the bastard and Sarah found each other, that would be the end of *him*.

This sounded like the kind of plan a person came up with when all their blood was going away.

The princess. She ran in with the page, but Keane had already lost track of her by the time he entered the room.

That was a complication.

Keane peered through the fencing at the hallway. Below him, the slinks swam in lazy circles in the water. They looked like small shiny-black river otters and spoke in soft mewling murmurs. Their quiet calls came together, pushing the louder sounds away. The mews chased up and down in slow rises and falls, strange and beautiful and...

A loud knock woke Keane when his head fell against the fence post. The damnable man-eating water shits below were singing at him.

In the walkway entrance, feet shod for long travel stepped into view. A nondescript man in plain clothing moved quiet as a breath into the room. Keane would never have looked at him twice if it hadn't been for the warbow he carried.

It took a lot of strength to pull that kind of weapon.

There went another plan. He half-hoped that Sarah could just charge up, catch the arrows out of the air, and stab them all back into this asshole before he could even scream. But Sarah told him she couldn't catch anything that came out of something bigger than a little hand bow, and this was definitely not one of those.

Keane nodded off again. This time he caught himself before he hit the fence. The slinks continued their song, and he felt the strength draining out of his limbs as his body succumbed to the weird soporific.

Fuck a ghost-owl in the armpit, he really knew how to pick a shitty hiding place.

The man with the warbow smiled at the floor, his eyes glittering with reflected orange light from the emberflies. He stepped in Keane's direction.

The blood that ran down Keane's leg left a black smeary trail from him to the entrance which now led the hired killer straight to him. There was no way even Sarah could make it to the plain-dressed man before he shot one of the two of them. And Keane couldn't wake up enough to so much as crawl away. Every bit of energy he had, he used to keep his eyes open so as to watch his murderer walk around the slink enclosure, raise his warbow...

"You're not the one I want," he said. "Where's the big woman? I done shot all the guards, right? She's the only one left on my list."

"Uh," Keane responded. His head rolled to one side. Each eyelid weighed a good fifty pounds. As they fell shut, a small shape coalesced out of the orange gloom behind the killer, and reflected light flashed off of steel in a violent arc.

"*Faah*," the man shouted as he let go of his arrow. The deadly projectile thunked deep into the fence next to Keane's face and cut a dozen hairs from his head. The bowman spun and cracked Princess Megan across her nose, who twirled into a heap.

That was all he had time for, though. Sarah ran full tilt from the middle of the room and launched herself off of a fencepost. As the killer's eyes flew open in surprise, she collided, elbow first, into his throat. With her full weight on him, he crunched to the stone floor. His big bow skittered away.

Keane popped upright, fully awake. Sarah's dive from their enclosure shut the slinks up and sent them scurrying back to the rocky holes on their little island. He pulled himself to his feet and hop-dragged over to where the princess stirred.

"Are you all right?" he asked. He found himself terrified that she might be injured. From the entrance, men shouted, and heavy-booted feet trooped down the walkway.

The castle guard.

Megan sat up, blood running from under her hand and down her chin. "I thig he broge by doze."

"Can I come out now?" the page called from behind a tall cage filled with tiny yellow-eyed bats.

Relieved laughter bubbled up from Keane as the room filled with serious and well-armed castle guards. She would be fine. Better than fine. Now they had a shared danger, an experience to bring them together and...

Guards grabbed Keane and bore him to the ground, bringing

another shriek of pain when someone stomped on his injured leg. But still, he couldn't stop laughing.

"Stobbit! Datz da man ober dere." Megan pointed with her other hand at the unconscious would-be killer underneath Sarah, who sat on him with her legs crossed. Megan's dagger still protruded from the man's lower back.

"I have him," Sarah said. "But we *were* going to feed him to the bear upstairs."

A guard helped Keane up. Still chuckling, Keane ripped the leg of his hose, trying to remove it and make something he could tie around his wound. The stitches in his leg were torn open and felt on fire.

"Your Highness," he said. "I'm really happy you're not hurt."

The black scowl she turned on him pierced his chest and chilled his blood. She spun on her heel and stalked back up the long spiral walk.

"She was behind the emberflies beside the entryway," said Sarah. "Wish I'd thought of that, but I was trying to hide the boy. After that, I was just trying to stay hidden until he got close enough to grab. Or until she stabbed him in the kidney, anyway."

"I don't... Sarah, what did I do?"

Sarah's lips turned up in a half smile, and she walked to Keane's side. She watched the little princess storm away, brown curls bouncing behind her. Most of the guards followed, and the rest pretended not to hear what was being said around them.

"I don't know," Sarah said. "I *love* it when my intended laughs at my injuries. Especially when he tells me I'm not hurt while I'm bleeding all over my dress. But, of course, I'm not a princess. There could be a difference."

"When I write my book about how to talk to younger women," Keane said, "I'm devoting the chapter on ugly sarcasm to you."

"Pff. As if you could write." She helped lift him off the fence and onto his one good foot.

Six guards remained behind to escort Keane and Sarah out of the menagerie. They stood in silent disapproval beside the entrance.

"This is really odd." Sarah stared around the room and held Keane upright. "I mean, *really* odd."

"What's odder than me deluding myself into thinking I could make that woman like me?"

"Well," Sarah said, inhaling deeply and opening her eyes wide, "you wouldn't think about it at first glance, and even then, it might not occur to you unless you could call them, but there shouldn't be this many emberflies here."

Keane frowned in concentration. "I don't get it. I know most people who can do it at all can only call them one at a time, but couldn't they just have a bunch of people on emberfly duty all the time?"

"No," answered Sarah. "There's too many. The emberflies disappear after a few days. There'd have to be a constant line of people coming in and out all the time, and it still wouldn't be enough. Plus, these columns are the right shape, but they're set into stone.

"I think these emberflies were summoned all at once and have been here since this place was created."

The two mercenaries stood there and considered what that might mean. Only demons had this kind of power. Did Greenshade employ one in its construction crews?

Or was there a demon in the court, right now?

"I don't think we're gonna escape," Keane whispered.

"Come on," Sarah replied, voice low. "There's always tomorrow."

31

ELI GETS HIS WISH AND IMMEDIATELY REGRETS IT

ELI

Low whitecaps lapped against the forward hull of *The Floater* while Eli oiled his well-kept short sword. In his first battle, Eli went in with a length of board to use as a shield and a fist-sized rock for his blade. Fifteen years old and drunk as a lord, he had been knocked unconscious at first contact with the enemy. When he woke, he picked this very blade off the first dead man he saw. It took good care of him in the intervening years, and he took good care of it.

He was sentimental that way.

"You sure love on that gray hunk of metal for a man who says he hates killing." Harden sat on one of a row of crates lined up against the starboard wales next to Eli. He leaned back and propped himself up with his elbows on the worn railing that ran along the wale top. A breeze blew along the wide brim of his leather hat, and Harden closed his eyes and smiled.

"You know, if it weren't for the horrid food, I could almost see myself becoming a sailor. This is really a pleasant way for a man to spend his life."

"Sailing ain't for you." Eli lifted the blade and turned it in the sun. He lowered it again and oiled the other side. "Not unless there were someone to stab and steal from at the other end. Peaceable living just ain't in you."

"Probably right," Harden said and squinted from under his hat brim. "Maybe a pirate then." He closed his eyes once more, head leaned back.

Eli chuckled. "Maybe, but I doubt it. We been on this damn tub two full days now, and I ain't understood a single word any one o' these bastards has said. You're too old to be learning new languages."

"Still younger than you." Harden pulled his lips back, showing a lupine grin. "They call me old man because I'm the boss. They call *you* that because it's true."

"Did you have a purpose for this visit other'n making me wish I'd let Darkling murder you?"

Harden's grin went out like a candle dropped in a rain barrel. He blew out a long sigh.

"Yeah, I did. I want to talk about Sarah."

Eli's brows shot up, and he leaned forward, looking back at his lord marshal. He casted around to see if anyone was close enough to listen in. It was late afternoon in mild weather without a cloud in the sky. Most sailors and soldiers had found a stretch of board to curl up and nap in. Those few up and about had actual duties to attend to and little interest in sticking their noses in where they would be likely to lose them.

"Alright. Let's talk."

"I wasn't going to promote her," Harden said. "Even though she'd make a fine captain, and I was... anticipating an opening."

Eli made a soft noise that was almost a laugh. He cleaned his blade and sheathed it.

"When we first got her—what was she?" Harden asked. "Eight? Nine years old?

"She was fifteen," Eli answered. "And big as any man in the company."

Harden frowned. "I forgot. It feels... it feels like she was smaller."

"It *feels* like you think you're her goddamn father," Eli said. There was no anger in it, but still, the comment came out sharper than Eli intended.

Harden's eyelids opened a slit, and he cut his gaze to his captain. "I don't need an adopted daughter."

"No, you do not," Eli agreed. "I wonder though. Sometimes I feel like I done a whole lotta evil in this world. More'n a person's share. I suppose if I could feel like I done one thing right to set against that, at least I'd *have* a thing to look back on and say I ain't done all bad. Maybe that's how you feel too."

"I almost did, Eli," Harden said. He leaned forward, now resting his elbows on his thighs and staring at the sea across the main deck. "If not for that fucking Keane."

Aware that Harden couldn't see his face, Eli rolled his eyes. "As long as we're baring our souls and all, what's your headache with that boy anyhow? He's a pain, but he had potential. He ain't no worse'n plenty, and he's better'n most. Fine mercenary. Good with a sword, not completely stupid—"

"He's not good enough for her," Harden interrupted. "And he's stuck to her like he was dog shit in her hair."

"Come again?" Eli asked. Maybe he was wrong about Harden feeling like a father to Sarah.

"She's not meant for a mercenary's life, Eli. She's special. Something different. You know what I mean."

She was a hell of a soldier, but Eli doubted that's what Harden meant.

"I'd saved some money, and I was going to give it to her," Harden said. "Give her a fresh start somewhere new, far away from all this horribleness. But then there's Keane. She'd take him with her. And he'd take the life with him. No matter where she went, he'd be there to drag her back down into the muck and blood and ruin everything all over again."

Eli understood. "You wanted better'n that for her."

"I did," Harden answered. "And because of that, I tried to remove Keane from the adding, and then she ran away with him."

"Almost like she don't appreciate you murdering her best friend on her account. I don't expect many girls would care for that kinda help from their real fathers. This seems like one o' those situations where if you love a person, you gotta let 'em go out and make their own mistakes. Learn who's good people and who ain't."

Harden sat up and met Eli's gaze.

"I will carve that boy out of her life if I have to burn the world down doing it." His face twisted in anger. "She is special, and she will be happy. No matter how many people have to die for it to happen."

Eli slapped his hands down on his thighs and rubbed them against the leather leggings, generating some heat. He stared at the horizon. At least that explained the reason for the big boat trip to Vastard.

Harden was out of his damn mind.

But then, hadn't that been what Eli was here for all these years? Harden always had a bit of an edge to him. Didn't really fit in with normal folk. He needed Eli to navigate the parts that bumped up against the rest of the world. Let the lord marshal be canny, be angry, be crazy, and manage it into something productive. Hopefully lucrative.

Might be a tall order this time.

"Well, then," Eli said as he stood and picked up his rags and sword-oil bottle, "if we're gonna burn down the whole damn world we oughtta get to planning it. Got three more days to land, and another four to Vastard. And things are likely to get a lot less quiet then. The more we got to show when we arrive, the better off we'll be."

Harden came to his feet and squeezed Eli's leather-coated shoulder.

"Thank you, Captain Eli. What would any of us be if we did not have each other to rely on?" With a wide smile on his face, Harden went belowdecks to his room to gather his maps.

Eli watched him go.

"Same thing we are *with* each other. Buncha goddamn idiots."

32

THE FOURTH TIME'S THE CHARM

KEANE

Hidden away in the upper reaches of Forest Castle, Keane and Sarah sat in a small gallery overlooking an open courtyard some twenty by thirty feet, with colored diamond shapes painted at either end. If there were a purpose to the yard, it escaped Keane, but it was a good place to hide from everyone else who lived here.

Keane, blood spattered across his gray doublet, gripped the long bench on which they sat. Sarah leaned forward, forehead creased in concentration, as she picked teeth out of a broken-off chair leg she held. More blood coated her boots.

"If I had an ox's asshole for every way that went wrong, I could put every brothel in this fucking city out of business overnight," Keane said. He glowered into the clipped grass below. "Seriously, what the fuck does it take for a thief to walk *out* of luxury and opulence? How many times is it gonna take for us to get outta here?"

"You sound angry." Sarah pried another tooth free and set it on the bench beside her.

"Oldam's craggy god cock, Sarah! Yes. I *am* goddamn angry. How are you not? You want to get out of here more than I do. Two weeks ago, we get stopped by a would-be assassin at the menagerie, four days ago a bunch of drunk nobles' brats looking for a brawl are wandering by the castle wall at the same time we're creeping out a second-floor window—that we scouted for a *week*—and then there's today. What the hell was that?"

"They were clowns," answered Sarah. "They were in the castle to celebrate the fourth birthday of Duke Hubrane's grandson."

"Doesn't his grandson live in March Castle?"

"Yeah," Sara said, picking at a stubborn bit of broken enamel. "That *is* weird."

"And why would clowns celebrating a child's birthday attack a pair of passersby on sight?" Keane folded his arms and frowned at Sarah. "Any clever thoughts there?"

"Someone is onto us." She sat up straight and stretched her back, put down the chair leg, and gave Keane her full attention. "And they're gauging our strength."

"That's right. Someone is onto us." Keane climbed to his feet and leaned against the railing that separated the courtyard from the gallery to stand face-to-face with Sarah. "But they aren't testing us. What would be the point? I know you think Hubrane is behind all this, but he doesn't care how strong you are—he only wants you dead."

"Then who?"

"It has to be Finnagel," replied Keane.

"No," said Sarah. "That doesn't make sense. Why would he help us with the Tyrraneans and give us advice about the duke only to try to murder us—clumsily—a few weeks later?"

"Well, he straight up murdered all of those Tyrraneans, so helpful *and* horrible." He crossed his arms. "He did give us advice about how to stay out of Hubrane's way, and now suddenly, all the people trying to kill us are amateurs and dumbasses? *And* they only show up when we're trying to escape?"

"Finnagel's spies," Sarah said. She glanced around them.

"Yeah. We already know he's aware we aren't Prince Despin and his bodyguard, and for whatever reason, he wants to keep us close. Not let us get away. So every time we try, he throws a bunch of expendables in the way to stall us until the guards show up. And think about it. None of our attackers has even tried to avoid the guards after they went for us. Almost like they're *not afraid* of getting caught."

Sarah raised a brow. "Seems unnecessarily complicated. Why not just let us in on whatever his plan is and ask us to stay himself?"

"I don't know," Keane answered. "Maybe we wouldn't like his plan. Maybe he hates clowns. Maybe he's just a sneaky old fuck who's so used to thinking sideways, he never thought of asking us to our faces. Personally, I don't care."

"There's nothing we can do about it either," Sarah said. She scratched the side of her head and straightened her braids in their leather sleeve. "No way we can move against him without him catching wind, and then he's got us by the balls."

"He's got me," Keane said, holding up a finger. "You don't have balls."

"So I get to go free?" Sarah asked, a half smile on her brown face. "What am I doing hanging around here with you, then?"

"I thought you liked my personality," Keane said.

"I do." Sarah stood and picked the chair leg and teeth off the bench. "You're a cuddly kitten. A cuddly, super-irritating, noisy kitten that everyone else wants to drown."

Keane grabbed the bigger woman in a fierce hug.

"Thanks. I really needed that."

33

THE FRIENDLY LANDS OF VASTARD

ELI

E li, Harden, and the remaining fifteen mercenaries chosen for this voyage landed at Korris, close to the Western Crags. Korris was a small village on the shore of the Beacon Sea that never seemed to do enough fishing, growing, or trading to keep itself afloat. It was run by a wily old Darrishman named Jackleg Pete who liked to keep traffic through his town moving at a brisk pace. In and out before anyone had the opportunity to cause trouble.

The ugly clapboard hamlet served as the northern gateway to Vastard, and none of the people headed that way were the kind you wanted hanging around.

They would have been more like Eli and Harden in that regard.

Harden decided to keep everyone's heads down and just move through without stopping to say hi, and Eli agreed. They even almost made it.

A recent rain turned the rutted streets to mud in the faded village, and Harden led his men east toward the Little Gods Mountains and the pass there to the Yellow Sea. Bennah, Harden's old nag, and Clinker, Eli's well-trained stallion, followed on short tethers. Korris's buildings were already behind them, and ahead of them, the bright sun reflecting off of the wet road made them squint. Scrub covered the hills to their right, and the Beacon Sea lay dark, blue, and serene to their left.

Even the Battered Soldier, the faded green tavern Jackleg Pete used as his base of operations, was almost out of sight.

"Harden Grayspring, is that you I see trying to slither out of town without so much as a wave hello? That's just impolite is what that is."

Eli tensed and turned. In the road behind them, flanked by a pair of dirty and hard-looking thugs stood Crestor Frain, Jackleg Pete's right-hand man. Crestor showed his browned teeth—it would not be right to call the expression a grin—and hooked his thumbs behind the leather strip that served as his belt. His greasy yellow hair stained the shoulders of the threadbare red shirt that pulled tight over his paunch.

"Crestor," Harden said, pushing back the brim of his hat. "No disrespect intended, but we had no business in Korris, and Pete has taken great pains to let everyone know that folks aren't welcome in his town unless they have a reason to be there. So, if you don't mind, we'll be on our way."

The situation was more delicate than it seemed. While Harden had the numbers, Crestor represented the power in this region, and just killing him would set the forces they were here to deal with against them. Eli knew that sucking up to this fat weasel must be burning a new hole in Harden's ass, and he was pretty sure that Crestor knew it too.

The fucker sure seemed to be enjoying himself enough.

"It would be Jackleg Pete's business you should be worrying on there, *Lord Marshal*. And it would be his business to know every witless bastard that steps through our fine village." Crestor turned his head and spat on the road. One of his thugs drew a carving knife and ran a finger up and down the blade. "But then, he already knows you been in and out, so no count to concern yourself there."

Harden clapped his hands and rubbed them together. "Well, thank you for the visit. Bye, now."

"Nossir, I don't think so." Crestor's lips slid over his teeth like a dying snake in rotten lamp-oil. "See, it's old Eli there who still has business in Korris. Business what wants him to stick around awhile."

"Crestor, you goat-fucking coward, just what the Undergates are you pissing on about?" Eli's face reddened as he shouted. "What business'd anyone possibly have with *you*? I'd sooner put my tongue up a..." He trailed off when he caught Harden's black glare.

"That is, uh." Eli took a step back and drew in a deep breath. "How can I help you?"

"Orena's in town," Crestor said with a sinister leer. "You remember Garullo's little sister? She'd love to say hi while you're passing through."

The thug with the knife in his hand snickered.

Eli deflated. Garullo had been an evil-tempered loudmouth decades ago in Vastard who ended up on the wrong side of Eli in a very public duel. At the time, the man had been big and fast and deadly with his steel, but Eli has been young, drunk, and full of piss. He took great pleasure in humiliating Garullo before killing him mean and bloody. The sister, Orena, had not taken kindly to the whole thing and swore to slap Eli in the face with his own innards.

It was a loose end he'd always meant to tie up somehow but never had the chance to do it.

Looked like he'd get it now.

"Go on ahead," Eli told Harden. "If I get out of this, I'll meet up with you in Vastard. And if'n I don't, then I guess you'll have two captaincies to fill."

Harden shook his head and pinched the bridge of his nose. "I assume Orena does not yet know that our good Eli is here yet?" he asked Crestor.

"As a matter of fact," Crestor said, turning his head to one side, "she does not."

"How much not to tell her?" said Harden.

"Ten gold crowns would do." Crestor grinned wider, turning Eli's stomach.

"Sir, no." Eli stepped in front of Crestor. "You can't give this sheepshit our *gold*." The lord marshal's look shut Eli up. He stepped back out of the way.

"How much to kill her?" Harden asked Crestor.

"One hundred crowns."

Harden's brow rose. "What? Why so much? She breathe fire or something?"

"Lord Marshal," Crestor said with a slight bow. "I married Orena twenty years ago. She is my *wife*."

"Ah." Harden rubbed his chin between thumb and forefinger. "I'll give you thirty."

"Eighty."

"Thirty-five."

"Sixty."

"Forty and a bottle of grog for your grief."

"Done."

After the transaction was finished and everyone had gone their separate ways, Eli approached Harden.

"Sir, I gotta thank you for that. No one never did nothing like that for me. I—"

"The forty's coming out of *your* share," Harden said. "And two bits for the bottle."

As Harden stalked off, Eli couldn't help but chuckle. If he'd known how much it was gonna cost him, he'd have let Garullo win the damn duel.

The mercenaries moved across the pass through the Little Gods Mountains and into the high dunes of the Yellow Sea. After a few days' travel through the desert, they left the dunes and entered a particular set of foothills in the Eastern Crags.

With long tracks that dimmed behind them in the windswept sand, the group closed in on their destination. Eli wiped sweaty palms against his cloak and pulled a stained white ghutra forward to protect his face from the sun. In his estimation, there was no place in the Thirteen Kingdoms more dangerous than Vastard. His palms didn't sweat from the heat.

"How soon?" asked Harden. The lord marshal and his captain

rode the only two horses. The rest expressed relief amongst themselves at trading fine sand for rocky ground.

"Watch station is there." Eli pointed up at what looked like nothing but more rock. "They'll jump us soon's we get past the outcrop just there."

As the head of Wallace's Company, Harden had made occasion to visit Vastard in the past. After all, the place was its own tiny kingdom run and populated entirely by mercenaries. It would have been rude not to drop in and pay respects. But Eli lived here once and knew how they operated.

"Everyone, keep your damn weapons out of your hands," Eli said over his shoulder to the men. His voice came out in a sharp hiss. "They're gonna try'n rattle you, and if you draw, you'll catch an arrow in the throat for your trouble. These watch bastards have contests for the most idiots killed. Don't be one."

Behind him, grim-faced freemen nodded. The brothels of Vastard were legendary among the sell-swords of Andos. No one wanted to be the one to prong the deal now.

"Stop where you stand, and piss in your boots, you miserable flocks of beetles." Atop a stony pile not two hundred feet distant, a Darrishman in brown-scaled armor and long wrapped braids waved a spear over his head. "Ze man who doesn't bend over and take himself in ze mouth is getting ze beating from me. We are understanding?"

Eli exhaled a breath he did not realize he was holding, and the tension drained away from him. The dark-skinned man standing on the rocks was named Pan, and he was a friend.

Not everyone here was.

"What the hell did he just say?" came a voice from the mercenaries behind Eli, destroying his newfound calm. "I'll cut out that..."

One of Darkling's men strode out from the main group, sharp metal in his hand and murder in his eye. But before he finished his thought, a pair of arrows hit him out of nowhere, knocking him to the ground.

"Sorry to ask," Pan shouted from atop his rocks, his red-and-yellow wrapped braids swinging in the wind. "But can you look and see what color fletchings are on ze killing arrow? Zere's some money involved."

"Call off the games, Pan." Eli rode forward, his arms outstretched and his hands empty. "It's me."

Amusement battled with disappointment on Pan's face. An instant later, a broad welcoming grin broke out like a sunrise over a mountaintop.

"Eli Whister! You shoulda spoke up first. Mighta saved your man."

"It's all right," Harden said, riding up beside Eli. "He wasn't one of our favorites. Come on down and we'll talk."

Three minutes later, the expedition from Wallace's Company found themselves surrounded by three dozen deeply frowning men in desert clothing and armor, scimitars in their hands. The rest of Eli's group kept their hands well away from their weapons.

At the front, as the sun dipped beneath the Western Crags behind them, Pan clapped Eli on the shoulder. With Eli and Harden off their horses, the Darrishman stood a full foot taller than the captain.

"It's hard to believe you haven't killed Harden Grayface yet, Eli." Though he spoke to Eli, Pan stared Harden in the face.

"Gray*spring*," Harden said.

"Never happen," Eli replied. "Then I'd have to be in charge. I'd rather sit on my sword."

"You are ze strange sort of man," Pan said, letting his arm drop. "But is zere any uzzer kind in zis life of ours? Perhaps not." He took a step back and straightened. "Welcome to ze Fourteenz Kingdom."

"Your business is with me." Harden's voice was just above a growl. "Not my men."

"So now zere is business?" Pan asked. "Ah well. No one ever comes to Vastard just to say hello."

"I need soldiers," Harden said. He removed his hat and scratched at his damp scalp. "Real fighting men. Not farmers and fishermen."

Eli returned to his mount and unstrapped the battered cash box.

"How many?" asked Pan.

Harden told him.

Pan's bright-as-the-sun smile returned. "Do you have money?"

Box in hand, Eli stepped up and opened the lid.

With practiced movements, Pan lifted each tight leather bag out of the box, looked inside, and weighed it in his hand. His brow creased together.

"What's in that box is a drop of what's on the other end of the take," Harden told him.

"Where is ze target?"

Harden told him that, too.

Pan's head rolled back, and he boomed with laughter. Around them, the desert-cloaked mercenaries of Vastard returned his mirth and sheathed their scimitars.

"So we have a deal?" Harden had to shout to be heard over the freemen. Even their own men were laughing now, though Eli doubted they understood why.

"A deal like zis requires ze approval of King Oppah," Pan said, his grin wide and happy. "But coming from the great Harden Grayface, I suspect ze answer is yes."

"Gray*spring*," Harden said.

34

DYSFUNCTION FOR DINNER

KEANE

K eane sat for the family meal, a weekly occurrence that he had been obligated to attend as soon as his leg healed. The wide dining hall had the same greenish cast to the stone as the rest of the castle, all the way up to the vaulted ceilings. The long table, with King Rance at the head and Queen Loffa at the foot, could have seated twenty. Instead, Keane and Princess Megan made up the rest of the party, just to the right and left of the queen. A huge tapestry depicting Forest Castle, before the Stone Tower had been built to replace the original, covered the wall in front of him. The colors were faded, the tapestry in the shadows, and the whole thing looked oppressive as if it were trying to smother the wall behind it. A pair of guards and the master butler hovered at the edges, completing the scene of aloof indifference.

Sarah positioned herself against the far wall so that she and Keane could see each other. She stood, hands clasped behind her back, and watched the room.

That impression might have been Keane's mood, though. To distract himself, he closed his eyes and inhaled. Over the scents of the food, he smelled the princess's flowery perfume as well as that of Queen Loffa, which smelled to him like sweet almonds.

It had been almost a month since King Rance stabbed Keane in the leg. No more assassins came in the night, which he and Sarah attributed to them quitting every room Secretary Duke Hubrane entered—it gave him little opportunity to be irritated by Sarah's continued being alive. Also, the pair stopped trying to escape, and the attacks by ill-placed bowmen and wandering packs of strangers had declined.

Except for trying to win the favor of Princess Megan, an effort that so far bore little fruit, Keane was almost bored.

The death rate among travelers from Tyrrane's capital of Dismon slowed to a trickle, and while the subject continued to make Keane jittery, no one seemed to assume he and Sarah had anything to do with it. They appeared not only to be in the clear but also free of those who might recognize them. Sarah had decided not to broach the subject with Finnagel. That Lady Roselle thought the spymaster capable of such a thing meant he was extremely dangerous, and whether he was involved or not, he didn't seem like the kind of person to be leveling accusations at.

Though Keane stayed aware of any further evidence of a demon in the castle, none presented itself. If the hellish creature were ever here, it must be long since departed.

The food at these dinners was almost always pedestrian. King Rance had a taste for dinner breads, though Keane doubted that the actual street food of the Darrish kingdoms typically held bites of lobster, steak, and wine-soaked mushrooms—nor were they fried in butter. Captain Lowger, the surly Darrish giant, once told him that it was a mark of status in Egren for the wealthy never to have even touched a dinner bread. It made Keane smile to think of the image-obsessed king finding out that one of his favorite meals marked him as a commoner amongst the caste-conscious Darrish.

Sullen silence interrupted only by the clinking of cutlery was usually the best that could be hoped for; the king had a habit of sudden and capricious rages at the table which often resulted in Megan stalking off to take her dinner elsewhere.

Tonight did not seem to be a night for silences.

"Who does she think she is, sending me apples from Arlea?" King Rance asked, waving his fork in the air. Every time he moved, his folded-over hair, thin and light as breath, fell back and forth. A typical conversation could leave him looking like he'd just woken up after sleeping in a tornado.

"Is that supposed to be a gift? It's an insult—that's what it is. We grow the best apples *anywhere*, right here in Greenshade. Everyone says. Apples from Arlea. You know, Ambassador Dana sends bottles of salt-bloom to her family. For the fish. Doesn't even pay for it. Me, I don't say anything. I'm not that kind of man. But she could be up in stocks if I wanted. Just saying it. Up in stocks."

"Your Majesty," Keane said, taking advantage of one of the few breaths that slowed the king's fulmination. "If I may?" The lull in attempts to murder Keane and Sarah had him increasingly on edge. He felt as if someone—Duke Hubrane—was trying to get him to put his guard down.

They needed some kind of preparation.

Sarah, standing against the wall opposite with the other servants, looked at Keane, her eyes wide. He never spoke during these dinners. King Rance made a face as if discovering a fat roach dung in his potato soup.

"Ah, what is this? Secreed, why is he talking?" the king asked Secreed, his master butler and chamberlain. "You know I get a sour stomach when he talks." Secreed had been the elderly servant who had announced everyone when Keane and Sarah first arrived. Keane wondered what King Rance's reaction would be to finding out his chamberlain was one of Baroness Roselle's lovers and spies in the castle. The thought was almost enough to bring a smile to his lips.

"Sorry, sir," Secreed said and walked over to stand beside Keane. The stiff old butler straightened the hem of his formal servant's jacket as he spoke, "His Majesty requests that you maintain silence during these meals, for the proper digestion of all—"

Keane turned, reached up, and stuffed a prawn in Secreed's face. "I want my bodyguard to be armed, sire. I think we've earned the trust of—"

"And judging by her unfortunate and continued presence here in my home," the king said, "I'd say she hardly requires a weapon to defend herself, wouldn't you? If she needs a sword, she'll have a sword. Trust me."

Keane bit back his reply while Secreed dutifully chewed his prawn. Any further comment would invite an explosion. The last time that happened, Sarah had been met with a pair of huge Norrik warriors as she prepared for sleep and had been forced to beat them both to death with the footboard from Keane's bed.

The bed had *still* not been repaired.

"Megan, are you excited about your marriage next month?" Queen Loffa asked.

Everyone at the table turned to look, the queen's conversation taking them all by surprise. Most evenings, she did nothing but eat small helpings of whatever vegetables were being served and was silent unless addressed directly. The only time she ever spoke of her own accord was with Baroness Roselle, and the lady was taking dinner tonight with an "acquaintance," doubtless one of her many paramours.

Keane found himself wishing he had the station here to dine wherever he wished. Being a prince in another country's castle looked a lot like being a prisoner, even if the food was better.

"Um... not really," Megan answered. The queen, maintaining Megan's gaze, nodded gracefully. Not for the first time, Keane thought of Queen Loffa as being like one of the gazelles from Sedrios housed in the menagerie below. Her every motion flowed, poised and beautiful. Of course, the comparison between queen and animal went beyond the quality of their movement. They both inhabited cages, and neither seemed smart enough to notice.

He sympathized.

"Well you *need* to be excited about it," the king said. "Every royal family in the Thirteen Kingdoms is gonna be here to *watch* you be excited when you marry your Pavi-tainted, deadbeat prince."

"*Every* family?" asked Keane. Would it be too much to ask that

Prince Despin's family not attend his royal wedding? But articulating the thought, even in his head, *did* sound kind of stupid.

The king ignored him. "Do you know what I'm spending on this? You are gonna have the best, most spectacular wedding ever. Not because of this half-breed." He pointed to Keane with a fork. "*His* father isn't paying for anything. It's because you are *my* daughter. And *I* have the biggest weddings anywhere."

"Like when you married my mother?" Megan asked, face reddening.

"Your mother was a whore," King Rance replied, turning the fork on his daughter. "She was lucky to be under my roof as long as she was. I still have a hard time believing how generous I was to take her in to begin with."

"Generous?" Megan asked, putting down her knife and fork. "Is it generous to lock your wife in the Night Tower for five months? Is it generous to take her clothes and her blankets, and let her freeze to death up there? I suppose I should hope for a less generous husband for myself."

"I would bring you *extra* blankets," Keane whispered to the princess. He tried to understand how the ruler of an entire nation could be such a petty and vindictive person, but he just couldn't get his brain around it.

Megan shot him a withering look.

"I mean, I would never lock you in a tower?"

King Rance smiled, finally looking over at Keane. "I'd say you've got your work cut out for you, boy. You know it was this kind of talk that led me to divorcing—"

"Murdering," Megan interjected.

"—her mother. But I don't have to do anything about this harridan-in-training. Just hand her off to the first snot-nosed royal with a hard-on and an important daddy who comes to call. That's what I call smart dealing."

To everyone's surprise—including his own—Keane found that he had stood from the table and was staring, face contorted by anger, at the king.

"Do not speak about her like that," he said, voice shaking.

The pair of guards standing in the corners of the room behind Rance bristled. Sarah, tight as a bowstring, tensed for battle.

"She is my fiancée," Keane continued, mastering himself, "and I would be a shitty husband if I didn't answer such insults"—he paused, swallowing—"just as you are a shitty father for making them."

There was a deathly pause as the room held its breath. King Rance reached out, picked up his wine glass, and took a drink. He set it down and looked at Keane, his brows coming together in distaste.

"You know those stories about the young suitor who finally gains his father-in-law-to-be's respect by standing up to him, and the father-in-law *doesn't* throw him out of the dining hall window for being an insolent loser?" the king asked, his voice measured and calm. "Well, you are *not* in one of those kinds of stories."

Keane looked around, weighing his options. No one was yelling... yet. Sarah nodded toward his chair, willing him to sit. Loffa smiled and picked up a single brown bean on the end of her fork. Megan scowled and shook her head at him. The king just watched, waiting to see what Keane would do next.

Frustrated by his powerlessness, Keane sat down in his chair. King Rance smiled and took another drink.

Opposite him, Princess Megan stood and stepped away from the table.

"I think I have lost my appetite," she said, casting Keane a glance he couldn't interpret. It didn't seem to be loathing, which was a step in the right direction. She turned and walked toward the door to the right of the awful tapestry. Keane found himself lost in the formfitting gray dress she wore, shiny satin flowers working around her muscles and curves...

King Rance waved her off nonchalantly as if the princess had been waiting for his approval. The door slammed shut.

The silence stretched out, the noise of King Rance's chewing the only sound in the hall. Keane jumped when the queen spoke again.

"Where did Megan go? I wanted to ask her if she was going to enter the archery contest this year. She's very good, you know. She wins every time."

Keane looked at Queen Loffa, whose attention drifted back to her plate. He turned to the king, who stopped eating and now sat glaring at Keane. The king leaned forward over his plate, propped up on his elbows.

"Excuse me. I, uh..." Keane stammered, pushing back his chair and standing again. "Good night." He turned and left the hall through the door behind him. Even with Sarah following, he felt the push of the giant tapestry's regard, as if it were reaching for him, wanting to smother him along with the wall behind it and everything else in its dreary world.

35

SARAH DECIDES WHO NOT TO HAVE SEX WITH

KEANE

B ack in the gallery above the odd little courtyard, Keane reclined on a long wooden bench and rubbed at his thigh. It was fully healed now, but the scar still itched. Sarah sat on the bench above him. This was the one place in Forest Castle they were relatively sure they weren't being spied on.

"I never considered defying the king's authority at his own dinner table as a way to get into his good graces," Sarah said, head cocked to one side while she stared down at the grass and courtyard walls below. Her posture was one of careful consideration. "Have we been doing this wrong up until now?"

"I don't give a shit what that lout thinks of me," Keane said, feeling angry and kind of loutish himself.

"You might if he orders Hubrane to send more assassins," Sarah said. "I mean, *I* don't mind. I can always use the exercise, but you get upset."

"Dammit! Oldam crap in my head and call it brains," Keane said. "I... I didn't think. I'm sorry. And don't talk that way. Those assholes only need to get lucky against you once. Shit. Maybe Finnagel will talk to the king for us as long as we aren't trying to escape. The man is a wizard when it comes to calming that fat-assed box of bees down. I just wish..." He didn't finish his sentence. What was it he wished, anyway?

"What?" Sarah said. She put a muscular hand on his forearm. "Do you still wish we could get out of here? Do you wish we knew what Finnagel was thinking? Or do you just wish you knew what *you* were thinking?" She lowered her voice. "You know I'm here for you, but I think we should consider some more creative means of escape. There's a sewer we could drop into from the—"

"She's miserable." Keane sat up and looked sideways at Sarah. "I just can't leave her here. I don't know why. I've never felt like this before. And whether she's willing to admit it or not, she *needs* me."

Sarah closed her eyes and turned away, nodding. From outside, a great confusion of bird cries erupted from the menagerie below them and settled down again.

"I guess it isn't like we have anything better to be doing." Sarah sighed. "I was going to build a sewer-kayak out of dinner tables and wax candles, though. It would have been special."

Keane stood and walked to the window. "King Rance killed Megan's mom and then married that—*really attractive*—simpleton. He's horrible to Megan every day in every way he can think of. I think... I think that I can help her. Somehow." That somehow felt a lot bigger to Keane than he thought it would. He would stop trying to figure out how to escape the castle. Finnagel was always two steps ahead anyway. This would be his new project. He was going to rescue the princess.

"Probably be easier if she didn't hate your guts," Sarah said. "Wow. Deja vu. I'm positive I've said that exact same sentence to you before."

"Probably," Keane said, "but I'm used to women hating me. Besides, I think I've figured out the problem."

"Oh?" Sarah asked.

"It's you," Keane answered.

Sarah's eyebrows shot up. "Me? What did I do? I'm nice. People like me."

Keane smiled at her obvious pique. *Faced off against three armed men with her bare hands and everything is fine, but she gets upset when a nineteen-year-old girl doesn't like her?* He pushed the smile back off his face.

"Finnagel told me that because of my reputation, the *prince's* reputation anyway, everyone in the castle assumes I'm sleeping with you."

Sarah burst into laughter.

"It's not a joke," he said.

"Sorry," she said, wiping her eyes. "How do you think Finnagel figured out you weren't the real prince before we ever got here?"

"I dunno. Spies? That's a whole different conversation. Right now, we need to fix this 'you and me' issue." He made a wide circular motion toward Sarah with one hand. "Then I can get Meg to trust me."

"It's Meg now, is it?"

"It will be," Keane said with a quick grin.

"So," asked Sarah, "do we have a plan here, or should I just pick someone else in the castle and start having sex with them?"

Keane's grin widened, and he gave a slow shrug.

"Oh, come on," Sarah said, standing. "*That's* the plan? I have to... I can't believe this."

"Not just some random guy," Keane said.

Sarah tapped her chin. "All right. I guess I *do* have a few candidates who might do. Have you seen Bencham? He's one of the guards on the evening shift. He's usually in the lower keep. He's all smooth and muscly, like a big, strong baby."

Keane mimed retching.

"Oh great. I suppose *you* have an idea who this lover of mine should be. Do I find out now, or would you rather I just take off all my clothes and go wait in the closet?"

When Keane did not immediately answer, Sarah's expression darkened.

"It doesn't even have to be real," he said in a rush. "We just need Meg to *think* you are having a relationship with someone else and that I'm good with it. See?"

"Won't work." Sarah crossed her arms. "The princess thinks you sleep with everyone. Why would she be concerned with just me?"

"Roselle said that I'm followed pretty much everywhere and every*when* I go." Keane sat up on the bench and twisted to face Sarah. "You are literally the only person I am ever alone with. Megan knows that. You're the only one I *could* be having sex with. The reputation works in our favor here. As soon as she understands that I'm not chasing after anyone else, she'll *have* to know that I'm only here for her. Then the three of us can get the hell out of here together."

Sarah frowned. "No way *that* can go wrong," she said. "So, who am I to be having all this fake sex with?"

"Lady Roselle thinks it should be Finnagel," Keane said. "He's young enough for it to be believable, but mostly, he's willing to be in on it with us. Reliable allies are thin on the ground in Forest Castle, and bringing in someone new may not be a good idea." Keane tapped at his chin with a forefinger. "Well, maybe not reliable, exactly, but his goals and ours line up on this since it keeps us in the castle. Plus, there's always the chance that if you are attached to Finnagel, Hubrane may officially stop trying to kill you. You may even get your sword back. Or maybe not. Hubrane seems to *really* hate Finnagel."

"Maybe I can keep an eye on Finnagel instead of the other way around," Sarah said. "The baroness knows about this too?"

Keane grinned and shrugged. "Baroness Roselle seems to know as much as Finnagel himself."

Sarah gave a great stretch, her brawny limbs going rigid, then relaxed. "Sure," she said, "why not? Hardly my first choice, but things could always stand to get more interesting around here."

36

KEANE AND THE PRINCESS PLAY "TOSS THE CARROT"

KEANE

The next day, Keane walked into the kitchen looking for an apple to eat. Hidden to one side sat an attached dining hall for the servants, and he liked to hide out there on occasion when no one else was using it.

The large kitchen hummed with perpetual activity. Tall and square, unlike the peaked ceilings of the upper castle areas, the chamber conjured images of warmth and food, comfort and safety.

And sometimes a little bit of terror.

Cook, a tall, bony banshee of a woman with a perpetual scowl, filled the kitchen with shouted orders and deprecations, enjoining the staff to further speed and efficiency. A constant smudge of flour decorated her cheek—one that no one was ever brave enough to tell her about.

Snatching an apple from a basket in the furiously busy kitchen, Keane ducked Cook's scorn and dove into the servant's dining hall. He was brought up short, however, by Princess Megan, already sitting at the long, dark wood table, chewing on a raw carrot.

"Oh!" said Keane. "Sorry. I just... I don't want to bother you. I'll, uh... I'll go."

"No, stay," she said, indicating the bench opposite herself. "I suppose if we are to be wed, we should be able to remain in the same room with one another without being forced."

That was as close as she had ever come to saying something nice to him, and Keane found himself grinning like a loon as he fell into the chair. This girl, a child really, had some sway over him he could not understand. He was older than she and no stranger to the fairer sex. Yet somehow, the princess transfixed him. He realized he had barely looked at other women since arriving here.

The princess's blue dress with its wide neckline, showing off her shoulders and neck, her hair, loose and dark like a waterfall caught in time, the smell of flowers—he was a mouse under the hypnotic gaze of some exotic snake. Immobile, staring...

"What?" she said, rubbing her nose. "Why are you always looking at me like that? It's creepy."

Keane woke from his rumination with a start. He hadn't realized.

"Sorry," he said. "I've just... well, I've never been betrothed to anyone before. It's new for me too."

"Shackles chafing a bit?" Megan asked, taking another bite of carrot.

"I guess," Keane said, then realized what she meant. "What? No! I mean... no. That's not it at all. It's just... I'm sorry. About dinner yesterday."

She looked at him, her perfect features unreadable beneath the gentle fall of her dark curls. "I guess it wasn't your fault. You're just stupid. Nothing you could have done about that."

"Not the first time I've heard that," Keane admitted.

Megan almost smiled. "Not that it will do *you* any good, but it was kind of nice to have someone on my side. No one else is willing to stand up to him."

A warm burn lit in Keane's stomach and spread north and south across his body. He was on *her* side. The warmth passed over his crotch and his face at the same time, making him blush intensely.

Realizing he had already fallen to staring at the delicate hand with which Megan held the carrot and imagining that hand touching his face, Keane shook his head and asked, "How does Loffa stand him? I've known brutes like that in my life. They aren't often kind to women behind closed doors."

"He hits her all the time. I'd say she must be used to it, but I'm not sure she even knows. That's another way she's better than my mom was, you know. My mom always hit him back."

"But how can a queen even be treated like that?" Keane asked. The Andosh were infamous across the Thirteen Kingdoms for their terrible treatment of women, but this was so disrespectful. The woman was a *queen*.

"She's a slave," Megan said. "She's been... conditioned."

"Oh," Keane responded. From where he sat, he could see the line of Megan's side, from underneath her arm to where it curved out of sight below the tabletop. Her pale blue dress was tight against her torso, and he pictured running his hands along her, burying his face in her hair, breathing her in...

"Not like my mother," Megan said, putting the half-eaten carrot down on her napkin. Even now, Megan's face betrayed very little emotion. "*She* was a real queen. Smart, confident—everyone looked up to her."

"What happened?" Keane asked. "I mean, I know what he did, how he killed your mother, but why?"

The princess rolled the carrot back and forth under one slender, well-formed finger. She did not look up as she answered. "Murghall, the king of Oulan—they call their kings something else there, San... somethings—he sent Loffa to my father as a gift. I guess he sends women to a lot of kings as concubines or whatever. My mother didn't like it and told the king as much. I think he got mad at her about it and locked her in the Night Tower until she froze to death. Then he married Loffa. Greenshade needed a new queen."

"That's horrible," Keane said.

Without thinking, he reached over and put his hand on Megan's arm. She did not pull away.

"What was her name? Your mother, I mean."

"Keliah," Megan said, looking up at Keane.

Keane's eyes widened, and a smile spread across his face.

"Something funny?" Megan asked.

"No, it's just," Keane said, "it's just that I knew a Keliah once. She was a barmaid in... Rousea? "She was nice. You'd have liked her."

"Did you like her?"

There was something ominous in the princess's tone, but Keane couldn't figure out what it was.

"Yeah," he answered. "Sure. We all liked her. She was good at her job and nice. Like I said."

"Do you think I don't know what a *nice* barmaid means?" Megan's brow rose. "I suppose she was *nice* to all your men that night. Or was she *nice* to everyone at the same time?"

"That's not what I meant," Keane said, his hand up in front of himself. How did a princess get such a dirty mind? "She was a fine woman. Never spilled a drop of beer. That's all."

"Am I to believe that Prince Despin of Tyrrane remembers the name of every serving wench who brought him a beer without spilling it? For that matter, what were you doing in Rousea? I thought your family were all paranoid shut-ins?"

Oh. He had forgotten he was Despin. For just a moment he had spoken to her as himself—as Keane. It felt so natural and right, he had not considered how his comments might sound coming from the prince's entitled and philandering mouth.

"I already told you," Keane shouted, his reserve crumbling, "my family and I don't get on well. I'm not their favorite. I hated being at home and got out as soon as I could." That part was all true, anyway.

The princess leaned back on her bench and drew in a breath. She blew it out in a long sigh and let her shoulders slump forward. Her eyes came up, and she sat straight-backed once more, looking Keane in the eye.

"This is ridiculous. *You* are ridiculous. I know you have a past, and it is unimportant." She tucked an errant curl behind her ear. "Please, if you would—if you *can*—tell me something about yourself that doesn't make me want to drop you in the ocean."

This was what he had been waiting for, an opportunity to say something for himself. To refute all of the horrible rumors swirling about Prince Despin. To show that he was not that person. To tell the princess that he was worth loving.

"Um."

He had nothing.

Keane was staring right at Megan with his mouth still open when she threw the rest of her carrot at him and bounced it off his head. By the time he regained his equilibrium, she was storming from the room. He turned to the door just as it slammed shut.

He dropped his head and shook it.

"How am I so *bad* at this?"

37

BARONESS ROSELLE BABYSITS SOME IDIOTS

KEANE

K eane winced against the bright sunlight as he opened the door for himself and Sarah onto the summit of the Stone Tower. Half of the tower's peaked roofline was left open to the air as if sliced down the middle and left unfinished. Gigantic curving timbers framed the open side and allowed sun and rain onto the gently graded portion of the roof, which along with the huge wrap-around terrace that protruded from the southwestern edge of the tower, held the grand High Garden.

The "garden" was a tiny forest, carefully tended and manicured by groundskeepers, that looked over the city several hundred feet below. From the southern side, you could see the Cattle Streets with Fish Hill at the far end, the offshore ship houses, as well as the shining Beacon Sea beyond.

It was the kind of view that screamed "remember your place" to anyone it looked upon.

High Garden itself was made of fully-grown white oak, chestnut, and holly trees, with undergrowth limited to occasional clusters of shaped bushes. The ground was covered in clipped grass and mulch, and the sounds of scurrying chipmunks surrounded them. Keane knew there was a family of foxes that lived in High Garden, too, though he had never seen them.

He thought the place was ridiculous; why not just go outside?

But it *was* beautiful.

Keane and Sarah followed the outer wall of the terrace for several minutes until they came to a place where that wall rose up and curved over, creating a shelter for a long marble bench. Within sat the Baroness Roselle Tralgar, feeding nuts to a quartet of brassy chipmunks chittering on the grass in front of her. The largest of these, a full foot long with a deep red-brown back, yellow sides, and black-and-white stripes down his spine, voiced his disapproval every time Lady Roselle tossed a nut to one of his fellows—this despite the fact that his own cheeks already bulged like overstuffed cabbage sacks.

The lady wore a fetching gown of red with deeper red velvet panels, black fur trim, and, as always, a fancifully matching hat.

"You brought Sarah," Lady Roselle said, her face lighting up. "I'm delighted. Please, come sit with me, both of you."

With Lady Roselle in the middle of the stone bench, Sarah and Keane took seats to either side of her. As they did, Keane spotted Queen Loffa, who reclined on the grass at the far edge of the clearing and fed a band of smaller chipmunks. Her blue and white skirts spread out around her in a large circle, and the little rodents ran all over it, chasing the food she dropped. The queen smiled wide and gave a silvery, somehow lyrical-sounding laugh at the chipmunks' antics. Her yellow hair shone in the sunlight.

"Thanks for letting us join you here, milady," Keane said. Lady Roselle had been tutoring Keane in proper speech for a castle since he first awoke in the surgeon's bed with a knife wound in his leg, though he still messed it up.

"Not at all, my prince," she answered. "Though when we are in private, you may call me Roselle. And I shall call you Despin."

Keane grimaced. It made sense to always call him by the prince's name, but it also made him exhausted like he was always on stage.

"Roselle," Sarah said with a smile and an incline of her head.

The baroness frowned, pursing her lips. "I suppose I should just give up trying to get you to curtsy like a proper lady."

"Curtsying requires a dress, I believe," Sarah answered. "Or at least a skirt."

"I suppose I should just give up trying to get you to wear a dress like a proper lady," Roselle said.

The two women smiled at each other. Their banter had a comforting, affectionate quality to it that relaxed Keane. While their methods were drastically different, both Sarah and Roselle affected their own landscapes similarly.

Neither were people to be trifled with.

"Have you given any thought to what we talked about?" Keane asked Lady Roselle. "Do we have any allies here? Or at least people we don't have to worry about?"

Roselle shot Keane a quick frown over her shoulder and returned her attention to the chipmunks. "The king hates you. Secretary Hubrane would have you dead if he could and return the crown to his own family. I don't *think* he would kill the king to do it, but you never know. The queen seems to like you."

"For what that's worth," said Keane, scowling.

"The queen is a dear, sweet woman," Roselle said. "You should remember that."

"Ow!" Keane shouted, reaching back to rub the back of his head where Sarah had reached around Lady Roselle to cuff him.

The big woman just smiled at him.

"I'm feeling a little outnumbered here," he said.

"You should remember that, too," Sarah told him, prompting a laugh from Roselle.

"I swear, I learn to like you more each day," Roselle said, patting Sarah on the knee. "At any rate... where was I? Oh yes. Allies. Princess Megan is likely the most honest human being I know, which is probably bad for the two of you. Your boyfriend Chancellor Finnagel can certainly keep a secret"—Roselle nodded in Sarah's direction—"though as I've mentioned, I feel like he is already keeping more than a few."

"Finn isn't really my boyfriend, and you know it. But on that subject, what about Secreed?" Sarah asked with a primly innocent expression.

Roselle ignored the implication and answered, "Secreed will do as I say, although I would prefer not to place him in any compromising positions. Which leads me to a question I've been wanting to ask the two of you."

Out on the lawn, one of the smaller chipmunks darted onto the queen's palm and sat up. Grinning, she lifted it and made cooing sounds.

"What is your plan here?" Roselle continued. "No one is more compromised than I am by your presence, as I have claimed to know you. I thought you were just going to grab some gold and run. I intended to tell people that you decided to flee both your own hateful father and the marriage he tried to trap you in, but you're still here. Why is that?"

"I want to save the princess," Keane blurted out. He hadn't meant to be that blunt, but he couldn't think of anything else to say. Besides, it was the truth.

"Save her from *what*, dear?" Roselle asked, leaning in close to Keane and looking him straight in the eye.

Roselle's directness flustered Keane, but he did the best he could. "Her father. He's horrible."

The baroness sat back and looked at the chipmunks in the sun. They chittered at her for more nuts, and she absently tossed them a few. When she spoke, her voice was low, and she kept her gaze forward.

"King Rance is a horrible man," she said. "That is entirely true. But I want you to listen carefully to me because I mean what I say. There is no path for you to save Megan from her life here that does not end with you—and quite possibly me—on a headsman's block. Nor, I believe, would she want you to. The princess does despise her pig of a father, but she loves Greenshade. She serves her role as best she can for her people. If she puts up with you at all, it is because it is her duty. Megan may be young, but she is strong and proud. She does not need to be rescued."

Keane sat silently, digesting this. He felt embarrassed and out of his depth. For the most part, he just felt worthless.

"Wait a moment," Roselle said. "Were you planning to go through with the *marriage*? Is *that* why you're still here?"

"Um..." Keane began.

Rising, Roselle stepped forward and turned, facing them both. The ring of chipmunks scattered into the brush, chittering angrily. "That is a *terrible* idea. It's dangerous, foolhardy, and horribly unfair to Megan."

"Thank you," said Sarah. "I've been telling him the same thing."

"More foolish than sneaking into a certain baroness's tent in the middle of a pitched battle and chatting with her about her marital problems?" Keane asked.

"*Yes!*" both Sarah and Roselle answered together.

"Oh," Keane replied, shrinking backward. That had sounded like a conversation ender in his head.

"What about you, dear," Roselle said, taking one of Sarah's big hands into her more diminutive ones and looking up into the fighting woman's dark eyes. "What do you think of all of this? You're every bit as affected as we are."

Sarah paused, her brow furrowed in thought. Keane knew that when the answer really mattered to her, Sarah liked to take her time with a reply. It was just one more way the two of them were different.

"Roselle is right. We need a plan," Sarah said. Her mouth tightened, and she squinted up. "We don't even know how we're going to get out the front door yet. I'm willing to try and make things better here if we can before we go, though I have no idea how. I *do* know that I don't want to be a mercenary anymore. I'm sorry, Keane. I'm not trying to pile on. I just think I want more than that for us. For me, anyway." She looked down and turned to face Keane.

Roselle rubbed the back of Sarah's hand, her brown Pavinn skin making the baroness's look even more pale by comparison. The baroness sat back down beside Sarah, putting her between herself and Keane.

"Oh, my dear," Roselle said, "you are an exceptional woman, and you are capable of exceptional things. Don't ever think that you are limited to fighting for your supper. But you are correct. The first thing is to figure a way to get the two of you out of the castle without bringing every member of the King's Swords down on your heads. Keane?"

"We've had opportunities before," Keane said. "We've been attacked and tossed back on our heels each time, but I'm sure we'll have another. We'll leave then. We just need to be ready." He felt dejected, stupid, and most of all, alone. He didn't want Sarah to be a mercenary if that made her unhappy. He couldn't think of any other kind of life that didn't make him miserable, and the thought of bringing Megan into the life that used to keep him happy just sounded stupid now. Had he really thought that would work?

Most of all, he felt the loss of the princess, whom he never even had and now never would. Could he have helped her? Made her life less of a prison somehow?

Probably not.

Keane, Sarah, and the baroness sat in silence watching the sun-kissed queen play with her gaggle of tiny animals, the three of them lost in their own—very different—thoughts.

38

SHOOTING MAT

KEANE

Warm summer breezes blew across the archery range, situated past Old Storage Road on the west side of town. It overlooked broad grain fields to the north and south and, just a little further west, a short cliff face beyond which cattle and horses grazed.

Keane leaned against a tall iron fence bordering a hedgerow that separated a small portion of the range for commoners and watched the princess practice. Though frustrated by his inability to connect with her, he found a little awe creeping in as he observed her shoot. Not for her skills, which were both surprising and impressive, but for the simple joy of watching her move and flex out on the line. Her dun-colored sleeves beneath a green vest were designed for summer comfort and showed off her feminine musculature. Sarah stood beside him, her arms crossed over her black and gray Tyrranean tabard.

"She's amazing," Sarah said, squinting against the bright afternoon light. "That's got to be a forty-pound pull at least. She's so tiny! See how she breathes into each shot? That's what I was trying to get you to do. You should watch her closely out here. You could learn something."

"I'm watching."

Sarah turned to Keane and then rolled her eyes.

He bit at a fingernail. "If we're going to leave, I'd like to be on civil terms. It'd be nice if she didn't hate me."

"I don't think she hates you." Sarah leaned against the iron fence next to Keane. "I think she strongly dislikes you in the best possible way."

"Explain to me how that's different next time I'm not paying attention to you." Keane scratched at the dark growth of beard on his chin. "We need a way to talk to her. An excuse to..."

Without finishing, Keane walked over to Princess Megan's archery instructor, a short man in his mid-forties with a broad build, green-and-yellow castle livery, and a bushy mustache that drooped with a regal sort of aloofness. He stood behind the princess and next to the return targets, observed her form, and made occasional commentary.

As he and Keane chatted, Keane glanced over at Sarah, who tried to shake her head no so only Keane would see. He did and grinned back at her.

The archery master called for the princess to halt and stepped out to her. They spoke while Keane waited. The girl made him happy and nervous and swimmy in the head, and he did not understand it. Women were not new to him; somehow, she was different.

But there was one thing he did understand about her.

"The princess has accepted your challenge."

She was proud.

"Would you care to go first?" Princess Megan asked Keane.

"No, no. You're already there. Go ahead, Your Grace." Keane smiled to himself as the archery master returned to his place.

Sarah cleared her throat to his right. He jumped, not having seen her approach.

"Maybe getting slaughtered in a shooting contest might earn you a couple of sympathy points." Sarah pulled her tabard and hauberk up at the shoulders and let them drop back into a more comfortable position. "But this looks to me like yet another opportunity for disaster."

While Sarah talked, they both watched Princess Megan land three shots in the center of the distant four-foot-wide coiled straw target.

"And she *will* slaughter you. She is *far* better that you are."

"Sergeant Sarah," said the archery master, "I have taken the liberty of selecting these bows for you to choose from. Would any of these meet with your approval?"

"What?"

Keane clapped her on the shoulder. "You're my second. Go second."

"I really should have expected that." Sarah's mouth curled up in her half smile.

"You really should have," Keane said. "I wasn't even trying to trick anyone. I just assumed you'd expect it of me."

Sarah selected an Egren-style recurve and three long bodkin-headed arrows. She walked away from the princess and Keane, chuckling.

"I come out here to be alone," said Princess Megan to Keane. She kept her eyes on Sarah. "I assume this is another ploy to curry my favor?"

"Would that be such a bad thing?" Keane asked. "You said yourself that we should be able to remain in the same room with one another if we're going to get married. Now we have all of the outdoors. I guess we oughtta be able to not crowd each other out here."

"No, that wouldn't be a bad..." The princess trailed off, watching Sarah shoot. "Where did she learn to do that?"

With slow, fluid movements timed to her breath, Sarah drew, paused, and let fly with her last arrow. As with the first two, it landed exactly one inch outside of Princess Megan's, each arrow of Sarah's paired with one of the princess's.

Keane walked toward the distant target but was stopped by the archery master holding another selection of bows.

"No, I'm not—"

"I insist," Princess Megan said, placing an implacable hand on Keane's arm.

"This is not going to be fun," he muttered aloud.

After Keane sank his final arrow somewhere in the vicinity of center target and the trio approached the target mat, the diminutive princess stepped forward and inspected the results.

Sarah spoke first. "You have taken the lead, Your Grace. Excellent shooting."

Megan turned narrowed eyes up into Sarah's unassuming face. "If we are going to continue doing this, you are going to have to actually play. I am not some idiot child in need of coddling. You may have lost, but you have done so with incredible skill and precision." The princess's thin-lipped smile was all challenge. "If you would advance Prince Despin's cause with me, then do your best."

Sarah shrugged.

What followed was a masterclass in bow work. And also, Keane was there. The archery master soon took a position in the south safe zone and just sat it out. Keane walked up and down the range between targets, but he knew he was not truly participating.

Princess Megan took an early lead, but Sarah clawed it back from her, inch by inch. Twice Sarah called for replacement arrows because the princess shaved the fletching off of hers, and once the big Pavinn warrior, excited by the game, broke her bow string. The replacement, a huge war bow with an ivory grip, put her next arrow through the mat and left only feathers sticking out.

The princess snorted in amusement, and soon all three were calling and laughing as the match, and then the next, progressed.

"Very nice," Sarah said, patting Keane on the shoulder. "You have a solid command on third place."

Keane's happiness overshadowed his poor showing with the bow. Here he was, enjoying his time with the princess, and *she was enjoying hers*. More than once he caught himself thinking that maybe they wouldn't have to go. Maybe they really could be happy here. But then he remembered Baroness Roselle's words.

He wasn't a real prince. Anything less than that would be a horrible disservice to Megan, and he just couldn't do it to her.

"Sergeant, I can't pull this thing again." The princess held up her bow. "I'm going to be sore in the morning as it is. What do we think the score might be?"

"To be perfectly honest, milady, in all the fun, the count completely got away from me." Sarah grinned and inclined her head toward Keane. "I do know he lost though."

Keane didn't feel like it.

"Prince Despin," Princess Megan said, "I thank you for the most entertaining afternoon I have spent in years." She handed her bow and quiver off to the archery master. "I look forward to our next outing."

The instant the princess was out of sight, Keane spun and punched Sarah in the arm. A huge grin covered his face. "We did it! We really did it! She doesn't hate me almost at all now."

Sarah rubbed her shoulder and nodded. "That we did. This has been a good day."

He knew what she was not saying. If they could determine a way past Finnagel, there wouldn't be a next outing. It broke Keane's bitter heart to think about it, but if that's what it took to ensure Megan's happiness, then he would do it.

39

THE WELL-LAID PLANS OF PICNICS AND MERCENARIES

KEANE

fter the events at the shooting range, Keane thought he would feel better about escaping. Instead, he fretted over how much more he had to leave behind. He calmed himself by nicking small items of either gold or gemstone around the keep and stashing them in the hole he made under his mattress. When it was time to run, he intended to be ready. After a week, he had built up quite a tidy pile of loot, and as of yet, no one appeared to notice.

On no fewer than four separate occasions now, Keane and Princess Megan had exchanged pleasantries without anyone yelling, storming off, or getting hit in the head with a carrot. Whenever he found himself in her company, he wanted to shout with joy, and whenever he thought of leaving her, he wanted to fling himself from the nearest window.

Sarah and Keane were meeting with Princess Megan and Chancellor Finnagel in the royal audience chamber which sat in the center of the Grand Arch, the largest of the flying halls.

These four flying hallways connected the towers of Forest Castle's keep far above the ground with wide arching corridors. Enormous buttresses supported them from the tower walls in a feat of engineering that was the envy of the Thirteen Kingdoms. The Grand Arch spanned the distance between the Monarchs and Crows Towers.

Square in shape, the audience chamber was lit during the day by a series of tall, thin, and arched windows that ran down its east and west sides, with dark red and blue draperies tied back. At the south end of the room, a short series of steps dominated, leading to a raised platform with a throne and two chairs, all three currently occupied.

The mammoth king, dressed in his gold and ermine robes of state, lounged on his oversized gilt throne. The queen, wearing a delicate green that set off her hair, sat straight in a wooden chair to his left, seeming to listen attentively to every speaker, though Keane doubted she had any real understanding of what was being said. Secretary Hubrane, in his typical white, sat in a taller chair to the king's right, muttering into his ear.

The middle of the chamber was crowded with a queue of people here to ask favors of the king. The sides were filled with nobles and merchants, making deals and pontificating quietly so as not to speak over their sovereign. Out of the windows lay the entirety of Treaty Hill, displaying a riot of fiery leaves as the tree-laden thoroughfares showed the colors of fall. Keane could pick out the groaning roar of water dragons in the menagerie. Must be feeding time.

The four of them—Keane and Sarah in cleaned and pressed Tyrranean military uniforms and Megan and Finnagel in a pale pink dress and yellow kaftan, respectively—stood in a far corner of the royal audience chamber. Keane was supposed to be listening to King Rance's monthly hearing of the citizenry's requests and petitions.

"If you don't want the courtyard," Megan was saying to Sarah, "and who would, you should try Imperial Park over in the Darrish Quarter. It's next to the embassy of Kos—the one with the big statue of the demon. Did you know that's a *miniature* of the real thing?"

"I did not," Sarah said. She smiled with real warmth at the smaller woman.

Sarah and Finnagel's "relationship" had hit the two-week mark, and so far, the princess seemed to have no suspicions about it not being authentic. The problem was that Keane was beginning to believe Sarah and Finnagel's relationship, too, and Sarah was being much too closed mouthed about the whole thing for Keane's liking.

That was not how you were supposed to spy on the enemy—if Finnagel was an enemy. Was he?

"Anyway, that's where I would go for a picnic if I were trying to get away," Megan said.

While the princess had warmed to Keane, she took Sarah as a genuine friend. They were not as close as Sarah and Roselle, but they seemed easy and chatty in each other's company. Watching them made Keane realize how much Sarah had lost by her life in Wallace's Company.

In that instant, he resolved that they would leave tonight. He had accumulated more than enough valuables to get them anywhere they wanted to go, and they already knew where Finnagel would be. Sarah would find a nice local boy and settle in, and he would find a nice girl.

His gaze lingered on the princess, dashing other thoughts from his head. How had he never noticed how beautifully she breathed before?

Sarah leaned against the windowsill, the sun behind her. "What kind of wine should I bring? I don't know anything about what's good."

Letting the conversation about the picnic he wouldn't be attending anyway fade into the background, Keane caught Finnagel's attention and pointed up toward the queen. "What's Loffa's deal?" he asked. He needed a new subject that wasn't centered on his own failures. "I've been told something was done to her, but the subject always changes before I can find out what. Megan told me she was a gift from some king, but that's all I really know."

"Nothing is wrong with the woman that is not intended to be," Finnagel answered, hooking powerful thumbs into the belt of his kaftan. She is from Agran-ti, the capital of Oulan, and she was indeed a gift of their king, Sahansah Murghall."

"So why is she so... weird?" Keane asked. "It's like she's never in the same conversation you are."

"The royal slavers of Agran-ti utilize a particular form of behavioral conditioning on certain, select females," Finnagel explained. "They sell these women around the world to whoever can meet their prohibitive prices. The queen was captured as a child in a raid on Coldspine, in the islands off of Brittlepin if I remember correctly."

"So, the conditioning, what? Breaks their brains?" asked Keane.

"No, not really. Well, not precisely," Finnagel said. He narrowed his eyes as he gazed at the queen. "The master of a royal slave must have his every whim catered to. He may humiliate his slave, beat her, lend her to visiting dignitaries, and she will comply with puttylike pliability—all of which you may be certain has happened here with regularity. In certain situations, however—the bed chamber, for instance—she performs with abandon and creativity." Finnagel threw an assessing gaze at Keane. "But when a woman's voice is uncalled for, she is silent and... mentally absent."

Keane was horrified. He was beginning to wish he had never asked the question in the first place, but he was too far in to stop now. "That is *so* wrong," he said. "Megan said the king killed Queen Keliah to marry Loffa. Is that true?"

"Queen Keliah was a strong woman and a powerful queen. She, more than any other, was a match for her king. I believe he assumed, and for what it's worth I agree, that she would not have tolerated a royal slave in their marriage, and regardless, slavery is not legal in Greenshade. Keeping Loffa as his mistress would not have been a popular decision—and more than anything else, the king lives and breathes by what other people think of him. So, once Rance discovered that he liked the company of a woman who could not challenge him, he disposed of Keliah and married Loffa."

"Bizzith-non take him," Keane said, his voice low and angry. "I cannot believe how much I hate this guy."

"That's the roach-goddess, right? Pavinn pantheon?" Finnagel asked.

"Yeah," Keane replied. "Her body is made of the souls of the wicked turned into roaches. She tortures them inside her body for eternity. One of Sarah's favorites."

"Yuck," said Finnagel.

"Not half as disgusting as *that* sack of assholes." Keane nodded in King Rance's direction.

"I am rather surprised you knew so little about Oulani royal slaves, Prince Despin," Finnagel said. "I was given to understand that King Brannok, your father, had three in his castle." The compact Darrishman looked over at Keane, a sly smile on his face.

"We're not that close," Keane said. While happy to believe that Finnagel was, in general, an ally, Keane would be glad to be away from him. The man was insufferably smug.

"I have all the particulars together, darling," Sarah said. She sidled up to Finnagel and ran an arm around his shoulders. She was a full six inches taller than her faux paramour. "Ready to go for our picnic? I know *just* where to stop for the best supplies."

The picnic was their plan. Sarah would take Finnagel to someplace he would be unable to rouse his network of spies, make an excuse to step out for a few minutes, and then she and the waiting Keane would make their escape.

Keane already carried their pillowcase full of stolen loot in the shoulder bag he wore.

As Finnagel responded, Keane looked at Sarah, cut his eyes to Finnagel, and raised his eyebrows in question. Sarah shrugged back and smiled. Keane made a circle of his thumb and forefinger and ran his opposite forefinger back and forth through it, repeating his eyebrow-questioning. Sarah stopped smiling and crossed her arms.

Before the silent conversation could get any further, everyone in the room was interrupted by the doors to the audience chamber just behind Keane, which flew open with a tremendous *bang*…

40

MAKE A GOOD FIRST IMPRESSION

ELI

Eli ran to catch up as Harden flung the doors of the royal audience chamber wide, banging them against the interior walls—or one wall, rather. The other door caught a smoked-fish merchant in the face. The dramatic entrance had the desired effect, and while Eli jogged into the room, King's Guardsmen running after him, all eyes were on Harden.

"Hello, everyone," Harden said, sweeping his dusty hat off his head as he stepped back into a low bow. "I am Lord Marshal Harden Grayspring, and for the nonce, you are all my prisoners."

"Who *is* this?" King Rance shouted, his mane of wispy hair flying in several directions at once. "Guards, feed these people to the jungle cats. All of you, has anyone ever seen a guy get fed to jungle cats? You can watch these guys get fed to the jungle cats at sundown tonight. It'll be fantastic. I love those cats."

Beside him, Secretary Hubrane grew even more pale than normal.

Harden struggled with the guards and shouted, "Don't act like you don't know me, Collin Hubrane. And unless you want everyone in this room to know exactly how you and I came to be acquainted,

I'd expect to be treated with the respect due a man who just led an army of four thousand freemen to your door."

"Let him go," Duke Hubrane commanded.

The guards on Harden jumped back as if bee-stung.

It had taken a week and a half to pull it off, but Harden had led both the waiting Wallace's Company and the vast mercenary army from Vastard into Treaty Hill one and two men at a time. They now loitered all over strategic areas listening for the signal to attack. The standing army here in the capital would be caught by surprise and immediately overwhelmed.

While this was happening, Eli "recruited" a well-to-do merchant who did not wish to see his home burned down with his family tied to chairs inside. A small force of mercenaries—Harden and Eli among them—posed as his personal guard and walked right into the castle through the front door.

They were now perfectly positioned to give the city a right fucking-up.

Hubrane put his hand on the king's shoulder and said, "*Sire.*"

King Rance, who was working the crowd into a proper watch-a-guy-get-fed-to-a-big-goddamn-cat frenzy, lowered his arms and asked, "What did he just say?"

Eli shoved the frightened-looking guards off and gave his best killer's smile as another dozen mercenaries entered the audience chamber. There was silence, broken at first only by the calling of bonewheel gulls in their exhibit below, and then the first trumpet blasts of alarm and the shouts of soldiers from the city outside.

The festivities were beginning early.

"I have landed an army a few days north of here, King Rance," Harden said as he cast his gaze about the room. "One that I have gone to considerable trouble and expense to obtain."

It had taken all their money and a sizeable promise of future treasure to hire the thirty-five hundred men from Vastard, but in Eli's experience, Harden was a difficult man to say no to. In the end, he had gotten what he wanted.

"They have taken up positions all over the city. My *other* force," Harden said, looking directly at the angry and confused king, "has moved in from the north and west, and blocked off any hope of escape. Oh, Eli. I owe you a silver duke. They really *didn't* have any idea we were here."

"Told you so," Eli said with a smirk.

King Rance came off his throne, pointed at Harden, and bellowed, "We will fight you to the last man! We can never lose because Greenshade is *my* nation, and *I* am a—"

"What do you want?" asked Duke Hubrane, stepping in front of the frothing king and cutting him off, mid-bellow.

"Well, Duke, I think you'll find I'm as easy as a two-bit whore on that account," Harden replied. He gave a little tip of his hat to the queen, who stared at him with a prim smile and nodded as if he were just another noble paying his respects.

Harden raised an eyebrow but continued. "You can keep your gold and your... women"—he maintained his scrutiny of the queen, waving a hand back and forth, to which she waved gracefully back —"for now... You know, I gotta ask. Is that one of those slave-girls from Oulan? I've never seen one before. She is *very* pretty."

"You were saying?" Hubrane asked.

"Hm? Oh, right. Keep your baubles and whatnots. We only want the two people who've tricked you cretins into thinking they were Prince Despin and his sergeant bodyguard."

"What did you say?" Hubrane asked, speaking with slow deliberateness. Eli thought the man's breath would freeze a bottle of whiskey.

"Despin and bodyguard. They are imposters. Are we all speaking Andoshi here?" Harden's grin stretched all the way across his face, and he held out his arms in an exaggerated show of confusion.

"He wants the prince?" King Rance asked. "Why?"

"The two of them are traitors who owe me a crushingly great debt," Harden said, betraying a trace of irritation, "and unless you would like to owe that debt as well, you *will* turn them over... right... *now*."

"Imposters?" roared the king, finally catching up. "I knew it! I knew they were liars. I can always tell a liar. I have a sense. Find them immediately!"

Harden turned and winked. He'd told Eli that as soon as these ridiculous halfwits realized they'd been duped, they would stop resisting and do their best to throw Sarah and Keane back to the wolves. As usual, Harden had been right.

"No need, my king," replied Hubrane. "They are here." He stood and pointed to the corner of the chamber. Nobles and merchants alike skittered out of the path of the secretary's finger to reveal a surprised-looking Finnagel and a defiant-looking Princess Megan, alone in the corner.

Finnagel smiled and shrugged.

41

WHEREIN SARAH IS HEROIC, AND KEANE IS SELFISH—LIKE NORMAL

KEANE

Keane raised his hand, and both of them stopped and crouched behind a stand of brush. It was dusk, and he and Sarah were almost out of the city, which meant that they were beginning to run into the freemen Harden had placed on the roads. The soldiers would be there to prevent anyone escaping and gathering allies. From experience, Keane knew that the cordon would only last until the city was well and truly taken.

No one wanted to miss out on the rape and pillage, even if they were happy to skip the fight.

Sarah and Keane crept along a tiny trail that led out of an apple orchard and into the woods, yet there were at least fifteen poorly dressed men guarding it, several eating the apples they had pilfered from the farmer's trees. The men stood in the shadow of the trees, drinking, bragging, and laughing at one another.

"Do we go back?" Sarah asked.

"No..." Keane stroked his chin. "But be ready to run in case this doesn't work."

He waited until the flow of the conversation took everyone's eyes off of one of the apple eaters, and threw one of his own stolen apples at the back of a different man's head. He hit, dead-on, and knocked the man into the soldier in front of him.

"What the bugger?" the soldier shouted. He turned and shoved the dazed man into the apple eater.

"He hit me!" the man yelled. "Wiv an apple!"

Seconds later a brawl ensued with everyone either fighting or screaming at those who were. Keane waved over his shoulder, and he and Sarah ran through the twilight to the trees on the other side of the path, out of sight of the mercenaries. Keane's pillowcase full of gold and jewelry barely made a sound inside his pack.

After another hour, their trail led to a proper road, and being well past the company, they felt comfortable enough to make conversation. Sarah did, at any rate. Keane was anything but comfortable. To the west, on their left, grasslands stretched as far as they could see, interrupted by the occasional small farm. To the east loomed the first third of the Three Sisters Wood, dark and alive with night noises.

"You know Harden," Sarah said as they walked the field not far from the moonlit road. "All he really wants is the two of us."

"Yeah, I do," said Keane. "All he really wants is to torture and kill us. Well, *me*, anyway, and I *really* don't want to see that happen— which I will *have* to if he catches us—because I will be there getting tortured and killed."

"I don't think so," said Sarah. "I think that underneath it all, he honestly cares for us, Keane. I think we could make up with him. Go back to the old days."

"Did you forget that it's the way things used to be in 'the old days' that we're running away from? You don't want to be a mercenary anyway. How could going back to that be an improvement?"

"No," Sarah said. "I honestly don't want that life anymore. And it wouldn't be an improvement for me. But if there's a chance he'll back off, don't we have to try? Harden is going to kill *thousands* of people in Treaty Hill looking for us. How can we let that happen?"

Keane pointed at his feet, as he walked away from the capital.

"Funny," said Sarah, "but what if we could stop him? What if we could just go back in, say we were sorry, and have our old jobs back? No innocent people dead. Wouldn't that be worth doing?"

"Yessss..." Keane said, feeling conflicted. *Damn Sarah anyway.*

"Then let's do it," Sarah said. "Don't think about it, let's just turn around and go back. Just... turn around. Turn around. You aren't turning around."

"But... money," Keane said. He jerked a thumb over his shoulder at the backpack where he carried the pillowcase full of stolen gold.

"C'mon," Sarah said, "just think about it for a minute. You and I have not been good people. But we've also never had an opportunity to do something truly *good* before. Something to make up for all the other crap we've done. I want this Keane. Don't you?"

"No," Keane said, "I don't."

"You know something, Keane?" Sarah stopped in the road with her arms folded. "You're being a coward. What about that girl? Megan's just a kid. You know what'll happen to her if the company takes Treaty Hill and Forest Castle."

That did stop Keane. He had considered it but pushed the thought away every time it surfaced. He didn't want to think about it now, either.

"Sarah, you *know* what Harden wants to do to me. How will my death help Megan? How will *our* deaths help anyone? You think Harden will call off the goddamn attack if we hand ourselves over? The other captains will never hear of it. An army that big, you think they're not gonna want to use it? They can't afford *not* to. Please."

"You can't know that." Sarah pled now. "You can't. Harden has the other captains under control. You're just scared."

"Can you think of a good reason I *shouldn't* be scared?" Keane said, his voice rising. "Harden doesn't love *us*, Sarah—Harden loves *you*. Do you still want to know what he said to me that night? Do you? He said I was holding you back, keeping you from a husband, a life. He said I was *keeping you in the company.*"

Sarah's eyes shone wide and red.

"And you know what the worst part of it is? Apparently, he was absolutely right. If it weren't for me, you'd be off somewhere being happy. Harden didn't want to kill me so he could have you all to himself—he wanted to kill me so he could *let you go*. Let you make a real life for yourself. Only now, we've left together and set fire to all his plans, because here *I* am still screwing up your life!

"What was the best we could come up with if we got away? Go be mercenaries somewhere else? Because we never came up with anything better. And now there *he* is again, still trying to fix it." Keane turned his back on Sarah and resumed his walk up the road.

"*Fuck him*," Sarah said, anger in her voice.

Keane turned to her, surprised.

Sarah rarely cursed, and she was never angry. "Who does he think he is, making decisions about my life like that?" Sarah yelled now and waved her arms in precise gestures.

Keane discovered he was more than a little frightened.

"*I* decide who I am and what I want to do," Sarah shouted. "If I'd wanted a husband and children, I'd have had that. Long ago. I can't believe he thought that. Thinks that. Why couldn't he just leave me alone?"

"Right," Keane said. "You're the victim in all this."

"I'm *so* sorry, Keane. What he did to you, the *things* he said... But that makes it easy then, doesn't it?" Sarah said. "Fine. I'll go back alone. You run. That way you'll be safe and..."

"And what, Sarah?" Keane asked. He stopped and turned back around in the road, his feet solid on the beaten dirt, but his heart stared off a cliff. "You know Harden. You know how he takes these things. We aren't just thieves to him—we're *traitors*. Look at what he's already done to find us. You think he's going to give up on killing me just because you came back? That's not him, Sarah. It never has been. He's *crazy*."

"You're not even going to try and go back and save those people?" Sarah asked.

He knew she was at the edge, and he didn't know how much longer she would be able to control her anger and disappointment. Sarah always seemed so serene. These were uncharted and terrifying waters.

She stared into his eyes. "The city... those people don't deserve what's going to happen to them."

Keane stepped closer. He tried to sound calm and reasonable, but it was difficult with the need to scream and run trying to burst from his chest.

"They have an army. We don't even have a goddamn *table knife*. The captains are *going* to use that army. Think about it, Sarah—we don't know how much was in that box, but it sure as Oldam's nipple rings wasn't enough for four thousand mercenaries. They *have* to sack Treaty Hill. It's the only way everyone gets paid, and getting paid is what a mercenary is all about, right?" Keane took a step back and held out his hand to Sarah. "You and me, we gotta go. Go be shit-eating farmers or some stupid thing like that."

"I will always love and care for you, Keane, no matter what," Sarah said. Her voice cracked as her control slipped away. "And that 'no matter what' has already included some blindingly stupid decisions. But I think that today—right now—is the first time I have ever been ashamed to call you my friend."

Keane nodded and turned away, walking off into the night.

After a few moments standing in the road and watching him, Sarah followed.

42

NEVER FLEE MORTAL TERROR ON AN EMPTY STOMACH

SARAH

J ust north and west of Treaty Hill lay the town of Crosshouse. It was a medium-sized town that existed on trade from the capital that ran into the rest of Greenshade and Tyrrane. A place of dim-lit taverns and rotting warehouses, Crosshouse enjoyed a reputation as a town where men who would rather not be seen in Treaty Hill came to make deals and find morally flexible entertainment.

Its many pubs and whorehouses stayed open all night and all day too.

Sarah and Keane sat opposite each other in the *Red Window*, nursing their ales and ignoring one another. They had walked most of the night to get here and were tired as well as angry.

If she looked him in the face, she was afraid she might put a fist through it.

The large common room was theirs except for one lonely career drinker at the bar and the barkeep, an older woman with a stoop and white hair, who also served as the cook.

An uneaten plate of traveler's rolls, Keane's favorite, now sat cold at his elbow, and his pillowcase full of treasure rested on the bench next to him. At least he had sense enough to feel bad about walking away from the inevitable disaster that was taking place in Treaty Hill.

The front door swung open, and a thin man in mail with a stained yellow and green tabard yelled in a halting shout, "Proprietor! I require any food you have and cups for water. As fast as possible."

The barkeep looked up. "I'm not the—"

Lieutenant Falt ran in, reached across the bar and clutched the keep by the collar. He shouted in as commanding a voice as he could muster, "I don't care if you're the owner, the keep, or the town drunk. I'll have that food and I'll have it now!"

"He's gotten a lot pushier since he led our carriage to Treaty Hill," Keane said to Sarah.

"Wasn't our carriage," Sarah replied as she looked over her shoulder at the lieutenant.

"A'right," the old woman said. "What's the hurry?"

Falt drew himself up to his full height, which was about the same as Sarah's, and said, "I am leading the Swift Shields to find and capture the giant brigand, Burgen. He has led a gang of bandits on a trail of wanton and violent debauchery across the whole of Green-shade and is a threat to all and sundry. Crosshouse is our last opportunity to provision for some time, and we must be off. So where is that food?"

While the lieutenant talked, Keane pushed back his bench and stood. What was he doing? Easing his conscience by sending someone else to go fight his battles and even die on Keane's own behalf?

The thing that bothered her the most was that she sort of understood his point of view. There was no guarantee that they could do anything to rescue anyone, and everyone would come to the same end as if Sarah and Keane had not thrown their lives off a cliff.

"Do you always stop to explain yourself to a nearby barkeep when you have a job to do, Lieutenant Falt?" Keane asked.

His voice cracked a bit, but Sarah doubted Falt noticed.

"What the devil?" Falt spun around. The knob on his neck that served as a chin sported a week's growth of beard. "Who are... I... Prince Despin! What are *you* doing out here?"

Keane inhaled deeply, held it, and spoke in a rush. "I have just arrived to take command of the Swift Shields and lead them back to Treaty Hill. A mercenary army led by the blackguard Harden Grayspring has laid siege there, and we are required to break it."

Sarah's mouth fell open.

She thought Keane looked a little surprised, too.

The color drained from Lieutenant Falt's face. "That's *horrible*," he said, falling back into his habitual slouch. The capital city... Between you and me, Your Grace, I'm your man to round up a few bandits here or there or settle a squabble about which chicken belongs to what farmer, but breaking sieges and rescuing cities is above my pay grade. I can't believe you're taking over for me!"

From her seat across the room, Sarah chimed in and said, "I believe you speak for all of us, Lieutenant Falt."

Falt leaned back and saluted Keane. "Lieutenant Falt, turning over command of the Swift Shields Unit of the King's Swords to you, Prince Despin Swifthart! Your orders, sir?"

Keane walked around the lieutenant and to the bar. He stared at its dark surface and traced invisible lines and curves over stains and around the deeper pits in the wood.

"Right," he said. He nodded, his lips pulled back in a tight smile.

Sarah knew that look. Keane was seeing an advantage, something they could use against Harden and his army.

Even as she thought it, she knew what it was. They *knew* how the mercenaries worked—how they thought.

Like cowardly and evil assholes, mostly.

Keane spun around and caught Lieutenant Falt by a bony shoulder. "Burgen is a distraction meant to draw your forces away from the city. Send ten men on horseback to deal with him. The rest are with us. I will lead the Shields to Treaty Hill. Harden... uh, the mercenaries have men on the roads to block the exits. We will smash them and rescue Forest Castle from their unwholesome depredations."

The smile wouldn't come off of Sarah's face.

"Yessir!" Falt said, with the enthusiasm of someone who had never participated in large-scale combat before.

"Good," Keane said. He returned to his and Sarah's table. He lifted his tankard and finished off the remaining ale.

Sarah looked up at him and smiled. "What happened to not wanting to throw your life away to save the hill? I thought that was stupid."

"Well, I didn't have an army then, now did I?" Keane responded.

When Sarah smirked at him, he said, "Oh just take the win. I'm sure this is all *your* fault somehow."

43

SARAH AND KEANE RUN INTO TROUBLE WHILE SIGHTSEEING

KEANE

"There were soldiers here guarding the road out of Treaty Hill," said Sarah, looking down from her borrowed horse to the tracks in the dirt. The road in question made a broad curve through the trees, small bits of sunlight finding the ground here and there, appearing and vanishing in the breeze. "I think they went south."

"Toward town," Keane said. "I guess it's time for the after-party."

He spun his mount about to look up the road at the lieutenant and the long column of infantrymen behind him. The line of six hundred soldiers followed the road through the trees and long out of sight.

"Lieutenant Falt," Keane said, "I want you to divide the men into three sections of two hundred each—the middle one here, one a half mile east, the other a half mile southwest. The sergeant and I are going to do a little scouting and determine the best time and place to attack. We should be back within three hours."

He sat up straight in his saddle, pulling Prince Despin's military crest flat across his chest.

"And if you're not?" asked Falt, hunched in his saddle.

Keane frowned. "Do you have a horn we can borrow?"

Falt swung a bony leg over his horse and dropped to the ground. He rummaged through a saddlebag and turned up a curved instrument made from a ram's horn and tied to a loop of leather. He handed it up to Sarah, who put the loop over her shoulder.

"You're going to be fine, Lieutenant," Sarah said to Falt. The soldier looked up at her, his eyes round with fear.

"If you hear that horn," Keane said, "then the time for you to enter the city and attack the mercenaries within has arrived, and I want the Shields in this to their nutsacks. If you haven't heard from us *or* the horn within three hours..." he trailed off, looking to Sarah. What *could* he tell Falt to do if he and Sarah were dead?

"We've probably been forced to ground," Sarah continued for him, "or had to make an escape from a different direction. In that event, proceed with a plan of your own choosing. You will be responsible for the reclamation of Treaty Hill, Forest Castle, and the royal family themselves" She paused. "And you'll be fine."

"What she said," Keane finished. It sounded a lot better than any of the things he had thought of.

"Please don't die." Falt looked terrified.

Keane tried and failed to suppress a grin. "Come on, let's get this disaster started." He slid from his horse and walked south. Sarah hopped off her own steed and followed.

"Won't you need the horses if you have to run away?" asked Lieutenant Falt, holding the reins of Sarah and Keane's borrowed mounts.

"Can't hide behind a bush or a barrel on horseback," Keane called over his shoulder with a wave. "You be good now."

Once they were out of earshot, Keane laughed. "Laid it on a little thick, didn't you? We'll be lucky to get that boy within a hundred miles of a fight now. '*You will be responsible.*'"

"We can't coddle him," Sarah said, grim-faced. "He needs to know what to expect if he's going to lead those men into combat."

Keane cut her a glance and snorted. "Horseshit. *You* just thought it was funny."

Sarah burst into laughter, holding herself erect on Keane's shoulder. "Slago's teeth, yes!" she said. "Did you see his *face*? I thought I was gonna lose it."

"Of course, that means we have to succeed here." Keane frowned, as he pondered. "Our only backup plan is a guy who has trouble ordering dinner in a tavern, and that backup plan sucks."

"I'm glad you changed your mind," Sarah said.

"Worried about your boyfrien—*oof!*"

After Keane was able to breath and walk upright again, Sarah said, "So, to prevent me having to gut-punch you again, I suggest we discuss strategy. We have six hundred men against four thousand. Did you have a plan?"

"We are better armed, trained, and enjoy the element of surprise," Keane said as he tried to coax breath back into his lungs.

"That sounds like a no. Those numbers break down to twenty of their men for every three of ours," Sarah replied.

"That is kind of a lot," said Keane. "I was thinking we would sneak in, and maybe something would suggest itself."

"Speaking of sneaking in, we should ditch the gray-and-blacks here." Sarah pulled the Tyrranean tabard over her head and tossed it into the trees. Keane did the same, leaving him in his comfortable old leathers and her in her mail hauberk and cloak. They both wore standard-issue long swords from the Swift Shield's supply since they had yet to get their own weapons back from the castle.

"You smell smoke?" Even this far in the trees, the familiar scent of a burning city tickled Keane's nose.

"For a while now," Sarah answered. Neither of them needed comment on what the smell meant.

"What about that?" Sarah asked.

"Oh. Uh..." Keane unlimbered the pack with the pillowcase in it and set it on the road with a small clatter. "We bury it... I guess?"

Sarah rolled her eyes. "All right, but let's be quick about it. We are kind of on a schedule here."

Several minutes later, they had buried the loot next to a head-sized stone in the woods, and Sarah flashed several trees to indicate the correct spot, peeling the bark so that three flashes pointed from three trees directly at their treasure. Keane kicked leaves over the freshly turned earth.

"That oughtta do it," Keane said.

The pair walked a bit more through the wood, trying to enjoy the sunshine and the green as if it might be their last opportunity to do so. This wasn't much different than that trek through the trees a couple of months ago, back when he and Sarah had been simple mercenaries and thieves. Of course, then they had been running *away* from Harden and his gang of thugs and not toward them like suicidal moths into a lantern's bell.

As they came to the end of the trees, Keane recoiled from the sudden stench of smoke. "Oldam shit a custard pie."

Further ahead, the woodsroad became Coach Street, which in turn ran right into Treaty Hill and further on to the Country Gate, ultimately opening into the Quarters. From where the two of them stood, it seemed that the entire city was ablaze. Though it was early afternoon at the tree line, Keane gazed into a black and orange night of flame and smoke, crashes and screams, and the laughter of mercenaries with no one to master them.

"Kinda like Gullhome," Sarah said, her words just above a whisper.

"Lot bigger than Gullhome," Keane answered. "And we're on the wrong side of it." He considered a moment. "*And* it isn't so cold you have to snap off your piss." He recalled the white-haired old demon that lived in the tower of that snowy coastal town and the merciless purple wizardfire he'd let loose amongst the freemen of Wallace's Company—until Sarah put an arrow in his noggin.

Keane coughed on the smoke. The nearest burning building was still a mile away. No, this was going to be a lot worse than Gullhome.

"Listen," said Sarah. "I think we might've caught a break here."

Keane stood with his head turned. He heard screams and shouts, the roar of flames, drunken laughter and... singing.

"They're done taking the town, except maybe for a few pockets. Now they're just *enjoying* it."

Keane thought on that a while, and as he did, a slow smile spread across his face. He'd been down in that particular cesspool more than a few times himself.

"They're already bladdered." His smile turned to a grin.

"And getting more so as we speak," said Sarah. She pulled out the sword Lieutenant Falt gave her and cut at the air a few times with it. "They must think that Burgen's diversion is keeping their backsides safe. Let's go in and pick our spots. We might have a chance yet." She frowned. "What idiot made these swords? The grip is round."

Keane rolled his eyes and shook his head. A round grip could make it harder to keep the sharp side of your sword pointed the right way unless there was a guard to guide by or a flat pommel, both of which these swords had. Although Keane judged it ought to have made him feel *more* anxious, seeing Sarah's nervousness had the opposite effect.

"Here." He pulled out his own weapon and handed it to her, point down. "Trade."

After exchanging weapons, Sarah scowled at Keane. "They're exactly the same, jackass."

Keane shrugged and grinned at her.

"I can't wait to kill someone who's holding a better sword with a proper grip." Sarah stared into the smoke and flame. "I want to be comfortable when I stab you."

They both laughed at that if only to stave off their jitters.

As they approached the city outskirts, Sarah spoke up. "Keane, we still haven't discussed what we're going to do with Harden."

"That's putting the crabs before the whore, isn't it?" Keane asked. "We have to survive ourselves before we can kill him."

"I don't want to kill him," Sarah said.

The two of them had entered the first outlying homes and stables of Treaty Hill and were bent behind a fence, looking up the road. The farmland around them had been miraculously untouched. Nearby, a tiny herd of cattle stood huddled under a wide oak tree, lowing in fright.

Keane turned and stared at Sarah. "What?"

"Harden isn't a bad man." At Keane's horrified expression, she shook her head and began again. "All right. Yes. He is a horrible, awful, despicable person. Which is why I don't want to kill him."

"Naturally," Keane said, "that sounds like perfectly reasonable crazy-person logic."

"He's a terrible person who finally had a good impulse. He wanted what *he* thought was better for me, but no one has ever shown him how to do anything like that. That's why"—Sarah waved an arm to encompass the burning city—"all this. He thought he was doing good."

Keane just stared. He wanted to argue, but his brain rejected the idea so thoroughly that he didn't know where to start. He couldn't understand her point of view at all.

"Puckered stone butthole of Oldam almighty, Sarah, are you out of your *mind*? Look around you. If this is what a *good* impulse looks like on Harden, then we're better off with the evil ones." He clapped a hand over his eyes and dragged it down his face.

"This," Keane waved a hand toward the screaming, crying, smoke-choked city, "is just collateral damage. This"—he pointed a thumb at himself—"is what he's after. If you let him live, I die... and I'm not even sure what happens to you."

Sarah sighed and looked up the street. Keane followed her gaze. A woman, naked and dirty, ran across it, out of the smoke on one side and into it on the other, pursued by rough laughter. That was the face of war. Keane thought of Megan and wanted to run and do something, but he had been here before. Running out and getting themselves killed now by attracting attention wouldn't help that woman or the thousands of other people they were here to save.

Sarah looked back at Keane and pulled him close, embracing him.

"I just... I mean, we never had a lot of friends, you know? The thought of killing someone I used to think of as one is—" Sarah caught Keane's glare and stopped.

"You're right," she said. "Sorry, not a friend. Murderous bastard who deserves it."

The pair of them wound their way into the city through wild-eyed mercenaries, wailing and bloody townspeople, and thick smoke that stole their breath. Bodies folded into the crying city everywhere, draped wherever they lay over stepstones, handcarts, and each other. The stink of burning hair and flesh competed with the released waste of the dead and disemboweled.

Sarah moved like a predator, sure-footed and dangerous. Keane slinked along behind her, moving from shadow to shadow, even if there were no way to see through the haze.

"I always forget how exciting these things are," Keane said.

Sarah started to reply but swung her blade to the side and caught an incoming sword-stroke on her cross guard.

"I can't believe you're here," said a mercenary, as he stepped out of the smoke.

Keane sort of remembered him from Wallace's Company. Not a name, just a vague impression of avarice and stupidity.

Pretty average.

The mercenary's face was flushed red, and the shoulder of his leather coat was burned away. He pressed his attack against Sarah, short sword banging again and again.

"I can't believe *I'm* the one who's gonna get the reward!"

Sarah, one brow raised, effortlessly blocked his drunken attacks. "You do know there's only one of you?" she asked him as she knocked away another stroke and slapped him on the cheek with the flat of her blade. "Go away."

Another five men, armored in stolen pieces of leather and metal, appeared out of the haze behind Burned Coat. They brandished blades and grinned like bonewheels circling a fresh corpse. Sarah's attacker had not yet spotted Keane, who was pressed against the corner of a ruined wooden building. Not able to find a rock to fling, Keane removed his shoe and threw it at Burned Coat's head. The man ducked the shoe, taking his eyes off of Sarah for the smallest fraction of an instant.

Sarah's sword arm blurred in front of her.

"I asked nice." Sarah stepped back calmly and lowered her blade. Burned Coat fell backward into a man with a bloody bandage over his scalp. As he fell, his head knocked against Head Wound's chest, and dropped off of his neck, splashing blood everywhere. The mercenaries stopped and stared.

Sarah's decapitation of their leader had happened so fast, none of them even realized she had struck.

"I don't recognize any of you idiots," Keane said. He stepped forward and took in the group of dirty, patchwork-armored men with a wave of his sword. "I assume you're from Vastard, *and* I assume you don't know any goddamn better. What's-his-name here should have"—he indicated Burned Coat on the ground—"but I think he was pretty drunk, so we won't hold it against him. Anyway, you're gonna be very disappointed in just a minute, as soon as you realize what a life-endingly stupid decision this is."

"That one said you was worth a reward," Head Wound said, pointing at his dead comrade. Sweat streamed down his face, carrying blood from beneath his bandage onto his grubby shirt. He pointed at Keane and Sarah with his hatchet. "You got lucky once, girlie. Don't count onnit happening again. *Get 'em!*"

The mercenaries came in one at a time, each waiting for the one in front to take the attack and then trying to dive in before the backswing. Mercenaries, as a breed, were heroic drinkers and even more heroic retreaters, but rarely were they heroic combatants.

Head Wound made a chop at Sarah with his hatchet, who dodged right.

"Nope," she said and ran her sword down through his forearm and into his leg. She stepped inside his reach and delivered a punch with the force of a sledgehammer to the side of his face. As he fell, she caught the dagger from his other hand and yanked her sword free of his leg and arm.

Keane lost track of Sarah's fight when he inadvertently attracted the attention of two others by laughing. They looked over at him and leered—a short Pavinn man with a frayed orange sash covering his head, who held a knife in one hand and a length of chain in the other, and a tall Andosh, covered in furs and scars, who looked as if he had just stepped off of a raiding ship from the Troll Coast. That one hefted a long-handled axe that Keane thought might have been a few inches taller than he was.

"Whoops," Keane said as the two rounded on him.

And the fight was on.

Big Axe swung at Keane's head, while Orange Sash whipped the chain around his left leg. Keane managed to duck the axe blow but immediately had his foot yanked out from under him. He fell onto his back, spoiling an intended comment about size-compensating axes.

The next axe swing scythed for Keane's neck, so he rolled forward and pulled against Orange Sash on the chain to give him some extra lift and jumped, bowling right into the shorter Pavinn man. When they both rolled to their feet, Orange Sash's hands were empty of both chain and dagger. Keane jumped again, flashing a grin of his own and this time thrusting his sword into the small man's chest. Orange Sash clutched at the sword blade while Keane put his foot up and kicked him away, straight into the oncoming Big Axe. The tall Andosh merely grunted and smashed Orange Sash in the face with the butt of his axe, knocking the smaller man out of the way.

"Try not to be so careless with your weapons next time," Keane said to Orange Sash's corpse, "and maybe I won't kill you again."

It was at this point, with a gasp, that Keane realized that Orange Sash's knife, far from having been dropped, was protruding from his leg about an inch above where King Rance stabbed him. With the realization came the pain, but Keane planted the foot and braced for Big Axe's charge, regardless.

"I bet you were a bully as a kid too," Keane said, tensing.

Instead, the big Andosh went down with a howl as Sarah ran up from behind and chopped his hamstring, the gristle retreating upward into the leg with an audible *snap!* Sarah leapt onto Big Axe's back and brought Head Wound's dagger down into one eye, ending him and the fight.

"Told you," Keane said to Head Wound's corpse. He looked around at the dead men lying in the street. "I bet you guys feel pretty stupid right now, don't you?"

"You're hurt," Sarah said.

Keane looked over at Sarah and shifted his weight. A quick stab of pain shot up his leg and into his hip, making him grimace.

"You would tell me if there were some kind of secret agreement that everyone was supposed to stab me in the goddamn leg, wouldn't you?"

"Nope," Sarah said, her generous lips pulled back in a wide smile. Her face and front were sprayed with blood. "But I am supposed to report it to the authorities if you figure it out. My reward is half an orange." She tore the shirt off of Orange Sash, who seemed the least filthy of the group. "Let's get you bandaged and moving again. We're close to the walls."

44

KEEP YOUR FRIENDS CLOSE, UNLESS YOU OWE THEM MONEY

KEANE

By way of occasional glimpses through the smoke, they were able to stay on track to the castle, although before long, they didn't need to see it. Loud, drunken cheering was coming from within the first wall, leading them right through the Country Gate.

"Should we send in the troops?" Sarah asked, lifting Lieutenant Falt's horn.

Keane shook his head. "Not yet. We don't even know how many people Harden has, much less where they are. If he's kept any reserves Falt'd be chopped up like a chicken in an asshole made of axe heads. Let's do what we came to and get the lay of the land first. Starting with the big party up ahead."

"An asshole made of axe heads?" Sarah made a mock-retching sound. "What is *wrong* with you?"

"What? I thought it was evocative."

Keane felt the need to disguise their appearances a bit, and he now wore the orange sash on his head in what he felt was a fetching and rather piratical fashion, while Sarah wore the Andosh raider's steel helm that covered not only her head but also the top of her face and nose.

They slipped through the Country Gate unmolested and within touching distance of a freeman Keane owed ten pieces of silver to from a game of draughts. Keane marked his location in case he had a chance to kill the little bastard before he could demand his money back.

To the right of the gate, three hundred yards or so in, was the wide square in front of the Rousland embassy, behind which they had evaded a warbow-armed assassin on their trip to the menagerie with Megan.

Harden wouldn't kill the princess, would he?

No, he wouldn't. Not first, anyway.

That thought put even more speed in Keane's limping gait.

From within the square's twenty-foot high walls, the pair could hear the shouts and laughter of mercenaries. The air was clearer here, a wind blowing from the Beacon Sea carried much of the smoke out of the yard. As he approached the wide opening in the front wall, Keane saw hundreds of drunken freemen milling about, perhaps even a thousand. And at the far side of the walled yard, on the sprawling portico in front of the white marble embassy building itself, stood the great Lord Marshal Harden Grayspring, surrounded by his other captains. The mercenary leader was wearing King Rance's crown over his hat.

A chopping block stood front and center, and a pile of bodies lay strewn down the steps in front of it. Captain Lowger cleaned his big scimitar on a dirty cloth, red blood dripped off of his ropy black forearms and down his bare dark chest. A line of terrified nobles and courtesans stood captive under the portico roof behind the colonnade. And in front of the nobles, Chancellor Finnagel, Queen Loffa, Baroness Roselle, Secretary Hubrane, a bleeding King Rance, and...

Megan.

Keane started forward, but Sarah grabbed his arm.

"Slow," she mouthed to him beneath the din of the freemen.

They moved with care, not attracting attention, through the crowd and toward the steps where Megan stood. Keane felt like every part of him would shatter and fly apart if he did not charge up there screaming and brandishing his sword, but he tried to focus on Sarah and moved only when and where she did.

Up front, Keane could hear the goings-on, and he found himself distracted by the spectacle of it. Harden swept around the king, taking little pokes at the large man with the tip of his cutlass. The old mercenary's wide-brimmed leather hat and long, once-purple coat lent him the air of a circus ringleader.

"Freemen of Wallace's Company and mercenaries of Vastard, I welcome you to the grand sacking of Treaty Hill." A shattering din arose from the crowd and quieted again when Harden held up a hand. "Take what you want. Take everything and everyone you want. But do so quickly and be gone on the morn. Today's actions will not go unnoticed, and every able-bodied sword in the country will be on their way here come tomorrow to cut bloody vengeance on us and ours. At sunrise, we will return to the ships, and we can all go where we like. You should have been told already, but drink makes us forget, and forgetting makes us die."

The crowd murmured bored assent.

"So, Your Majesty," Harden shouted, adopting the cadence of a grand theatrical speech. "It is time for another head to roll. Our good Captain Lowger seems to be getting bored." Harden raised his arms and shouted to the crowd. "How about Captain Lowger here, hey? Anyone *ever* see better head chopping in all their days?"

Keane could see Megan through the jumping and shouting men, standing resolute despite the bodies and blood, the steps in front of her littered with over a dozen heads already. He stopped himself from looking for familiar faces among them.

That kind of horror could wait.

"So King Eggan Rance," Harden continued while Keane and Sarah crept closer with agonizing slowness. "I believe it is finally your turn at the block. Do you have any last words for your adoring crowd?"

King Rance, his fine gold and purple robe torn and bloody, an obvious boot print on one side of his face, turned to face the screaming crowd. He held up his arms for silence, which caused the mercenaries to double their din. Laughing, Harden waved the volume down so the king could speak.

"You have come here because Greenshade is the wealthiest nation anywhere, and Treaty Hill is the greatest jewel any mercenary could pluck." Smattered hoots and applause. "But this guy, he could never lead you to real glory. Not like I could." King Rance jerked a thumb at himself, while Harden put a hand over his own mouth to contain his mirth.

"You wanna be a *real* army? Fight *real* wars and overthrow *real* countries? Trust me, no one will pay you like I will. You will be the best..."

Harden shoved the king aside and put a hand to his ear, prompting fresh screaming from the freemen. He waved them down again.

"Apparently, our great king does not know any mercenaries, hey!" Harden shouted. "A freeman doesn't want a *steady job*. A freeman doesn't want to *fight*. A freeman just wants to *drink* and *fuck* his way through life! A freeman just wants to be *free!*"

Keane had to clap his hands over his ears at the tumult.

The old monster might be a demon from the pit, thought Keane, *but he was a demon who knew his audience.*

"But King," Harden yelled once the clamor had subsided, "because you were respectful to the men—and because you were entertaining to *me*—I will let you live just a bit longer. Just a bit, mind you. You have only to do one thing for me. Choose the next one to die. That way..."

King Rance whirled and pointed to his daughter, cutting off Harden's speech. "Her!" he shouted. "Take her instead of me. She's useless."

Keane's heart was in his mouth. He had fallen behind Sarah, and he struggled through the surging and stinking throng with his head down and his elbows up. The orange sash around his head helped disguise him, but not as much as the extreme inebriation of the soldiers themselves.

They were never going to make it in time.

The horn! Keane looked down at his waist. *No... Sarah had it.*

If they blew the horn now, they may possibly stop the killing on the portico, or they could be no more than a momentary distraction. Falt *might* hear it, but even if he did, which did not seem likely, there was no way he could be here in time to be of any value. Keene needed to figure out a way to make whatever he was going to do count as much as possible, and he needed to figure it out now.

He made greater use of his elbows and knees while he fought his way through the crowd. As he did, he came upon one of Eli's squad commanders who turned and stared at Keane in open-eyed surprise. Keane kneed him in the stomach and folded the tan-faced young man over, then clubbed him in the back of the head with a clenched fist.

Several nearby freemen laughed their approval at the unexpected violence.

Up on the portico, Harden ambled up to the king, threw an arm around his shoulders, and turned the big man to face the crowd once again.

"You would have me slaughter Princess Megan, your *own daughter*, right here in front of your very face, just to save your neck for another few, miserable minutes?" Harden asked.

The king nodded, his jowls bobbing up and down. Harden raised a hand until the crowd quieted. Keane was forced to slow down again just to avoid notice. He thought the effort would kill him.

Harden brought his other hand to his breast. "I have been the leader of Wallace's Company for twenty-something years."

"Twenny three," shouted Captain Eli.

"Twenty-three years," said Harden, not missing a beat. "I have been responsible for the murder of not hundreds, not even thousands, but *tens* of thousands of men in my career." He stepped away from the king, arms clasped behind him, and walked to the other side of the portico.

"But I—*even I*—could never *begin* to touch the heartlessness of kings." He flicked a finger toward the king. "Captain Lowger, make him shorter."

A pair of burly men—Keane recognized them as two of Lowger's lieutenants—grabbed the king by either arm and dragged him to the block where Captain Lowger waited, a faint scowl on his face. Keane knew the big Darrishman would be enjoying his grisly task and that he would never let it show. Lowger thought contentment got in the way of being an evil, brutal fuck.

Apparently, he was wrong.

Secretary Hubrane broke ranks and rushed forward, yelling his outrage at Harden in his most stentorian voice. In response, Harden kicked the white-haired duke in the stomach and shouted, "We have another volunteer!"

It was then that Keane realized that, of all the captives, only Finnagel did not look like a man in mortal danger of his life.

He looked expectant.

A powerful hand grabbed Keane by the elbow and yanked him to the right. He fought back, but it was Sarah. She pointed to the portico, where the king was being forced up and onto the block.

"I see it." Keane craned his neck, trying to see around the thousand or so soldiers boisterously celebrating in the courtyard. If he could find a way to get behind Harden and his men to where the captives stood with their backs against the Rousland embassy wall, maybe he could... something.

Keane leaned into Sarah and spoke into her ear. "There's an alley that runs behind the embassy—where that frost cock with the warbow first attacked us. If we can get over the rear wall and attack Harden from behind, the prisoners can run into the building."

Lowger's men shoved the king to the ground in front of the block while Hubrane screamed for Harden's attention.

"And then what?" Sarah asked. "They'll just come in after us and kill everyone. What else have you got?" Just as he looked to her whenever the fighting started, Keane knew that Sarah looked to him for the planning. The only problem was, he didn't have one.

"Wait for my signal." He hoped to think of something clever between now and when that might happen. "And be ready."

Beneath the raider's helm, Sarah set her jaw in a determined line.

In one hand, she gripped the hilt of the borrowed sword. In the other, she held the horn.

Lowger walked to the block, his scimitar in both hands. The tall Darrish captain raised the blade high, not seeing the conniption that Hubrane was having behind him. Harden stepped forward and raised a hand for Lowger to wait.

"What is it, Collin?" Harden turned and asked the secretary.

Hubrane, in a rage, spat the words, "The imposter prince! He is here, and his cow bodyguard, too! They're over there!" Secretary Hubrane's hands had not been untied, and he hopped up and down trying to point to Keane with the top of his head.

Panic ran through Keane's heart like a dagger of ice. He ducked behind the mass of mercenaries in front of him, and Sarah simply turned around as if looking for the people Hubrane was trying to point at. Both of them became invisible to anyone on the stage.

"Oh, come *on*, are you *kidding* me?" screeched Collin Hubrane, Royal Secretary and Duke of the Western Marches. "They are *right there!*"

"Where?" asked Harden.

"Right..." In glances between stinking and stumbling bodies, Keane watched Hubrane dance in a circle as he tried to point with the fingers tied behind his back. "They're right there... I can't point! Untie me, you frost-cocked simpleton!"

"Untie you, Collin?" Harden said. "You know, I think you may be trying to trick your old lord marshal." And so saying, he drew his cutlass and drove it through the old man's guts. As Hubrane fell to the marble, Harden said, "Better get moving, Lowger. That one's not gonna last long."

Captain Lowger raised his scimitar and brought it down, severing the king's broad head from his shoulders with a soft thump. The crowd of mercenaries, most of whom had never witnessed the execution of a king before, went berserk. Without stopping to clean his blade, Lowger indicated that Hubrane should be placed on the block too.

Hubrane's decapitation was hardly necessary at this point, but Captain Lowger was a completist.

"Now?" mouthed Sarah.

Holding up a finger, Keane mouthed back at her, "Just a second. We're almost out of assholes."

Harden's two men pulled the bleeding Hubrane up, and after they kicked the king's body off the block and down the stairs, threw him onto it. Showing an uncharacteristic creative streak, Lowger stood sideways and took the secretary's head one-handed.

This was it. He still had no plan, but if he put it off any longer, people he *did* care about would start to die.

"Do it."

45

WHERE KEANE MAKES HIMSELF THE CENTER OF ATTENTION... AGAIN

KEANE

With the noise of the assembled mercenaries, at first, no one noticed the resonating tone of the horn Sarah held up in the air above her head. But its reverberating sound continued to gain volume, and as it did, more and more of the crowd fell silent. Soon enough, Keane and Sarah stood in an open circle, surrounded by confused men holding their ears.

She blew tone after sonorous tone, and when she was done, the entire city seemed quelled except for that familiar mournful honking from the menagerie.

A look of equal parts hope and irritation crossed Princess Megan's face when she located the source of the disruption.

That seemed about right.

Harden looked out over the crowd with one hand blocking what little sun was making it through the smoke. "That was dramatic. Hang on, is that actually Sarah and Keane? Oops. Looks like Collin wasn't lying after all. Sorry, Collin." Harden cast a contrite look toward the secretary's head, then smiled and waved at Keane and Sarah. "Well, if you wanted to say something, I guess now's your chance. Fellas, why don't we let these two come on up?"

He waved to the back of the courtyard. "Someone go check and make certain these two weren't signaling anyone out there."

A long, sad breath escaped Keane. There wasn't anyone out there who could help them. Not in time.

Harden's eyes held the customary red glaze of a career alcoholic well into his cups. Drunkenness might give Keane a tiny edge over the crafty old mercenary. Harden suffered less deficit when bladdered than most men, but he did tend toward unwarranted certitude in his own ideas. Maybe that would be something to work with.

Oh, great. *Now* Keane started to plan.

The crowd parted in front of them and left an open path to approach the portico. Keane looked at Sarah, and she nodded back to him. She walked and he limped up to their deaths.

As they reached the steps, scattered screams and the sounds of fighting broke out beyond the courtyard wall. Mercenaries turned and looked around themselves, eyes wide and nervous, trying to make out the source of the combat.

"Prepare for attack!" Eli shouted to the crowd. "Draw your fucking swords, you cowardly bastards!"

The first of the Swift Shields reached the entryway into the court-yard, hacking into frightened freemen who tried in vain to flee. More mercenaries tried to run further in, only to be stopped by the crowds in front of them.

"Dear baby Oldam's bitty stone cock, he's here," Keane said as he reached for Sarah to support him. "He didn't wait in the woods. Falt is here!"

The jittery lieutenant must have used the smoke and noise to advance far enough into the city to hear when Sarah blew the horn and then came running. It was the most foolish, most *wonderful* thing, Keane had ever imagined.

Finnagel smiled as Harden roared and drew his cutlass. The drunken and unnerved freemen fought with each other in their haste to escape the walled-in square, and Keane saw Lowger flick his scim-itar to the side, slinging blood. Eli came up on the left with Vancess in tow. Any one of these men would have been a match for Sarah, which meant that Keane needed to get creative, fast. He limped backward and the pain in his leg—showing *very* poor timing—ballooned from awful to excruciating.

Behind the frightened nobles, guarded by a single, black-bearded mercenary, the door into the embassy hung ajar.

Sarah went left, forcing their opponents to split up. They didn't want to chance letting either of them through.

"Eli, with me," Harden commanded. "Lowger and Vancess, on Sarah. *Don't* kill her." He glared his glassy red gaze at Keane. "I've been itching to hurt you for months now, boy. And I am not by nature a patient man."

An inward smile creeped up behind Keane's mouth. Harden was thinking like a drunk and angry man, not like the tactical intellect he was.

Of course, the likelihood was still that Keane would end up dead.

Captain Vancess snapped his blade to his chest in a salute, acknowledging Harden's command. Lowger growled deep in his throat.

Harden advanced on Keane and loosened his arm by cutting the air side to side. Eli drew his wide-bladed short sword and a dagger. Keane had seen that plain-looking sword cut down over a dozen men with his own eyes. The old man was a surgeon with the thing.

Keane stood on the portico steps, holding his sword with one hand on the pommel and one hand halfway up the blade. His fingers felt the leather straps of the sword's grip, and he used his forefinger on the guard to guide the blade. Round grips really were not practical —Sarah was right about that. Also, the sword had not been oiled and showed a dusting of rust. If he lived, Keane would have a word about proper construction and maintenance of swords with Lieutenant Falt.

Not that it would likely come to that.

Harden came in with an experimental thrust, which Keane was able to easily bang away. Smiling, Harden maneuvered right. The point of the attack wasn't to immediately kill Keane but to wedge him over to Eli where the old warrior could get behind him. Keane danced right instead, around Harden, to keep the mercenary leader between himself and Eli, while he made the pain in his leg scream.

"You know," Keane said, as he grit his teeth against his flaring leg, "some people might think all this is a bit of an overreaction. I don't even have your stupid box of coins anymore."

Harden took a step back, lowered his cutlass, and laughed. "You think this is for a wagebox? Boy, this is for Sarah. You're just in the way. Always have been." Harden's breath carried the heavy scent of wine over to Keane.

Behind Keane, the square had become a meat grinder as the mercenaries chewed each other to pieces trying to both run through —and away from—the single front opening in the wall where the King's Swords were cutting their way in.

Keane ranged out further right and moved sideways up the steps to cross Harden in front of Eli again. He came around behind the chopping block and, in that instant, turned and broke for it, bolting straight for the princess.

"Bye!" Keane yelled over his shoulder to Harden.

"Wha—*oof!*" was all that Megan managed to say before Keane snatched her up off the ground and ran to the huge double doors of the Rousland embassy. His leg shrieked in agony the whole way.

He lunged straight at the surprised mercenary guard in front of the doors, chopping into his sword arm, and the man's mouth made a surprised O within his dark beard as he watched his blade clatter to the marble flagstones.

Keane sprinted past, shouting with effort and pain. Inside, he dropped Megan to her feet and shoved the big doors shut with Harden and Eli less than twenty paces behind.

The dim ceiling of the entrance hall echoed back Keane's steps and exertions, and twin stairs swept left and right along marble walls toward distant corners. A broad upper landing ran between those far corners along the length of the back wall. Statuary, paintings, and tapestries had all been shattered and torn by the freemen in their gleeful looting. Bodies of guards and diplomats lay on the floor where they fell, lit only by the front windows, which were shaded beneath the broad overhang covering the portico outside.

It was a gloomy place to die.

46

WHERE HARDEN GETS MAD, AND KEANE GETS STABBED

KEANE

The Rousland embassy doors had been torn open by rampaging freemen and would not now close fully, much less lock.

"Get upstairs," Keane said to Megan as he looked out of the space between the ruined doors. Harden and Eli had stopped, and the lord marshal was whispering hurried instructions to his captain.

Megan moved as fast as she could toward the stairs, but it was dark, her footing was treacherous, and her hands were still tied behind her back. Keane stared, for once not finding himself inappropriately distracted by the way the skirt of her dress clung to her backside. He could not allow *anything* to happen to her. Keane tried to peek outside when he realized that Harden and Eli had stopped talking to each other outside the door.

Megan froze and looked up. "Here they come," she said.

Keane hobbled into position. "Hide."

Harden and Eli each shoved one of the doors aside and jumped forward, swords at the ready. Keane had placed himself to the right of the doorway and caught that door, swinging it back with all his might. There was a *whack* and a curse from Eli—and the sounds of a man being knocked to the floor.

Then Harden was on him.

This time, the old man came on fast and hard—cutting, sweeping, and jabbing. Only by continuing to stumble out of reach, with no thought to offense, was Keane able to survive without more than a grazing slice on his right wrist.

This was not going to end well.

Keane raised his blade in both hands and pushed aside another swing. "Wow, you seem really angry."

The two of them moved past the left stair where Keane noticed that Megan had dropped, unmoving, alongside a pair of corpses. He felt pride for her. That girl had nerve.

"Angry?" Harden said. "Over you? Did you do something I should be angry over?" He made a sideways chop at Keane's neck and forced him to the bottom of the right stairway. "I'm just killing you. Stop trying to make it personal. Not everything is about *you*, you know."

Harden swept his broad hat off his head and tossed it to the side. It landed on Megan, who did not react.

Eli got himself up and moving and stalked swiftly up the left-hand side of the hall, even as Keane backed away to the right. They both set foot on the opposite stairways at almost the same instant.

"So, where's Darkling?" Keane asked, moving crossways and up over the wide stairs. "Have a falling out?" As he went, he stepped over a corpse whose neck had been raggedly cut and had sprayed crimson over a broad swath of the polished wooden steps, leaving them slippery. He didn't give a damn about Captain Darkling, but he needed to play for time, distract Harden until he could think of something brilliant.

And perhaps piss Harden off and goad him into doing something stupid.

"We wanted different things," replied Harden, going for a series of overhand cuts intended to slow Keane down and put pressure on his injured leg. It did, and Keane grunted with the effort of simply remaining erect.

"Let me guess," said Keane as he hobbled back again up several steps, "you wanted a family and he wanted to concentrate on the business?"

"Yeah, actually. It *was* something like that." Harden tried a thrust, but his footing wasn't secure on the bloody steps, and Keane nearly stabbed him in the hand. Should have stabbed him. There was a pause. Even drunk, Harden was still the better swordsman.

Harden's lips peeled back in a slow, thin smile.

"I assume you murdered him," said Keane while he came around and up the steps to Harden's left. Eli had gained the landing above and was crossing it to the top of the stairs above and behind Keane.

Not good. *Very* not good.

"See? This is why I *have* to kill you." Harden lunged up the intervening stairs and whirled his blade in a complex set of jabs and cuts that forced Keane to halt and defend himself, batting crazily at Harden's blade. "You are just too observant and intuitive for your own good. Never let an enemy who really knows you live. That's my advice to you."

"No offense," said Keane as he kicked at Harden and scored a shallow cut along the lord marshal's thigh when he dodged aside, "but anyone who ever spent more than ten minutes with you would have been able to call the trajectory of *that* relationship. You kids were never gonna work out."

"Behind you!" screamed Megan from the darkened floor of the hall.

Without looking, without even thinking, Keane reversed his grip on the hilt of his sword and stabbed behind. He felt the blade bite deep into Eli's leg but had to yank it back and jump to the side to avoid Harden's sudden attack. Eli grunted, and Keane slipped. His foot slid off of a step and threw him off balance. He fell with a thump into a sitting position, his blade angled awkwardly beneath his legs.

Harden raised his cutlass in a killing blow but hopped back a step and caught Eli, who tumbled over Keane and down the stairs. The wound in Eli's shin turned his lower leg black in the shadowy light.

Keane flipped over and ran gasping on all fours up the remaining stairs and into the carpeted gloom. He could hardly believe he was still alive. It was all very exciting—if he could get his mind off his and Megan's upcoming deaths.

"Kill that little Pavi shit," Keane heard Eli say. Harden propped his injured captain up against the balustrade and followed Keane to the landing. Outside, the sounds of fighting drunks intensified, punctuated by shrill screams, commanding shouts, and painful wails.

The Shields were in the courtyard in force.

Harden peered about for Keane in the dark but addressed his comments down the stairs. "That was very brave of you, girl. Stupid, but brave. I was going to have Lowger chop off your pretty little head... *pop* and done. But you've vexed me, and I think that deserves some special—"

Keane leapt out of the shadows and swung a powerful cut which Harden ducked. But the cut was a feint for a pommel-strike which struck Harden a glancing blow to the shoulder.

"Ow," Harden said. "That was clever."

"Thanks so much," Keane answered. "I can't tell you how much your approval means to me."

They fought back along the balustrade between the two staircases, Harden always advancing and Keane retreating, looking for openings.

"You know what really gets me about all of this, boy?" asked Harden, unexpectedly stopping and pointing his cutlass at Keane's face.

"A sudden and crushing regret for not being a more responsible father figure to your men?" Keane asked.

"By Oldam's gritty granite feet, Boy, don't you *ever* get tired of hearing yourself talk?"

"You're asking *me* that?" Keane responded. Harden feinted low and tried to stab Keane in the face, but Keane swiped up and knocked the flat of his sword into Harden's wrist, coming close to dislodging the old man's cutlass. Before Keane could capitalize on it though, Eli, from the stairs, flung his dagger into Keane's left arm.

"*Goatfuckingsonofawhore!*" screamed Keane. He rolled away from the balustrade and left Harden to recover his grip. Keane felt heavy velvet where he thumped over into the lightless back wall and yanked at it, pulling himself to his feet. It came free and exposed a long, high window that illuminated the landing. Dark carpet, some chairs, a sofa, and a pair of corpses were now lit in dull oranges and reds. On the other side of the window and below him, the alleyway separated the embassy building from the high outer walls of the castle, lit by smoky late-afternoon sunlight.

There was the sound of an explosion from outside and screaming. Despite his immediate danger, the only thought Keane had was whether or not Sarah was all right.

"That looks like it hurts," Harden said. He walked to Keane's right along the window.

"That's what I said when your mother... shit." Behind Harden, Eli was coming up the last steps, a makeshift bandage around his leg and murder in his eye.

The top step creaked.

In the tiny portion of a second it took him to register the fact that Harden was glancing aside, Keane ran the lord marshal through the guts. Harden whirled and stabbed Keane in the chest and fell over backwards.

"Ow, you... dick," said Keane. Harden's cutlass protruded from his ribcage. "Fuck you so *very* much." Keane's knees lost some of their strength and knocked together. He felt the need to cough but had trouble drawing enough breath.

"Eli," Harden said from the floor with a sound like a croak. "He's still talking. Kill him so he stops talking."

"Back... off... you... evil old prick," Keane whispered. He looked sideways, and the floor started to pull up to his left. He saw Princess Megan, her hands somehow free.

In her grip, she clutched a table knife.

Keane decided to fall down too.

He could hear as people entered from below and ran up the steps. The first to the top was Sarah, who bled from a dozen tiny cuts, her borrowed longsword gripped tight in her hand. Up the other side came Captain Vancess, his helmet gone and his gleaming armor dented and scuffed. His right roundel was torn off, and a trickle of blood ran from the shoulder down his side.

Vancess took in the scene around him and turned to Sarah. He held out his rapier and saluted her, bowing low—which fight was *he* in? Then, against expectation, Sarah returned the gesture.

Captain Vancess turned and fled.

"Ah, fuck," Eli said.

Sarah turned to Eli, her sword raised and her eyes narrowed. Her every movement signaled death. The old mercenary's brows went down, and he took an involuntary step backward.

Chancellor Finnagel came up the stairs and strode to Sarah's side.

"Let us go, girl," Eli said. "Please. I can turn him around. I know I can. Just let us go."

"No, he can't," croaked Harden from the ground.

"That bastard *stabbed* me in the *chest*." Blood gurgled up between the words of Kean's complaint. He coughed, and his vision grew dim.

"Don't let him..." Keane wasn't sure if he was still talking or if he only thought he was. The last thing he remembered before everything went black was Finnagel with a reassuring smile for Sarah and his hand on her shoulder.

47

WE'LL JUST GO THEN

ELI

Keane finally shut up which Eli figured ought to make things simpler. He hoped so, anyway. A short man in a gold-colored Egren kaftan came up the far stair and stood by Sarah, and ex-King Rance's daughter—Meegan? Mehan?—dropped her knife and went running to Keane. From outside, Eli heard the King's Swords as they hacked their way into the square while drunk and panicked freemen tried to chop through their own to get out. It was a charnel madhouse.

"He doesn't look good, Finnagel," the princess said, a note of genuine distress in her voice.

"Can you help him?" Sarah asked the short Darrishman, who smiled and nodded in response. Eli thought Sarah looked surprised. "You're a spy *and* a healer?" she asked.

"No," he said, cocking his head to the side. "Well, maybe. I can handle this, at any rate. He'll be fine."

Eli wasn't feeling all that good himself. Ten minutes ago, they were on top o' the world. Now he was begging for their lives. It made him think of an old Andosh saying. *Murderers kill men; heroes kill everyone.* It meant that if you murdered a man, you went to the gallows, reviled by the world. But if you murdered a thousand men, you got a title, a piece of land, and the admiration of the people.

Andosh proverbs possessed a fixedly surly bent.

Looking at Harden and Sarah, Eli figured the Andosh had it backwards. Harden was no hero.

"Whaddya say, Sarah?" Eli pleaded. "You know Harden don't really want this. He's just stupid and hurting. That's all."

"I can hear you," came Harden's gravelly response. "I'm not dead yet."

"Please shut up, sir." If Eli could get Harden to let go of his need for control, make him trust just for a minute, perhaps he could get his friend out of here alive.

Sarah turned to look over her shoulder at Finnagel who crossed the carpeted floor to Keane.

"Yes, yes. I'm taking care of it." Finnagel knelt with the princess at Keane's side. "He's going to require some rest, but no worries. Poked a lung."

In the back of his mind, Eli realized the problem with this statement. Harden had killed Keane, the boy just hadn't caught up to it yet. Healing him now could only be the work of demons.

He decided not to mention it.

Sarah walked across the blood-soaked carpet to stand beside where Harden lay and faced him, sword pointed at his neck. Her body shook with each breath, and her face flushed dark in her anger.

"You and I are *done*, Harden," she said. "I let you go, and I never see you again. That's the deal. You stay away from me, and you stay away from Keane." To the side, Keane made a gurgling noise and blew blood bubbles. "Unless he dies, in which case, I will hunt you down and kill you personally."

It seemed like a more than reasonable deal to Eli. Sarah was cut up a bit, but he couldn't hope to beat her.

"Well, old man, what's your answer?"

"Nuh-uh," Harden said. "You'll never leave him, and he'll always lead you into trouble. The only way you'll ever let him go is if he dies. You should have... better."

Sarah stabbed Harden through the shoulder, wringing a low cry of pain from the lord marshal and a grimace from Eli. He felt pretty sure that whatever ultimately happened to Harden would happen to him next.

"Sarah." Eli put his short sword down on the floor. "I know you got no want to kill this man. If you did, he'd already be done. Lemme take him. Lemme talk at him once he's rational again. Alla this, what he's done, he done for you, fucked up as it is. He loves you, girl, like a daughter."

"I know that." Sarah stared into Eli, her eyes a cold precipice promising a fast and merciless death. "How much butchery and misery does that excuse, exactly?"

Eli had no answer.

"My life is my own," Sarah said, returning her attention to Harden. "You have no part in it. I have *always* chosen my own path, and I always will. I am not some farmer's daughter to be traded for a cow and a sack of beans. I do what I do and keep the company I keep because *I* want it. And *no man* may tell me differently."

Sarah moved the point of her broadsword back to Harden's throat.

This is insanity, Eli thought, *Harden's obsession come home to roost.*

The lord marshal was a shitty friend, but he was the only one Eli had. Could he stand here and watch Sarah gut him like a snake for the fire? What other option did he have? He wiped clammy hands on his leggings while freemen in the courtyard screamed.

At least Wallace's Company was gone. But what was that going to cost?

"Look at all of this—you think this is love?" Sarah went on. "You're crazy. You're... wrong. Evil. And the worst part is that you really *were* the closest thing I'd ever had to a father. How can you say you love me and then force me to live with killing you? Because that's what this is."

Tears welled in Sarah's eyes, but she held them back through force of will. And Eli had never seen a steadier blade than the one that hung over Harden's neck.

"You know," Sarah said, "it embarrasses me to admit this, but my whole life I've just been trying to live up to someone else's expectations of me. First Walder, then you... even Keane. At least he didn't expect that much. But you know what? I'm sick to death of it. I don't want to be a soldier, and I damn sure don't want to be a wife. I don't know what I want to be, but I'm going to decide what it is for myself, and *you aren't invited*. Do you think you can understand that and leave me alone?"

"I'll never... *ahhhgh*..." Harden said as Sarah stabbed him through the opposite shoulder.

"Goddammit, Harden, just stop," Eli's voice grew even more harsh than normal. "It's over. We lost. Only decision you got left is whether or not you die here. You wanna die? 'Cause I sure don't."

"I'll try again," Sarah said, her brows knit but her voice light—free even. "I'm going to do whatever I want no matter what you decide. Do you think you can understand *that* and leave me alone?"

"Please..." said Eli. There were no more arguments to make. All he had left was pleading. "Lord Marshal... she's gonna run out of arms and legs."

There was a pause as Harden digested this. "Hnnn," he grunted at length. "Yeah, all right. We go—we don't come back. I guess that does sound fair."

Sarah scabbarded the sword and ran to Keane, and Eli limped to Harden. "You're a stubborn son of a bitch," Eli said, ignoring his friend's groans as he pulled him up and swung one of Harden's arms over his shoulder.

Together they limped off, out of the embassy, and deeper into the smoke-filled city.

48

DENOUEMENTS AND STUFF

KEANE

This time, Keane awoke in his own bed—or Prince Despin's, anyway—alone, while the screeches of big bonewheel gulls and the grumbles of huge cats somewhere far below drifted in on the morning breeze. He lay and stared out the window, the thin white curtains with their lazy drift, the yellow-tinted sunlight cool in the beginnings of Autumn. He gazed up into the tall, arched ceiling of the room some fifteen feet above his head. Like most of the castle, the stone held that strange greenish cast. It was comforting once you got used to it. Made everything feel alive.

He felt his chest. There was a thin scar where—

A scar? Oldam's stone nipple-hairs, how long have I been asleep?

Keane leapt out of the bed, his leg giving him no pain, and ran to the window. The ruins of the city greeted him. Char and wreckage left dead holes everywhere, and the blackened skeletons of trees lent Treaty Hill a funereal mien that chilled him. Gray bonewheels spun their lazy circles over the areas of the greatest fighting while crowds of the dog-sized gulls bickered over the corpses of mercenaries on the ground. Here and there, poking out of the black and the haze, bright angles of fresh lumber showed perhaps a day, maybe two, of rebuilding.

This made no sense.

Keane dressed and left his room. The concern he felt over not knowing where Sarah was somehow doubled when he saw that there were no guards on his door.

He ran straight to Finnagel's rooms. The man knew everything, and he had been acting strangely during the confrontation with Harden at the Rousland embassy. *He would have to know where Sarah was, or if...* Keane shoved that thought down. He would be unable to take another step if he thought that Sarah had been killed without him there to help her.

The castle hallways were wide here, and people rushed to and fro. But the crowd parted for Keane. The morning sunlight blinded him every time he rushed past one of the arched hallway windows, but he ran on anyway without regard for who he might stumble into.

He rounded the corner and saw Finnagel's ironbound, oaken door. He strode to it, fist raised to knock on the oak, and froze. What if she really *was* gone? What if this moment, this instant, was the absolute last where he would not know she was dead? A mountain of guilt began to topple in his head, tumbling down slopes of irresponsible behavior to crush him.

"Well, don't just stand there like an idiot," came Finnagel's cheery voice from within, "come on in."

Some muttered words Keane could not understand came through the door, and then it swung wide. Sarah stood in the doorway and smiled.

"Oh..." said Keane, his voice thick. He lurched forward, grabbed her, and just stood holding her to him.

"I'd say it worked," Sarah said over her shoulder.

"I told you it would." Keane heard Finnagel reply.

"What worked?" Keane asked. He stepped back from Sarah with a sniff. The room inside was wide but low and circular. Intimate. There were several large, curved sofas in the Egren style and a few short tables, and the whole of it was well-lit with bright lanterns. Finnagel sat on a sofa, looking comfortable. He reached behind himself and tugged on a bellpull.

"Do come in. And Sarah, if you please?" Finnagel waved toward the door.

Keane walked into the relaxing chamber, and Sarah closed the door behind him.

"You're probably going to want to sit for this," she said.

Keane walked around the sofa opposite Finnagel and plopped down. The silk and velvet cushions felt wonderful. He might have to steal a few before he and Sarah left.

"We are going to discuss a few things which will come as shocks to you," said Finnagel as Sarah settled next to Keane. "It might take you a while to absorb them."

"Can I get a few questions of my own answered first before we start shocking me?" Keane asked. "Like did we win? And how long was I unconscious for?"

"The fight was yesterday," Sarah said. "We won. The mercenaries scattered when they heard another unit of King's Swords had arrived. They were too drunk to wonder how many soldiers we actually had. And you've been asleep less than a day."

"Good. That's good... but no. That doesn't... I don't understand. I've got a scar on my chest where Harden stabbed me. A six-month old scar, at the least. How does that happen? And where is Harden? Did I kill him?"

"You might have killed him," Sarah said. "I let him and Eli go. Vancess too. But Harden was pretty bad off. He didn't really look like he was going to make it."

Keane scowled at the thought of his old mercenary boss getting away, and Sarah raised an eyebrow. Uncharacteristically, he decided to let it go. She had saved him, and he had been unconscious. It was her call. Besides, he could use her broken promise to kill the evil old fuck to get whatever he wanted out of her for a long time. A half smile crawled up one side of his mouth, and he nodded.

Satisfied, she nodded back.

If Harden *did* come back, Keane could always blame her.

"Your other question has a much bigger answer," said Finnagel, frowning. He glanced to Sarah. "Are you certain about this?"

"Yes," she said. "But it wouldn't matter now, anyway. He's smart enough to figure it out on his own."

"I really hope the news isn't that I've woken up in the land of cryptic talkers," Keane said. "Because that crap would get thin *really* quick."

"I am a sorcerer," Finnagel said. "Even I don't remember how old I am, and I have been using magic to fetter King Rance's moods toward the two of you since you arrived. That is why you live. I have also used healing magics to cleanse your wounds and regrow the injured tissue. This is also why you live."

"So, you're telling me that the King Rance we all knew and hated was the one with magic shackles on his personality making him *nicer*?" Keane asked.

"That is not the most germane point here, but yes, that is the fact," answered Finnagel. "As I was saying, I have been working on your behalf since your initial arrival with Lieutenant Falt. Behind the scenes, as it were."

"Yeah," Keane answered, "you're a big ol' murderer. Thanks, I guess?"

Keane grew a little sick thinking of all the people who had died on his behalf. Finnagel had never consulted with him about it, but it would never have happened if Keane hadn't impersonated the prince. Hell, *none* of this would have happened if he and Sarah hadn't stolen that wagebox and run from Harden in the first place.

Of course, then it would have been *Keane* who was dead, and Sarah would be without him. No one would ever convince him that outcome was the better one.

"Well," Keane said, standing and grabbing Sarah's hand, "anyway, good luck on all your magical... ventures, and I hope you get on with the next king. Sarah and I will just be off now. Ta."

"You may certainly leave," Finnagel said. "No one would hold you here, but Sarah will not be accompanying you."

"What? Why not? What?" He turned and pulled on Sarah's arm, but she did not rise from the sofa. "Sarah, wizards are *demons*. We were both at Gullhome. You remember Gullhome? Purple fire?

Remember the way the bodies smelled? We stay here with that *thing*," Keane said, pointing to Finnagel, "and that'll be us, uh, no offense."

"None taken," Finnagel said with an expression that indicated otherwise.

There was a knock on the door.

"Enter," said the sorcerer.

A young serving girl in castle livery stepped in, and Finnagel waved her over. She leaned toward him, straight, straw-colored hair swaying forward, and he gave her a few whispered commands. Then she ran back out, closing the heavy door behind.

"I am staying here," Sarah said, "because I am to be Finnagel's apprentice. I am a sorcerer, too—or will be, at any rate." She crossed her legs and laid her hands over her knee. She looked so peaceful and confident.

So... happy?

Keane backed into one of the low tables and sat down with a thump. He raised a hand to his forehead. "Can we slow this down for just a minute? Wait... is this why you kept sending jackasses to get in our way when we were trying to escape? Because you wanted Sarah as your magic maid or whatever? What if someone—like me—had gotten seriously hurt?"

Finnagel glanced at Keane's chest. "You have been seriously hurt and are no worse for wear."

"That's not what I meant, and you know it," Keane answered. "Why all the theatrics and skulking around? Why not just walk up and ask us if we wanted Sarah to be a degenerate, demon-domestic slave girl for you?"

"That's not actually the job description," Sarah interrupted.

"I believe you have already answered the question." Finnagel drew his graying black eyebrows together and faced Keane directly.

"Neither of you were ready for the knowledge, and Sarah was not ready for the offer. You were already seeking to flee, and the discovery of my nature would have given you another reason to do so." The sorcerer's face softened. "And it was necessary for Sarah to say yes. She is a beacon to such as myself, and others may not be so kind."

This information did nothing to make Keane feel better about anything. It struck him as more manipulation.

But he couldn't argue with how happy it made Sarah. Or he wouldn't, at any rate.

"So, how does all this work?" he asked her.

"Finnagel explained it to me," Sarah said, eyes wide. She was obviously excited. "It's why I'm so fast and strong. Magical energy is everywhere, but only born sorcerers can use it. And if you're not trained to make spells and whatnot, it gets used physically. Because that's the easiest or it's following your will—or something like that."

"Something like that," Finnagel said.

"But he's going to train me, so I'll be able to do anything I can think of."

"Oldam's rocky asscrack, Sarah—he's going to train you to be a *demon*?" Keane asked.

"Do I look like a demon to you, boy?" Finnagel responded.

"More and more all the time," Keane answered. "What about me?" he asked Sarah. "Do I get a say in this?"

"Yes," she answered, "but I was kinda hoping you'd be happy for me. I think... I think this may have been the thing I was looking for. Something that's all mine. Something for me."

No matter how many times Keane tried to dodge this, it kept coming back to kick him in the stones. Would this be the thing that finally took Sarah away from him once and for all? And how selfish was it of him to even be thinking that way? He looked down at the table he sat on, running a hand across its smoothed-over knots and whorls. Though he felt stupid thinking it, Keane sympathized with the blackthorn tree the table had been made of.

No one had asked *it* if it wanted to be a table.

"Not all sorcerers are like the Demon of Gullhome, Keane." Sarah squeezed Keane's hand before releasing it. "Finnagel has helped Greenshade for ages. He was the one who summoned all those emberflies in the menagerie. *Permanently.* Not just for two or three days like everyone else."

Keane pursed his lips. "You've never wanted to be a sorcerer before. Why now?"

Sarah laughed. "You never mentioned wanting to dress up as a Tyrranean prince and have a stay at Forest Castle before either. I never thought about it because it was never a possibility before. It's like waking up one morning and finding out that you can fly. Wait a minute." She addressed Finnagel, "Will I be able to fly?"

"If you like," he replied.

Sarah snorted and giggled into the back of her hand.

"There is another point for you to consider," Finnagel said to Keane. He turned to the door. "Please enter!" There had been no knock.

The door opened. "I got your message," Princess Megan said, entering the room. Her eyes lit on Keane. "You're awake!" she shouted, her face full of joy, and ran to him.

The diminutive princess embraced Keane and pulled his face to her chest, where he remained, confused but unwilling to move. Instead, he closed his eyes and concentrated on the feel of the silver-colored silk against his face and the smell of flowers in his nose. His anxiety seemed to flow out of him as if pulled away by the heat of their contact. Well aware of how fleeting a happy moment with the princess could be, he determined to draw this one out as long as he could.

"It seems the young lady was quite taken with your heroics yesterday," said Finnagel, "both with your eagerness to stand between the vile mercenaries and her person and your actions to save Treaty Hill."

Princess Megan took Keane's dazed face in both hands, kissing him fully and at some length on the lips. Then she drew back and slapped him.

"That is for lying to me," she said, expression stern. "Don't do it again."

"Lying..." said Keane. Then he remembered the scene in the king's audience chamber when Harden and Eli had broken in and told everyone who he was. He winced with the memory. "No, wait. I can explain—" he started.

"No need," the princess said, backing away from him to sit next to Sarah, her fitted dress shimmering in the lantern light. She took one of Sarah's hands in both of her own and held it in her lap. "I know *all* about it. Sarah and I are best friends now, aren't we?"

At Keane's aggrieved expression, Sarah said, "I've never had a princess lady friend before. It's nice."

"I felt it was necessary for the princess to be informed fully of your adventures and identity before she made any decisions regarding you," Finnagel said. "But of course, you had no idea I knew you were, in fact, not a prince of Tyrrane." This last came with a knowing smile and a nod.

Keane and Sarah exchanged a glance. "I hope you weren't planning that to be one of your 'shocks,' Finn," Keane said. "We've known that since we got here. You're not very subtle when you're being smug."

Finnagel looked crestfallen. "You didn't know I was a sorcerer."

"We've had to move up your wedding," Sarah said. Keane stared at her and then at the princess.

"You're... I mean... I'm still getting married?" he asked.

"Of course," Princess Megan answered. "Greenshade still requires a king on the throne, and you *did* just rescue the capital city. The people *really* love you for that. Thank the Alir we have had Lady Roselle here to make the arrangements for us."

"King...?" Keane said, feeling lightheaded. "Can we slow this down again?"

"Yes, Your Majesty-to-be," said Sarah, enjoying herself. "Now as I was saying, we've had to move the date up a bit. We'd rather get you two married quickly and avoid the chance that any of Prince Despin's relatives might show up for it. Although apparently, no one from Tyrrane has arrived in a while, so we've gotten lucky there."

Something about that statement bothered Keane, but there was too much to worry about to pick it apart now.

"We'll just send out announcements that the whole thing is over with," Sarah continued, "and they'll never even have to leave Dismon.

We'll use the king's death as the official excuse. Got to get another royal butt in the chair. No time to lose."

"Moved up... to when?" asked Keane.

"Everything is set for tomorrow," Princess Megan said. "And call me Meg. At least when we're in private." She smiled. "That's what the people I like call me."

"Tomorrow... wait. What about all those people in the audience chamber? Everyone who heard who Sarah and I really are?"

"Between the princess and I," Finnagel said, having regained his composure, "it was relatively simple to convince them that Harden Grayspring and his mercenary company were perpetrating a ruse to capture you and ransom you back to your supposed family in Tyrrane. It was not a difficult sell to make them out as deceitful villains, what with the horrifying attack on our fair city."

Keane was at a loss. It just didn't seem right. He was a scoundrel, a thug, a mercenary. Hell, he had even been a murderer. How could this be his new life?

"But... you're so beautiful," he said to Megan. It was all he could think to say.

"You're just gonna have to get used to that," Sarah said as she jumped up and slapped him on the back hard enough to make him cough. "Just like she's gonna have to get used to what a jackass you are. Life's not fair, but you gotta take what you get, am I right?"

49

GETTING WHAT YOU DON'T DESERVE

KEANE

T he service was intimate and mercifully brief, and at the end of it, Keane was married to a queen and himself made a king. Earlier that morning, Queen Loffa had officially abdicated her duties to Megan so that the transition of power would proceed smoothly and without issue. The entire city was in mourning, and the abbreviated ceremonies seemed appropriate.

Lady Roselle was made the queen's official governess. No one knew exactly what privileges the title carried. Queen Loffa was hardly a child, but Keane had no doubts the wily baroness would turn it to her advantage.

The marriage took place in the castle's chapel, a mostly unused temple dedicated to the Alir from before the time when formal worship had been banned. The people were still allowed their gods. The shrines appeared here and there across the countryside, but priests were no longer allowed to acquire earthly power in the Andosh kingdoms since the fall of the Temple of the Sky. This chapel was a beautiful old reminder of what religion used to be.

Wooden representations of the Alir circled the walls to either side and flanked a larger stone statue of King Oldam, father of the gods. Lit candles burned along a pair of railings that circled the whole of the room. A trio of minstrels, somewhere out of sight, provided quiet music.

Keane also met Duke Collin Hubrane's two sons. Branch the elder —whom he liked—was a tall, reedy young man with a sallow complexion but a ready smile. Then there was Songham the younger —whom he did not—a small, thin man, with darting eyes and clever fingers. In the final ceremony of the day, Keane installed Branch Hubrane as the new Royal Secretary of Greenshade and Duke of the Western Marches. Afterward, the participants mingled in the speaking chamber, a low octagonal room with mirrored walls and cut crystal sconces. The whole chamber glittered like the morning sun over a glassy sea.

The ceremony, the celebration, and the wind down were almost over, and Keane found himself growing nervous over what was coming next. He had never cared for anyone the same way he did for Megan. Even Sarah, whom he loved more than himself, was not the same.

As his queen stood chatting with Lady Roselle and Branch's wife, Sigga, a Norrikwoman and the new Duchess of the Western Marches, Keane strolled over to where Sarah leaned against a greenish stone wall, watching the room. He had to look away from Megan to speak. Her brilliant white gown, covered in pearls and gauzy pieces of fabric that hovered about her like smoke, accentuated her shape and threatening to overwhelm his attention.

He stopped breathing every time he looked at her.

"You know, yesterday, I was utterly panicked over this moment," he said.

"Why?" Sarah asked. "I thought this was what we were hanging around for." Even Sarah wore a dress, a cool-green color with long sleeves that made her look like an actual woman. Instead of the braids she used to keep her hair back and out of her armor, she had allowed Lady Roselle's women to arrange her hair in a flowing mane of black. The whole was quite striking, if lost on Keane.

"Well, then I was being sneaky, wasn't I? I had the advantage. I knew who everyone else was, but no one knew who *we* were."

"Except for Finnagel, on both counts," Sarah said.

"Sure," Keane continued, "but now *she* knows me, you know? It's like I'm naked or something. Cock hanging out for her to see."

"Isn't that the point?" Sarah said with a smile.

"Kinda hating you right now," Keane said, "but the truth is I'm not sure *what* the point is anymore. Maybe just keeping her safe."

At that moment, Megan turned to look at Keane from across the room and smiled, and he felt his insides melt and go running into his feet.

Sarah glanced at the pair of them and rolled her eyes. "Gross," she said. "You two should just get married."

"Yeah," Keane said. He inhaled deeply, and his arms crossed over his chest. "She told me that she likes me."

"I'd say she does," said Sarah.

"Right... but... she *likes* me, and she cares for me. And I'm a big hero and all, but she doesn't love me. Not yet, anyway. This is about politics. Nineteen years old, and she's already more mature than I'll ever be."

"My boots were made yesterday and they're more mature than you'll ever be," Sarah said, grinning. "Relax. You're lovable. It'll happen."

Keane did not respond but stood watching while Megan make her goodbyes before walking to him across the dark green carpet. Beyond where he and Sarah stood were only the stairs leading up to the royal bed chambers.

"You know," Keane said and elbowed Sarah in the ribs as his beautiful wife approached, "I think we may just stick around here awhile."

50

NOT SO FAST...

BRANNOK II

Dreary gray clouds covered Dismon, which sat like a black crust on the plains below the Bitter Heights Mountains. Cold winds blew through the narrow streets, and bundled-up people made their way across the hard cobblestones. The tall buildings of the capital were made of heavy, iron-rich granite, and they rose into the sky, dark and somber.

It was a cold city from the ground to the roofs.

But they were strong—both the buildings and the people of Dismon—as was the man who ruled them. A tyrant in both fact and name, he was King of Tyrrane, Brannok Swifthart the Second.

Tall and fiery-haired with wide, powerful shoulders, Brannok's physicality matched his temper. He wore mail every day, a symbol of his domination over Tyrrane, and a shaggy brown cloak, the pelt of the bear he'd killed as a boy.

Deep within the black-and-rust-walled military fortress at the center of Dismon, which had served as the royal castle of Tyrrane for time out of knowing, King Brannok strode with grim purpose down dimly lit corridors leading to Angrim's antechamber—a journey which never pleased him. He did not go there without being summoned, and being summoned in his own castle made him cross from the start.

Adding to his displeasure was the knowledge that his wife, Moru, and two of his five sons currently in residence—Brannok III and Jason, as well as his daughter, Jasmayre—had been summoned as well.

What kind of state business required the participation of women?

Angrim was the immortal soul of Tyrrane and had been here since Jarl Hoggurd Tyrrane the First of the now-mythical nation of Oldsnow wrested the country away from the Darrish Empire. He was ancient, he was evil, and above all, he was *powerful*.

But damned if he wasn't a pain in the ass.

Brannok walked through the open doorway to the final flight of steps leading down to Angrim's chambers. The passage got colder the further down he went, and his breath puffed out in front of him. At least the cold mitigated the smell somewhat.

He passed a shivering guard and ignored the man's snap to attention. The soldier must have pissed Captain Thornson off in some manner to get stationed here. Angrim had been known to leave his guards as dried-up husks from time to time, no explanations given.

At the bottom of the black stone steps, Angrim's door lay open and dark. The smell of death was strongest here, but then the demon's chambers always stank of fear and rot. Brannok stepped through, irritated at his own reluctance.

Within, he joined his other family members, already frozen in horrified attendance along the upper balcony that ran the walls of the circular room some twelve feet above the floor. Brannok III, a younger version of the king, scowled down over the railing, while Jason, athletic, tall, and soft-hearted, glanced up to his father's entrance, showing obvious relief. Moru, his wife, a round woman with the weight of age on her, looked grim and cold, her face pinched and cheeks ruddy. Beside her stood Jasmayre. The girl's expression, as always, was unreadable. That one was, without doubt, the most clever and ruthless of his progeny, a fact alwaysh rankled the king every day.

She would have made *such* a fine son.

Leaning over the balustrade to look into the space below, Brannok saw Angrim, an unnaturally tall figure covered in black robe and cowl, standing to one side. The dimness of the lighting and the darkness of the stone made him indistinct, but his nightmarish voice, which Brannok had always fancied, sounded like metal claws on the inside of his skull, was anything but.

"*You are late, mote,*" Angrim intoned, the voice grinding on the king's soul. Of them all, only Jasmayre appeared unaffected by the ancient creature's utterances and unconcerned.

"I am king," Brannok answered. "That makes you early."

Angrim made a terrifying noise that Brannok thought might have been a laugh but sounded more like tearing metal.

"*As you wish, mote. Time is more your concern than mine.*"

It was only then that Brannok noted the bunched-up square of cloth in the center of the floor. It covered something and was the only thing down there not black. In fact, it was a dirty white. But such was Angrim's presence that anything else in the room with him faded away to obscurity.

"What is that?" Brannok asked.

"*It is what you are here to see, mote,*" Angrim said, yanking the cover away. A moment passed as Brannok's mind attempted to assign meaning to the form on the ground below him. Just as recognition sparked for the twisted shape, Moru gasped, and Jasmayre's brow drew down to a scowl. Jason looked dismayed while the two Brannoks, king and prince, narrowed their eyes, even angrier than normal.

"Where was this found?" the king asked.

"*West of Growinon, washed up on the north bank of the Greenshade River,*" came the terrible voice. "*This mote never made his way to Treaty Hill.*"

"How did he die?" asked the king, words tight and strained against his rage.

"*Neck,*" Angrim said. A thin, pale, and much too long arm drifted from the black and pointed to the twisted neck of the corpse. The body was rotted, flesh torn and eaten, one leg ending at the knee, but the steel band shone as bright as the day it was fitted to Prince Despin's arm.

Without another word, King Brannok spun and stalked out of the miserable dungeon, the vengeful cries of his two sons drowned out by the appalling laughter of the hell-beast that lived there.

Despin may have been his most worthless son, but he was Blood of Tyrrane, and that did not spill without grievous cost. There would be war in the Thirteen Kingdoms.

And it would come soon.

Here ends Book One of the Misplaced Mercenaries Series,

ACKNOWLEDGMENTS

There are so many people without whom this book—and the next five!—could never have been created. Each one is a linchpin on which the whole endeavor rested on in a different way. Books are big, time consuming projects with no promise of success at the end, and that cannot be done without the steadfast support of the people who love you.

I thank you all *so* much.

First and foremost, the thanks for this book belongs to my wife, Lena. There is no one who has provided more help, encouragement, and devotion than you have. Every day, whether I felt happy and support was easy, or insecure and it was hard, you were there. Whether I needed space, or a discerning ear, or just a hug, you were there. And above all, you were honest and loving.

Next I want to thank Kelly Colby, my editor and the owner of Cursed Dragon Ship Publishing, for taking a *huge* chance on me. You have been there when I needed you, with advice and the best kind of criticism, and have helped me to create a book that was, in the end, so much more than I could have made myself. I am proud to have been your partner throughout this experience.

I also want to thank the other editors who have been involved in this project, Joshua Essoe and Katharine Boggess. Joshua, you have been my story editor on every book of this series, and you were the first to encourage me to try and find a publisher. Your assistance and instruction can only be matched by your endurance on the telephone, while listening to me talk about Sarah and Keane. And Katharine, you not only helped me see through these character's eyes better than I ever could have without you, you were a terrific cheerleader, and gave me the backbone to pursue success in all the most uncomfortable—and necessary—ways.

My sister, Kristen, and brother, Brent, have been unstintingly kind and generous with their interest and emotional support. It means more to me than you will ever know. The writer has no words.

I'd like to carve out a special thank you to Kevin J. Anderson, Rebecca Moesta, Eric Flint, James A. Owen, David Farland, and all the people at the Superstars conferences. Year after year you have provided me with knowledge, nurturing, and inspiration, as well as a place to meet amazing friends and partners.

And really, this only scratches the surface. So many friends have been prevailed upon to read and give criticism. Roxanne Henkle, you have read everything, and keep coming back for more. We may not be related, but we are family. Jennifer Taylor, not only have you been there to give unconditional love and faith, you have been a mom for me when I needed one, and a true friend all the time.

To my poor, benighted friends who have been asked over and over to read and reread books for beta and advanced copy, Lloyd Brown, Devin Rollyson, Rook Watterson, Douglas Oosting, Courtney Walker, Thomas Fowler, Nic Patchett, Jason Harris, Ryan Koch, Brian McCray, Adam Czechowski, Julio Rodriguez, Toby Santerelli, David Drake, Justin Herzog, Mary Natwick, and Murshida Va—as well as those I've witlessly forgotten—I offer my heartfelt appreciation and condolences. I wish being my friend was easier, but you all know I am equally in your corners.

Finally, thanks to everyone who has picked up this book. If we ever meet, say hi and I'll be proud to shake your hand. When you put up your hard-won money, this book became as much yours as it is mine—in a figurative, non-legally binding way. I'm telling the story, but it lives in your head. We share it.

And that makes me a fortunate man.

ABOUT THE AUTHOR

Years ago Kevin Pettway looked around and decided that while there was plenty of amazing fantasy produced today, there was a definite theme to it, and the Red Wedding just wasn't funny enough. Resolving to address this critical oversight, he has produced the Misplaced Mercenaries series of books, which puts laughter back in slaughter.

Kevin Pettway has shaken the hands of several prominent authors whose names you might know, and has never had a restraining order filed against him—as of date of publication. Chief among his other accomplishments are taking first place in the Best Writer in His Own Household awards the last three years running. (Now that the funny dog has died.)

Kevin lives in Florida by the river in a house he always dreamt of, with a woman who is too good for him, and a pair of dogs who love him even when he forgets to feed them. (Unrelated to the funny dog incident.) Now he wants to be a writer because it is one of the few professions that will overlook his cursing with profusion and gusto in public.

You can find Kevin on FaceBook, Instagram, or his own website at www.kevinpettway.com. To file a restraining order against him, please call your local sheriff's department.

 facebook.com/kevinpettwayauthor

instagram.com/kevinpettwayauthor

ALSO BY KEVIN PETTWAY

Blow Out the Candle When You Leave

Preorder Book Two in the Misplaced Mercenaries series now! Set for Release in July 2020.

CPSIA information can be obtained
at www.ICGtesting.com
Printed in the USA
FSHW010634030120
65583FS